Coll e

MW01701835

Birds of New Zealand

Julian Fitter

Don Merton

Foreword by Rt Hon. Helen Clark

Collins

HarperCollins*Publishers*

First published in 2011
by HarperCollins*Publishers* (New Zealand) Limited
PO Box 1, Shortland Street, Auckland 1140
Published by arrangement with HarperCollins Publishers Ltd

Copyright © Julian Fitter 2011
Photographs © Individual copyright holders, 2011
Illustrations on page 20 © Norman Arlott 2011

Julian Fitter asserts the moral right to be identified as the author of this work.
All rights reserved. No part of this publication may be reproduced, stored in a retrieval system or transmitted in any form or by any means, electronic, mechanical, photocopying, recording or otherwise, without the prior written permission of the publishers.

HarperCollins*Publishers*
31 View Road, Glenfield, Auckland 0627, New Zealand
25 Ryde Road, Pymble, Sydney, NSW 2073, Australia
A 53, Sector 57, Noida, UP, India
77–85 Fulham Palace Road, London W6 8JB, United Kingdom
2 Bloor Street East, 20th floor, Toronto, Ontario M4W 1A8, Canada
10 East 53rd Street, New York, NY 10022, USA

National Library of New Zealand Cataloguing-in-Publication Data
Fitter, Julian.
Birds of New Zealand / Julian Fitter.
Includes bibliographical references and index.
ISBN 978-1-86950-851-7
1. Birds—New Zealand. 2. Birds—New Zealand—Identification.
598.0993—dc 22

ISBN: 978 1 86950 851 7

Cover design by Heike Schüssler
Edited and designed by D & N Publishing, Wiltshire, UK

Printed and bound in Hong Kong by Printing Express Ltd

Contents

Foreword

by Rt Hon. Helen Clark

New Zealand is known for its extraordinary birdlife. While many species have disappeared since human beings first arrived on our shores, we are fortunate indeed still to have a unique assemblage of birds, which attracts visitors from around the world.

I grew up on a farm on the border of what was then Pirongia Forest Park. From my earliest years, I have memories of the Tui, Bellbirds, Fantails and Kereru.

During my time in public life in New Zealand I also had many unforgettable experiences of seeing our extraordinary birds. A highlight when I was Minister of Conservation in the late 1980s, for example, was going to Kapiti Island. The glorious chorus of birdsong there was a sad reminder of what we have lost to predators in so much of the New Zealand bush.

During my time as Prime Minister, I visited the Kakapo rearing unit at Burwood Bush near Te Anau; went by helicopter to see from the air the habitat in the Chatham Islands where Don Merton and his colleagues worked to save the very rare Black Robin; walked in to the site on the main island in the Chatham Islands where David Crockett had laboured for decades to save the Taiko from extinction; stayed overnight on Tiritiri Island in the Hauraki Gulf where the reafforestation provides habitat for many species, including Kiwi; and participated in the release of Kiwi in Wellington's Karori Sanctuary.

I was also able to announce funding in 2007 for both the Maungatautari Ecological Island in the Waikato and the Rotokare Wildlife Sanctuary near Eltham in Taranaki – both aiming to give fully fenced protection to these natural areas to ensure the survival of rich birdlife there.

Don Merton's name has been synonymous with bird conservation in New Zealand for decades. He has dedicated his life to the preservation of our rare bird species, and inspired wide public interest in critical biodiversity initiatives. It is encouraging to see so many people and groups all over our country taking practical action to ensure the survival of our unique bird species.

This very compact book will be useful for New Zealanders and visitors alike. It is packed with information and photos, and offers advice on where to see birds. As my husband is an avid birdwatcher, I am sure the book will be in his backpack from now on!

I also hope that this important and practical book will help many more people to appreciate New Zealand's birdlife and become advocates for their protection and for the conservation of their habitats.

Don Merton – A Tribute

Don Merton is a name that is synonymous with bird conservation, worldwide. When he first started work with the New Zealand Wildlife Service in 1957 the idea of wildlife conservation was almost unknown; when he retired from the Department of Conservation in 2005, it was an accepted part of everyday life. In 1957 very little was known about the impact of introduced mammals on native birdlife, and even less was known about how to rescue birds that were in danger of extinction. Gradually, Don and his colleagues developed the necessary knowledge and expertise, largely by intuition and experimentation, a very practical New Zealand approach.

In the gallery of species saved from the brink of extinction, the South Island Saddleback, Kakapo and Black Robin owe a lot to Don. The survival of the Black Robin was a minor miracle, the species being down to five individuals with just one breeding female, Old Blue. Don and his colleagues used translocation and cross-fostering to ensure the survival of the species, which now numbers over 200 individuals. These techniques are now in use around the world and have helped countless other species to resist the seemingly relentless tide of human development.

His work with New Zealand's threatened bird species made Don a national icon and world-renowned figure in conservation circles. The people and wildlife, especially the birds, of Aotearoa New Zealand will be forever in his debt. He died before this book was published.

Kakapo *Strigops habroptilus*, Richard Henry, held by Don Merton on Codfish Island, November 2010.

Captured in Fiordland in 1975 by Don Merton, John Cheyne and John's labrador bitch Mandy, Richard Henry has spent the past 36 years on predator-free islands. Named after the visionary, pioneer conservationist and custodian of Resolution Island from 1894 to 1910, he was the last known survivor of his species from mainland New Zealand and was believed to be around 100 years old. Richard Henry Kakapo was found dead on Codfish Island on 24 December 2010.

RH's legacy: *His one female and two male offspring that hatched on Maud Island in 1998 may hold the key to the genetic rescue of a species suffering from chronic lack of genetic diversity.*

Acknowledgements

When I first arrived in New Zealand in 2005, I little imagined that I would be writing a 'Fitter Guide' to the birds of this very special Land of Birds, but those of you who have come across other 'Fitter Guides' will recognise the family style and I hope you will find that this is as straightforward and user-friendly as the earlier ones.

No book is ever the result of single endeavour, and this one is no exception; it has been possible only because of the help and support I have received from the whole environmental community in New Zealand, both individuals and organisations. You have spent years working, often thanklessly, to look after the natural heritage of New Zealand – keep at it, it's worth it!

Special thanks are of course due to my co-author Don Merton. Don has seen most of the New Zealand avifauna, and seen the good days and the bad, species rescued and species lost. I am deeply appreciative that he has agreed to help with this book and has put so much into ensuring that it is a book of which all New Zealanders can be proud.

Thanks also to Myles Archibald and Julia Koppitz at HarperCollins UK and Tony Fisk at HarperCollins New Zealand, for their help, faith and patience.

The real thank you has to go to the amazing native birdlife of Aotearoa New Zealand, for being so special, and so different. My one hope is that this book will do just a little bit to help you survive and prosper. You have had a rough 800 years and you deserve better.

Author's Introduction

New Zealand has long been known as 'The Land of Birds' and this was certainly true until the arrival of the first people less than 800 years ago. Since then some 41 species of bird have become extinct, the most recent in 1972, and even today several species are only surviving thanks to intensive conservation measures. These measures have set new standards and developed new techniques to help species survive the ferocious onslaught of man, the only species on the planet that appears hell bent on its own destruction.

While we have lost many species, especially of land birds, and the forest no longer echoes with the wonderful birdsong that it once did, the avifauna of New Zealand is still remarkable; much of it is not just endemic, but unlike anything elsewhere. The Kakapo, the world's largest parrot, and the Takahe, the largest member of the Rail family (Rallidae), are two flightless examples; other good examples are the two wattlebirds, the Saddleback and Kokako. All of these would probably be extinct by now were it not for recent intervention by dedicated conservationists.

New Zealand is a wonderful country for the birdwatcher, whether interested amateur or serious twitcher. Once you have found your way out of the urban areas and through the areas of industrial agriculture, populated as they tend to be by imported European or Asian species, then there is a wealth of opportunities to see the amazing native birdlife, be it in the surrounding seas, the harbours and wetlands, the lakes, the forests or alpine areas. New Zealand is a long, narrow country, so you can often access several of these habitats on the same day.

But you cannot travel in New Zealand today without being aware of the battle being fought between those who would preserve and expand the areas of wilderness and regenerate native bush and wetlands, and those who feel it should all be turned into industrial agricultural land or exotic forestry plantations. Sadly, in all too many areas, the latter are winning. While exotic forestry may be neutral in environmental terms, dairy pastures are a serious threat, not just to the biodiversity of the land itself, but to that of the country's waters and waterways. More threats are emerging too with the risk of conservation areas being opened up to mining; all of this 'development' has serious implications for native birdlife.

This book is not just a guide to help you identify the native birds; it is also a song of praise to those native birds and a wake-up call to look after them, to appreciate and protect them. We can only imagine what the birdlife was like before the arrival of humans but, having destroyed so much, surely we have the wisdom, and maybe more importantly, the common sense, not to destroy what is left. The early settlers can perhaps be excused for the damage they did, for that was a different age and they had little understanding of the intricate interdependence of all life forms. Now we know how important the ecosystem is to our own existence, and yet still we seek to destroy it.

Fortunately there are many examples, up and down the country, of sanctuaries and reserves, where the native species have a real chance, but unless these initiatives and projects and their sponsoring communities, organisations and agencies are supported, they will not succeed.

Go out, travel the country, visit the mountains, lakes and rivers, the sand dunes and the estuaries, the forests and the grasslands, enjoy and observe the birdlife and other wildlife, but above all look after it, cherish it, protect it.

Julian Fitter
Maketu, Bay of Plenty, New Zealand
February 2011

Stead's Bush Wren *Xenicus longipes variabilis*, a minute, near-flightless bird that became extinct in 1972 in spite of efforts by Don Merton and colleagues to save it. It would be nice to think that this was the last New Zealand bird to become extinct thanks to man's activities.

New Zealand and its offshore islands.

Aotearoa New Zealand - An Introduction

If you do not live in New Zealand, or Aotearoa to give it its Maori name, then some background information may come in useful, and may help you to understand this remarkable and very diverse country and its birdlife.

New Zealand is the largest (by landmass) oceanic archipelago in the world, its 270,000sq km broken up into three main islands, North, South and Stewart, and a large number of offshore islands, stretching from the tropical Kermadec Islands in the north to the sub-Antarctic Antipodes and Campbell island groups in the south. They lie right across the westerly wind belt know as the 'Roaring Forties' and have a very varied topography with high alpine mountains and massive active volcanoes. They are isolated from their nearest continental landmass, Australia, by the 2,400km of the Tasman Sea.

Geography and Geology

Geologically the archipelago straddles two of the earth crust's tectonic plates, with all of North Island being on the Australian Plate and most of South Island on the Pacific Plate. This makes for a very active geology with frequent earthquakes and volcanic eruptions. New Zealand broke away from Gondwana some 70–80 million years ago and has drifted gradually east, and is still moving. In 320 million years' time we should arrive in South America! This isolation from the rest of the world has resulted in there being very few land mammals in New Zealand, just two species of bat – a third species became extinct in 1973. The fossil record suggests that some other small land mammals did inhabit New Zealand in the past, but did not survive the various changes that have occurred over the last few million years.

Climate

The combination of an oceanic situation, a very varied topography with a long spine of mountains running virtually the length of the country, and the country's latitude has resulted in an unusual and very varied climate that can best be termed Oceanic Mediterranean. Northland lies the same distance from the Equator as does North Africa in the northern hemisphere, while sub-Antarctic Antipodes Island is so named as it is the nearest land to the antipodal point to London in the UK. The effect of the topography is to make some regions, such as the west of South Island, very wet, with rainfall of over 12m per year, while not far away on the east coast and inland rainfall may be less than 500mm. North Island, having a less dramatic topography, has a more even

One of the many amazing features of the New Zealand bush is the great variety of epiphytic plants that grow on some trees; they form veritable gardens in the sky.

NORTH ISLAND
174°
176°
178°
34°
36°
38°
40°
42°
Three Kings Is
Cape Reinga
North Cape
Great Exhibition Bay
Ninety Mile Beach
Mangonui
Bay of Islands
Cape Brett
Poor Knights Is
Hokianga Harbour
Kamo
Whangarei
Waipoua Kauri Park
Bream Bay
Little Barrier Island
Great Barrier Island
Tawharanui Peninsula
Kaipara Harbour
Tiritiri Matangi
Hauraki Gulf
Mercury Islands
Auckland
Coromandel Peninsula
Muriwai
Waitakere Ranges
Manukau
Manukau Harbour
Miranda
Thames
Mayor I.
Bay of Plenty
Waiuku
Whangamarino Wetland
Cape Runaway
Huntly
Morrinsville
White I.
Hamilton
Tauranga
Maketu
East Cape
Cambridge
Otanewainuku
Whakatane
Maungatautari
Kawhia Harbour
Rotorua
L. Rotorua
Kawerau
Ohiwa Harbour
Tokoroa
UREWERA NATIONAL PARK
North Taranaki Bight
Lake Taupo
Taupo
Gisborne
Waitara
Poverty Bay
New Plymouth
Wairoa
Mt Egmont Taranaki
Tongariro
Cape Egmont
Ruapehu
Hawke Bay
Mahia Peninsula
Stratford
Wanganui
Napier
Hawera
Whangaehu
Hastings
South Taranaki Bight
Cape Kidnappers
Rangitikei
Wanganui
Marton
Palmerston North
Dannevirke
Foxton
Levin
Cape Turnagain
Otaki
Mt Bruce
Kapiti I.
Masterton
Paraparaumu
Cook Strait
Carterton
Wellington
Lower Hutt
Cape Palliser
N
0
20
40
60
80
100 miles
0
100 km

168°
170°
172°
174°
40°
42°
44°
46°
48°
Cook St.
Cape Farewell
Farewell Spit
Golden Cape Stephens
Bay
D'Urville I.
Tasman Mountains
Arapawa I.
Nelson
Picton
Richmond
Blenheim
Karamea Bight
Wairau
Cape Foulwind
Westport
Buller
Spenser Mts
Inland Kaikoura Range
S O U T H
I S L A N D
Greymouth
Kaikoura Peninsula
Hokitika
SOUTHERN ALPS
Rangiora
Pegasus Bay
Kaiapoi
Okarito Lagoon
L. Coleridge
Waimakariri
Christchurch
Aoraki
Mt Cook
Canterbury
Hickory Bay
Ashburton
L. Ellesmere
Jackson Head
L. Tekapo
Plains
Banks Peninsula
L. Pukaki
Canterbury Bight
Olivine Range
Mt Aspiring
L. Ohau
Twizel
Timaru
Milford Sound
L. Hawea
L. Wanaka
Waitaki
Queenstown
Oamaru
Secretary I.
L. Te Anau
Lake Wakatipu
L. Manapouri
Clutha
Resolution I.
Mosgiel
Otago Peninsula
Taiaroa Head
Dusky Sound
Dunedin
Oreti
L. Hauroko
Gore
New River Estuary
Invercargill
Puysegur Point
Awarua Bay
Nugget Point
Foveaux Strait
Fortrose Lagoon
Codfish I.
Ruapuke I.
Stewart Island
Paterson Inlet
South West Cape
N
0 20 40 60 80 100 miles
0 100 km

James Cook

While Captain James Cook (1728–79) did not discover New Zealand, he can certainly claim to have put the archipelago on the map. Cook was a remarkable and able seaman and navigator, and he was also concerned, unlike many of his contemporaries, to develop good relations with indigenous peoples. He made three voyages to New Zealand, his first in 1769 after he had been to Tahiti to observe the transit of Venus. When he left there in search of 'Terra Incognita Australis', he brought with him Tupaia, a Tahitian chief, as an interpreter to help deal with any indigenous people that he might encounter. In spite of being able to communicate quite effectively, his first encounters with Maori were not a great success. On this first visit he circumnavigated the islands and produced a set of remarkably accurate charts. He made two further voyages, visiting New Zealand in 1773 and 1777. It was his favourable reports that attracted first sealers and whalers and later settlers to New Zealand. Joseph Banks and Daniel Solander accompanied Cook on his first trip, and were the first to describe the native fauna and flora, making observations and collections that are still used to this day. The first drawings and paintings of the unique birdlife of New Zealand were made by Sydney Parkinson, a trained draughtsman who was employed by Banks. The Black or Parkinson's Petrel *Procellaria parkinsoni* was named after him, while Cook's Petrel *Procellaria cookii* is named after Captain Cook.

Captain James Cook from a painting by Nathaniel Dance.

spread of rainfall, but even here it varies from over 6m to less than 800mm. On the sunshine front, many areas on both islands average over 5 hours and some well over 6 hours a day, year round; in contrast, London in the UK averages just over 4 hours a day.

The Flora

This unusual climate resulted in the main natural vegetation being a temperate rainforest where almost all trees and shrubs are evergreen and where birds are major pollinators. Before the arrival of the Maori, in about 1250CE, some 80 per cent of the country was covered in forest, the balance being permanent snow, alpine or wetlands. That cover has now been reduced to around 20 per cent with an accompanying loss of the biodiversity, especially to the birds that inhabited it. In fact the loss of birdlife is greater than the loss of forest thanks to the impact of introduced mammalian predators. Since the arrival of man, some 51 species of New Zealand's endemic bird fauna have gone extinct. Surprisingly

Ulva Island in Paterson Inlet on Stewart Island is an excellent example of a podocarp/broadleaf forest, where the introduced pest species have been removed.

some 28 species, including all ten species of moa, disappeared before the arrival of Europeans. The Maori managed this impressive feat partly by hunting, but more seriously by introducing the Pacific Rat or Kiore as well as dogs. They also managed to get rid of 25 per cent of the native bush, largely by careless use of fire as a hunting and land-clearance technique

Habitats

With its very varied geography and topography, New Zealand has a huge range of habitats; however, they can be broken down into four main types:

COASTAL AND COASTAL WETLANDS This includes a number of very extensive sheltered harbours with saltmarshes, mangroves in the north and large areas of mudflats, which attract huge numbers of native and migratory waders.

FRESHWATER WETLANDS Included here are some very sizeable lakes and the amazing braided rivers, which are in a sense a habitat of their own. There are few long rivers in New Zealand, a result of the shape and mountainous nature of the islands.

NATIVE BUSH This now covers only 20 per cent of the country and is home to most of the remaining native land birds. It can be divided into lowland and montane, with individual species varying and changing with altitude, but also into two major 'types': podocarp/broadleaf, which predominates in the North Island; and beech forest, which predominates in the South Island. The two types have quite distinct fauna and flora.

ALPINE AND SUBALPINE This is the area between the tree and snow lines, most of which is found in South Island but there are significant areas on North Island also. The fauna and flora here is very highly adapted and varied, but with relatively few bird species.

Maori Language and Pronunciation

The Maori language, te Reo, is experiencing a resurgence in New Zealand, and is increasingly used in general conversation. Many of the native birds are best known by their Maori names, and so it makes sense to have some small knowledge of the pronunciation. It is not the easiest of languages – it uses a small alphabet and virtually all words end in a vowel. Vowels are pronounced as in Spanish: *ah*, *eh*, *ee*, *oh*, *oow*; and the emphasis is either on the first syllable, or none. The letters *wh* are pronounced as a soft *f* and *au* is, as in French, pronounced *oh*. As an example, the town of Taupo is pronounced '*Toh..paw*'.

Human History

New Zealand was the last major land mass to be discovered by man. The Aborigines have been in Australia for 55,000 years, but the Maori, who are thought to have come from East Polynesia, arrived in New Zealand around 1250CE. The first European to visit New Zealand was the Dutchman Abel Tasman in 1642, but after a disagreeable encounter with the local Maori in what is now Golden Bay, he left without ever setting foot on land. The next European to arrive was James Cook in 1769, and it is from then that the modern history of New Zealand begins.

Initially, European influence was small, the people who came were mainly traders, whalers or sealers, and they mixed and intermarried with the local Maori. However, following the Treaty of Waitangi in 1840, large numbers of settlers arrived looking for land. Given the modest technology at their disposal, it is amazing what those pioneers achieved – the destruction of a further 50 per cent of the native bush and the draining of 90 per cent of the very extensive wetlands. It was only towards the end of the 20th century that this destruction ceased and groups and individuals started trying to rebuild some of what had been destroyed.

The huge increase in industrial dairy farming in recent years has seen the destruction not only of native bush, grasslands and wetlands, but also of exotic forestry, as here between Rotorua and Taupo.

Conservation and Alien Species

The New Zealand ecosystem is remarkable because we have a very good idea of what it was like before the arrival of humans, less than 800 years ago. While the destruction man has reaped in those 800 years is prodigious, it does mean that we still have areas that are close to what they were before man arrived, and therefore we have some hope of restoring it to something approaching its original glory, though sadly lacking a lot of its original avian inhabitants.

While some modest conservation efforts were being made by the end of the 19th century, the development of the conservation concept did not really take over until the last three decades of the 20th century. Even now, well into the 21st century, far too many people lack any appreciation of the real value of conservation and the conservation estate. New Zealand has, however, made huge progress and is a world leader in the development of conservation techniques and strategies.

As people came to appreciate the damage caused by introduced mammalian predators on the native biodiversity, so New Zealand gradually developed techniques for dealing with them. As a result, the country has pioneered methods for the control and eradication of invasive pest species. Living in a land with no major predators, New Zealand birds were singularly ill equipped to survive attack by the many different predatory mammals that were introduced. Many bird species were flightless and ground-nesting; they often had nocturnal habits, which was good protection against diurnal bird predators, but none at all against nocturnal mammals with a keen sense of smell. So it was that 23 species became extinct between 1800 and 1972 when the last Bush Wren died.

The conservation effort has been spearheaded by the Wildlife Service, now renamed the Department of Conservation (DoC). Initially the work was very hit and miss, but gradually staff developed techniques for helping species to survive

The introduced Black or Ship Rat *Rattus rattus* is, along with the Brown Rat and the Polynesian Rat or Kiore, the most destructive pest mammal in New Zealand. Here it is seen eating a half-fledged chick of a native Grey Fantail.

and recover. A classic example of this was the case of the Black Robin, a tiny all-black passerine found only on the Chatham Islands, 640km east of New Zealand. At one stage in the rescue operation, the species was down to five individuals and just one breeding female, Old Blue. In the process, Don Merton, Brian Bell and their colleagues invented and developed new techniques, including translocation, captive breeding and fostering, and triumphed so that there are now around 200 individuals. Since then, the techniques have been further developed to help the Kakapo, Kokako, Stitchbird, Saddleback and other species, not just in New Zealand, but worldwide.

At the same time as developing ways of helping individual species to survive, DoC has developed ways of eradicating pest species, including goats, pigs, deer, rabbits, Stoats, Brown and Black rats, mice and the ubiquitous Brush-tailed Possum. This last is a serious problem, and there are estimated to be some 70 million possums in New Zealand with no natural enemies, all happily munching their way through some 140,000 tonnes of vegetation EVERY night – that's 5 million tonnes a year! This devastation of the native bush has a serious impact on native bird species that depend on it, particularly the flowering trees, for their food. Possum also predate eggs and, at times, nestlings.

While much of the DoC rescue effort has been concentrated on using offshore islands as natural sanctuaries, they have also focused on mainland areas, where intensive pest control has given excellent results, and at the same time they have encouraged the development of the 'pest-proof fence', another New Zealand first. These fences are safe barriers against all alien mammals and have been used in a variety of locations, especially on North Island, to help re-establish populations of native bird species.

Sadly, the conservation battle is far from won. Many people are ignorant of the true value of the native wildlife and the conservation estate and there is constant pressure to bring more land into the agricultural system or to mine the conservation estate. The key to the future is to educate, educate, educate, not just the children but the adults, especially people of influence, who ought to know better, to the benefits of the amazing wildlife of Aotearoa New Zealand. Birds, being probably the most obvious and attractive and photogenic animals, are a very good tool to use in that fight.

The DoC 200 trap is a key weapon in the fight against Stoats and other invasive mammalian species that have serious impacts on most native bird populations. Recently, an automatic gas-operated trap has been developed that will help to reduce pest numbers further.

Identification Notes

Scientific Names

With the development of genetic identification using DNA analysis, scientific names change quite frequently as subspecies are identified as distinct species, or new genera are created or sometimes lost through amalgamation with another. In this book we have used the names, both common and scientific, given in the fourth edition of the *Checklist of the Birds of New Zealand*, 2010, published by the Ornithological Society of New Zealand (OSNZ), as the definitive version.

Maori Names

Many native species have Maori names, and where these are in common use we have used them, otherwise we have generally used the English common name.

Abbreviations Used in Species Descriptions

P&R Population and Range: population figures are often quite approximate but give a general indication of numbers. Range is sometimes very specific, but there can be significant variation from year to year.

T&M Threats and Management: this gives a general indication of the most serious threats to species and specific steps being taken to conserve them.

BV Best Viewed: some of the best, but by no means only places to see this species.

ABP Annual Breeding Pairs, often a more reliable population indicator.

Populations

With endemic species the figures refer to known New Zealand populations; for others it is normally the worldwide estimate except where indicated to the contrary.

Breeding

Breeding information is generally provided only for those species that breed in New Zealand on a regular basis.

Distribution Maps

These are provided for all species that breed on, or are regular migratory visitors to, the three main islands. For other species, distribution is indicated in the text. Red crosses indicate points of very restricted range.

Measurements

Lengths are given in centimetres and a single figure indicates a central value within a range. We have used wingspan rather than the length of individual wings, as this is more practical in the field. The measurements provided are a broad indicator only, as individual birds may vary appreciably; in general, females are somewhat smaller than males, unless indicated to the contrary. Where male (M) and female (F) measurements differ significantly, both are given. Weight is very variable, depending on sex, time of year and even time of day, but it helps to give an idea to compare with other species. With some species there is very little accurate data available, or figures are taken from a small sample.

L Length, from tip of bill to end of tail – typically in flight
WS Wingspan – wing-tip to wing-tip
Wt Weight – this is the biggest variable, especially for migratory species
Tarsus and bill length – indicated for some species where this is relevant

Plumages

Some species have fairly straightforward plumage, others very complex, therefore descriptions will not try to describe in detail but to point out the salient features. If species that breed in New Zealand change plumage when breeding, the breeding plumage will be the main description; migrants that winter in New Zealand will be described mainly in non-breeding plumage. Key identification indicators are written in italics. The photographs show typical adult plumages unless stated otherwise.

Bear in mind that there are many intermediate plumage stages, not just between breeding and non-breeding plumage, but between immature and adult, especially in those species (e.g. albatrosses) that can take many years to attain adult plumage.

Introduced Exotic Species

While the introduction of exotic species is prohibited in New Zealand, there are a large number of exotics already here in captivity. Inevitably these escape from time to time – these have not been included in this guide. There is always a chance that you will see one of these escapees, which include:

Budgerigar	*Melopsittacus undulatus*
Cockatiel	*Nymphicus hollandicus*
Golden Pheasant	*Chrysolophus pictus*
Ring-necked Dove	*Streptopelia capicola*
Carolina Wood Duck	*Aix sponsa*
Mandarin Duck	*Aix galericulata*
Rainbow Lorikeet	*Trichoglossus haematodus*
Diamond Dove	*Geopelia cuneata*
Peach or Rosy-faced Lovebird	*Agapornis roseicollis*

Several species of gamebird have also been introduced with very limited success; these have probably died out, but you might see Grey Partridge *Perdix perdix* or Bobwhite Quail *Colinus virginianus*. These species have been included in the main identification section, and you should contact DoC or OSNZ if you do see one or any other introduced alien species.

Hybrids

A number of hybrid species may be observed, the commonest of which is probably the Grey Duck/Mallard cross, which is widespread. There are also a number of populations of feral chickens, descendants of the Red Jungle Fowl *Gallus gallus*, and small numbers of Chinese Swan Goose *Anser cygnoides* hybridised with the Farmyard Goose, itself a domesticated variety of the Greylag Goose *Anser anser*, which may also breed with the Canada Goose. These hybrids have not been included.

Vagrants

Being an isolated oceanic archipelago, New Zealand receives a large number of vagrant bird species, either blown off course by bad weather, or individuals or groups that simply get lost. All species accepted as genuine vagrants have been included in this book, but new species will inevitably appear from time to time and will be included in future editions.

Abbreviations

Two sets of abbreviations appear after each species title: the first indicates the species' conservation status – whether it is in any sort of danger; the second indicates its 'immigration' status – whether it is native, a regular migratory visitor or a vagrant.

Conservation Status

While DoC has its own conservation status table, this is complex, with 13 different categories, so for the purpose of this guide we have used the standard BirdLife International/IUCN classifications. These refer to the worldwide status of the species rather than its status in New Zealand:

CE Critically endangered – in immediate danger of extinction if action not taken
EN Endangered – population declining and liable to go extinct without action
VU Vulnerable – vulnerable and liable to become endangered if remedial action is not taken
NT Near threatened – not currently vulnerable but may become so if steps are not taken to remove existing threats
LC Least concern – no information available to suggest there is a problem

Status

All species will be identified as:

EF Endemic family – species of this family found only in New Zealand
EG Endemic genus – species of this genus found only in New Zealand
E Endemic – species found only in New Zealand
BE Breeding endemic – breeds only in New Zealand but non-breeders and immatures may be seen elsewhere
N Native to New Zealand – breeds here and elsewhere, and is found here year round
BM Breeding migrant – breeds in New Zealand but winters to the north
NBM Non-breeding migrant – regular migratory visitor but does not breed here
RV Regular visitor – non-migratory and non-breeding
OV Occasional visitor – seen regularly but infrequently
V Vagrant – occurs on a very irregular basis, often after storms
I Introduced or alien species
IP Introduced pest or invasive species

Some species listed as vagrants or occasional visitors may in fact be more frequent visitors, but not observed. The increase in interest in birdwatching and the availability of powerful spotting scopes and digital cameras means that identification of rare species is easier and more reliable than in the past.

For the purposes of this book, New Zealand includes the three main islands and their associated offshore islands, the sub-Antarctic islands of Snares, Auckland, Campbell, Antipodes and Bounty, and the subtropical Kermadecs. It does not include any part of continental Antarctica or Norfolk, Lord Howe or Macquarie islands.

Bird Topography

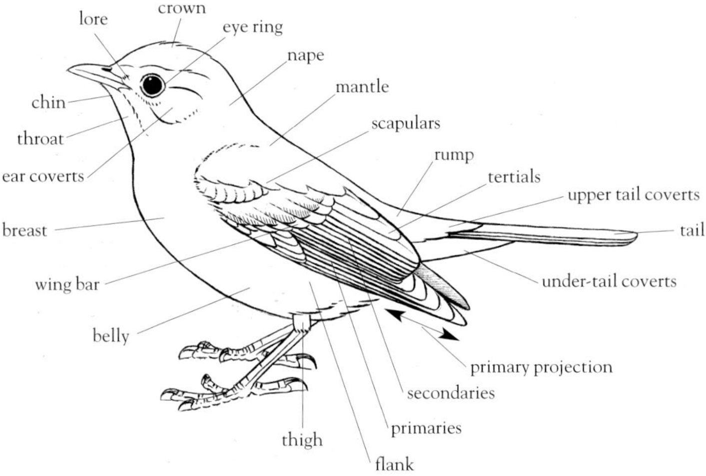

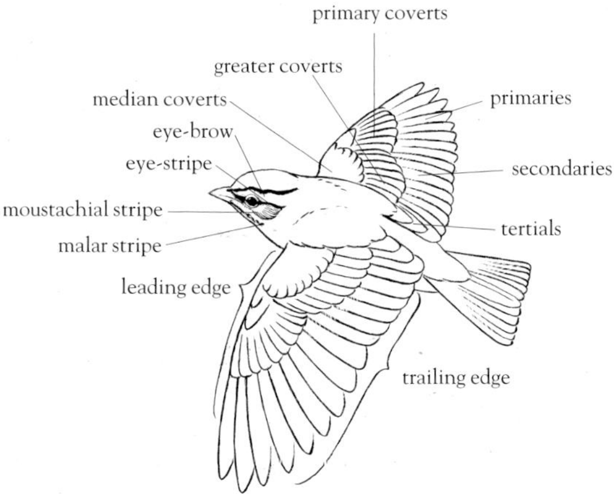

Seabirds

Seabirds constitute the largest group of birds found in and around New Zealand. While many species breed on remote offshore islands and are rarely seen close to the main islands, others are common inshore or within 10km (5nm) of the coast.

Albatrosses – Diomedeidae

New Zealand is the albatross capital of the world, with ten of the 22 species breeding here, though only one species breeds on the main islands. However, it is common to see several species within 10km of the coast. Populations are calculated as Annual Breeding Pairs (ABP).

GREAT ALBATROSSES This group includes the four species of wanderer and the two royals. The plumage of all four species of wanderer is not easily described as it changes with age, becoming gradually whiter. Males are generally whiter than females, and immatures browner than females. This makes identification very difficult, and at times impossible. Birds can be distinguished from other smaller albatrosses not just by their much greater size, but also by the way their wings droop down to form an 'M' shape, especially in light winds.

The Gibson Plumage Index was devised by Doug Gibson in collaboration with members of the New South Wales Albatross Study Group to help describe and identify Wandering Albatrosses. Low scores, i.e. 1,1,1,1 (4) indicate a recently fledged juvenile; high scores, i.e. 6,6,5,4 (21), indicate a mature adult male.

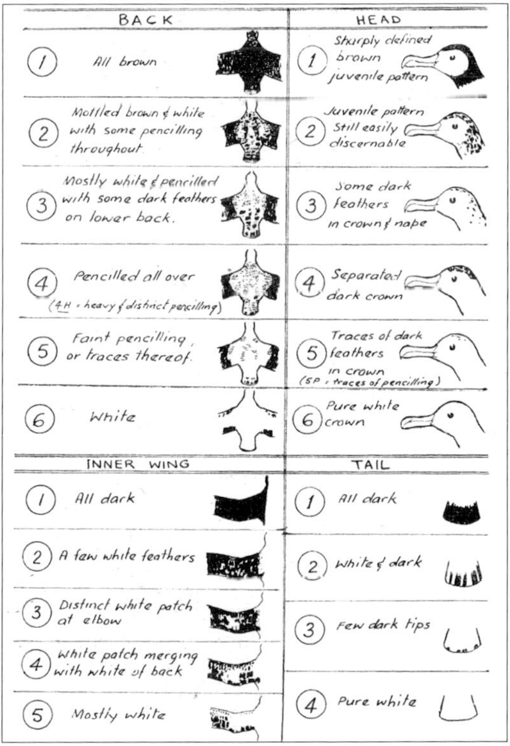

Antipodean Albatross *Diomedea antipodensis* **VU BE**

L 1.1–1.15m WS 3.0–3.25m Wt 5.1–8.3kg

A *huge dark brown and white* seabird with a *massive pink bill*. Plumage varies with age and sex. *Male (A) head* and *body white*, often with pink ear patch, brown vermiculations on mantle and rump, tail dark, sometimes dark cap, *upperwing near black*, white flecking near mantle. Bill huge and pink, *tip yellowish* and distinctly hooked. Legs and feet pinkish grey. Females (B) *much browner*, white belly and lower breast. Subspecies *D. a. gibsoni* both sexes whiter. Immature *largely dark brown* with white face, throat and underwing, becoming whiter with age. **COURTSHIP** A remarkable dance with outstretched wings and bill raised, variety of calls, coos, groans, cackles, etc. Immatures and non-breeders often gather in groups of up to 5 or 6 and display to each other; this practice is called 'gamming'. Mutual preening is also common, appearing to reinforce the pair-bond. **BREEDING** Biennial or less frequent breeder, first breeds aged 7–10. Nest a low truncated cone of vegetation and mud; single white egg December through early February, hatching mid-March through late April, fledging November–December. **FEEDING** Squid, particularly Giant Cuttlefish *Sepia apama* other cephalopods, some fish and carrion. Food taken from the surface or within a metre or so. **P&R** 11,000 ABP with 5,000 *D. a. antipodensis* on Antipodes Is and 6,000 *D. a. gibsoni* on Adams, Disappointment and Auckland islands in the Auckland Is group. *c.*10 ABP on Campbell Is. Breeding population levels appear stable. Some authorities consider *D. a. gibsoni* a separate species. Antipodes Is breeders forage east of NZ as far as Chilean and Antarctic waters. Auckland Is birds forage mainly in the Tasman Sea, and east coast of SI. **T&M** At risk from longline fishing activities, especially unregulated vessels in international waters. Feral pigs on Auckland Is and sub-Antarctic skuas may prey on eggs and small chicks. **BV** Kaikoura (SI), Bay of Plenty (NI) or offshore east and south of NZ and around breeding islands.

Male

Wandering Albatross *Diomedea exulans* **VU RV**

L 1.1–1.35m WS 2.5–3.5m Wt (M) 8.2–12kg (F) 6.7–8.7kg

The whitest of all albatrosses, *adult males can be almost all white*. Females and immatures less so. Significantly larger and whiter than Antipodean and Northern Royal, and lacks the latter's dark line along the cutting edge of upper mandible; *pink ear patches* sometimes visible on males. **FEEDING** Fish, squid, other cephalopods; a natural scavenger. **P&R** 8,500 ABP, mainly on South Georgia, Prince Edward, Marion, Crozet and Kerguelen islands. Circumpolar throughout the southern oceans between 35°S and 65°S. **T&M** Unregulated industrial fisheries. **BV** Offshore, especially to the south and east of NZ.

Northern Royal Albatross *Diomedea sanfordi* **E BE**

ALTERNATIVE NAME Toroa | L 1.15m WS 3.25m Wt 9kg

Larger and whiter than Antipodean but slightly smaller than Southern Royal. *All white apart from upperwing, which is all black*; underwing white apart from *dark trailing edge, and outer leading edge*. Sexes similar though female may show *small dark cap* after moult. *Bill large, hooked and pink with dark edge to both mandibles*. Immatures browner, becoming gradually whiter with age. **COURTSHIP** Typical noisy display at breeding ground as in all the great albatrosses; non-breeding individuals gam during breeding season. *See* Antipodean Albatross. **BREEDING** Biennial or less frequently, first breeding after 6–22 years. Nest a low mound of vegetation and mud. Single egg laid late October through late November, hatching mid-January through late February. Fledging September and October. On the Forty-Fours Is, breeds in dense Chatham Island Button Daisy *Leptinella featherstonii* vegetation. **FEEDING** Fish, squid and other cephalopods, occasionally crustaceans; scavenges near fishing boats. **P&R** 6,500–7,000 ABP, on the Forty-Fours and The Sisters in the Chatham Is. Small population on Taiaroa Head, Dunedin, is only mainland albatross colony anywhere. Circumpolar but much closer to nesting grounds while breeding. **T&M** Unregulated industrial fishing and possible habitat loss due to extreme weather in the very restricted nesting areas. **BV** Off Chatham Is and offshore south and east of NZ.

Southern Royal Albatross *Diomedea epomophora* **VU BE**

ALTERNATIVE NAME Toroa

L 1.07–1.22m WS 3.05–3.60m Wt (M) 9.6–11.5kg (F) 7.1–8.3kg

Largest of all the albatrosses. *Body, head, neck and mantle all white, wings dark at tips but becoming whiter inboard*, especially along leading edge. Underwing white with *black tip and narrow dark trailing edge*. Sexes similar, immatures darker on upperwing with some flecking on mantle and cap. Bill huge, hooked, pink and with *dark cutting edge to both mandibles*. **COURTSHIP** Similar to Northern Royal, slightly less exuberant. **BREEDING** Mainly biennial, occasionally annual and often less frequent. Nest is a low mound of vegetation and mud. Single white egg with pinkish spots at larger end, laid late November through December. Hatching mid-February through March, fledging October–November. **FEEDING** Large squid and other cephalopods, some fish; also scavenges, especially near ships. **P&R** 8,400 ABP, mainly on Campbell Is with small population in the Auckland Is. A few individuals have hybridised with Northern Royals on Taiaroa Head near Dunedin. Circumpolar but not to the north of NZ. Breeding adults closer to nesting areas. **T&M** Unregulated industrial fishing; possibly some loss of breeding habitat due to spread of natural woody vegetation (*Dracophyllum* spp.) through climate change limiting nesting areas. **BV** Around breeding islands and offshore to south and east of NZ.

MOLLYMAWKS A group of medium-sized albatrosses, mainly white underneath and black on the back and upperwings. The head, neck and bill coloration are distinguishing; underwing may also be significant in some species. Sexes are similar.

All are annual breeders and lay a single white egg on a mud pedestal nest up to 30cm high, which is reused each year. Courtship and display is similar in all species with bill rattling, tail fanning, gaping and bowing, often accompanied by loud vocalisations. Mutual preening occurs during and after courtship. Food is generally small fish, squid and other cephalopods, and most scavenge near fishing vessels.

Campbell Albatross *Thalassarche impavida* VU BE

PREVIOUSLY *Diomedea melanophris* Black-browed Albatross or Mollymawk

L 80–95cm WS 2.1–2.5m Wt (M) 2.75–3.8kg (F) 2.2–3.2kg

Body, head and neck white apart from a *black triangular area* in front of and extending behind the eye. *Tail black, upperwing black* with greying over the mantle, *underwing white with black edging*, deeper on leading edge. *Bill bright orange-yellow* becoming peach coloured at tip. Bright pink gape line visible only when feeding young or displaying. *Iris straw-coloured with white crescent behind it*. Immature similar but underwing darker, grey nape and neck, bill dull yellow with dark tip and iris dark. Black-browed Albatross differs in having a dark iris. **BREEDING** Egg laid late September through mid-October, hatching early February, fledging in April and May. **P&R** 23,500 ABP all on Campbell Is and its satellites. Mainly to south of NZ and Australia to 60°S, Tasman Sea and north and east of NZ. **T&M** Unregulated industrial fishing. **BV** At sea off southern and eastern NZ, including Kaikoura Peninsula and Bay of Plenty; also around breeding islands.

Black-browed Albatross *Thalassarche melanophris* E N

PREVIOUSLY *Diomedea melanophris* | L 80–95cm WS 2.1–2.5m Wt (M) 3.3–4.7kg (F) 2.3–3.8kg

Virtually identical to Campbell Albatross, but *underwing has more white with more clearly defined margin between black and white*. *Iris dark*. Immature underwing has less white, similar to Campbell Albatross. **BREEDING** Annual breeder, though some 30% skip a year; egg laid late September and early October, hatching late December, fledging April. **P&R** Most widespread and numerous of all albatrosses. Some 530,000 ABP, mainly in Falklands, southern Chile and South Georgia; in NZ a small number breed in Auckland and Campbell and Snares islands. Circumpolar to 30°S, and up west coast of South America. **T&M** Unregulated industrial fisheries; possibly the commonest scavenger behind fishing vessels and the most seriously impacted. **BV** Offshore south and east of NZ and around breeding islands.

Grey-headed Albatross *Thalassarche chrysostoma* VU N

PREVIOUSLY *Diomedea chrysostoma*

L 70–85cm WS 1.8–2.05m Wt (M) 3.1–4.3kg (F) 2.8–4.2kg

Body white, *head and neck uniform mid-grey with slightly paler forehead. Dark eye-shadow with white semi-circle of skin behind eye*. Upperwing and mantle black, underwing white with *very large dark band on leading edge* and narrower on trailing edge. *Bill black with bright yellow upper ridge, becoming orange-yellow at tip*. Bright orange patch at base of lower mandible enlarged when gaping. Immature has paler, more diffuse grey head and neck, underwing largely dark, bill black. **BREEDING** The only biennial breeding mollymawk. Egg laid October, hatching December and early January, fledging late April or May. **P&R** 92,000 ABP. Very widely distributed, in all three oceans. NZ birds nest on Campbell Is. Circumpolar, as far south as 64°S in summer and as far north as 15°S in winter, when it ranges as far as Peru. **T&M** Unregulated international fisheries. **BV** Offshore to east and south of NZ, especially Kaikoura, Bay of Plenty, and around breeding islands.

THE SHY TRIBE The following four albatrosses were previously described as a single species, *Diomedea cauta*, with four subspecies. They are now recognised as distinct species. All have a small bright orange patch at the base of the lower mandible, which expands along the cheek when gaping or feeding young.

Shy Albatross *Thalassarche cauta* **NT OV**

PREVIOUSLY Tasmanian Shy Albatross *Diomedea cauta*

L 90cm–1.0m WS 2.12–2.56m Wt (M) 3.9–5.1kg (F) 3.2–4.4kg

Body, head and neck all white apart from *light grey shading around back of head and dark eye shadow*. Upperwing and tail black, mantle grey and vermiculated, *primary shafts show white* when wing extended. *Underwing white with narrow leading and trailing edges and tip dark. Bill yellowish-horn colour with yellow tip*. Immatures head rather greyer, bill distinctly grey and with dark tip. Hard to distinguish from White-capped at sea, lack of yellow at base bill ridge may be diagnostic. Salvin's has greyer head and bill has pale yellow ridge and dark tip. **BREEDING** Islands around Tasmania and in the Bass Strait. **FEEDING** Known to swim-dive to 7.4m using wings. Fish, cephalopods and crustaceans, also scavenges. **P&R** 12,200 ABP. Mainly Australian waters and across Indian Ocean to southern Africa. **T&M** Unregulated industrial fisheries. **BV** Irregularly viewed, offshore to east and south, especially Kaikoura or Bay of Plenty.

Salvin's Albatross *Thalassarche salvini* **VU BE**

PREVIOUSLY *Diomedea cauta salvini*

L 90cm–1.0m WS 2.1–2.5m Wt (M) 3.1–4.3kg (F) 2.8–4.2kg

Body white, *head and neck mid-grey*, mantle grey with vermiculations, tail black. Upperwing black with white feather shafts showing at base of primaries when extended. Underwing white with narrow black leading and trailing edges and *dark thumbprint in armpit* where wing attaches to the body. Bill *greyish-horn coloured with pale yellow ridge and dark tip to the lower mandible*. Immature has greyer bill, grey on head and neck less complete. **BREEDING** Egg laid August–September, hatching early November, fledging in March and April. **FEEDING** Fish, cephalopods and crustaceans; a scavenger, little specific information available. **P&R** 30,000 ABP, almost entirely on the isolated Bounty Is; small colony of 1,200 ABP on Snares Is. East to South America and west to southern Africa. **T&M** Unregulated industrial fisheries. **BV** Offshore south and east of NZ, especially Foveaux and Cook straits, Kaikoura, Bay of Plenty and around breeding islands.

Chatham Albatross *Thalassarche eremita* **CE BE**

PREVIOUSLY *Diomedea cauta eremita* Chatham Shy Albatross

L 90cm–1.0m WS 2.1–2.56m Wt (M) 3.6–4.0kg (F) 3.1–3.9kg

Body white, *head and neck dark slate grey*, dark shadow around and forward of eye. Upperwing and tail black, underwing white with narrow dark leading and trailing edges and *thumbprint in armpit*. Mantle dark. *Bill yellow with dark tip to lower mandible*. Juvenile head paler and bill olive-brown with dark tip to both mandibles. Lower left photograph shows a chick. **BREEDING** Breeds only on the Pyramid, an isolated rock in the Chatham Is. Egg laid late August or early September, hatching late October through November, fledging late February though mid-April. Extremely restricted nesting area. **FEEDING** Fish, cephalopods and crustaceans; a scavenger, but little specific information. **P&R** 5,300 ABP, NZ waters occasionally, but mainly to the east of Chatham Is to South America. **T&M** Irregular harvesting of chicks by local people, and unregulated industrial fisheries. **BV** Chatham Is and offshore, especially to the east. Occasionally Kaikoura, Banks Peninsula and Bay of Plenty.

White-capped Albatross *Thalassarche steadi* **NT BE**

PREVIOUSLY *Diomedea cauta steadi* Auckland Shy Albatross
L 90cm WS 2.12–2.56m Wt (M) 3.3–5.3kg (F) 2.6–4.2kg

Largest of the mollymawks. Body, head and neck white with *pale grey wash around ears and back of head, resulting in a distinct white cap; dark triangle in front of eye*. Upperwing black with white visible at base of primaries. Underwing white apart from tips and very narrow black leading and trailing edges *and black 'thumbprint' where it joins the body*. Mantle grey and vermiculated, tail black. Bill large *greyish or horn coloured, ridge yellowish near base and tip greenish yellow*, dark tip to lower mandible especially in younger birds. Immatures similar but with greyer head and neck, bill greyer with dark tip. Difficult to tell from Shy Albatross at sea; Salvin's Albatross has greyer head and yellow ridge to bill. **BREEDING** Egg laid late November, hatching early February, fledging early June. **FEEDING** Fish, cephalopods and crustaceans; also scavenges. Frequently makes short plunge dives and often longer swimming dives. **P&R** 110,000 ABP, in Auckland Is with small population on Bollons Is in the Antipodes group. Mostly to the west across Indian Ocean to southern Africa. **T&M** Unregulated industrial fishing. **BV** Offshore to east and south of NZ and around breeding islands.

Buller's Albatross *Thalassarche bulleri* **NT BE**

PREVIOUSLY *Diomedea bulleri* | L 90cm–1.0m WS 2.1–2.56m Wt (M) 3.6–4.0kg (F) 3.1–3.9kg

Body white, *head and neck mid-grey, crown and forehead pale grey*, dark triangular eye-patch and *white crescent of skin behind eye*. Upperwing and mantle black, underwing white with broad dark band on leading edge and narrower one on trailing edge, wing-tip dark. *Bill black, with upper ridge and lower edge of lower mandible both bright chrome yellow*. Immatures head and neck paler, bill markings dull yellow and tip dark. Two subspecies, Northern *T. b. platei* (A) and Southern *T. b. bulleri* (B). **BREEDING** *T. b. bulleri* on Snares and Solander islands; eggs laid in January, hatching March or April and fledging early September. *T. b. platei* on Chatham and Three Kings islands; eggs laid late October, hatching January and February and fledging in June and July. **FEEDING** Small fish, squid, cephalopods; also scavenges and swim-dives to 1m or more. **P&R** 32,000 ABP: 60% are the Northern subspecies *T. b. platei* on the Forty-Fours and The Sisters in the Chatham Is and a small colony on the Three Kings Is; 40% are Southern subspecies *T. b. bulleri* found in the Snares and Solander Islands. West to south-west Australia and Tasmania, east to west coast of South America as far north as Peru. **T&M** Unregulated industrial fishing. **BV** Offshore to east and south of NZ, especially Kaikoura, Bay of Plenty and around breeding islands.

Indian Yellow-nosed Albatross *Thalassarche carteri* **EN OV**

PREVIOUSLY *Diomedea chlororynchos* Eastern Yellow-nosed Albatross
L 75cm WS 2.0m Wt 2.5–2.9kg

Smallest of the mollymawks. Body white, *head and neck pale grey with distinct dark eye shadow*. Upperwing and mantle black, underwing white with fairly *broad dark leading edge* and much narrower trailing edge, tips dark. *Bill black with bright chrome yellow upper ridge and tip, which narrows to a point at the base*. **BREEDING** Islands in the southern Indian Ocean. **P&R** 36,000 ABP. Indian Ocean and east as far as NZ. **T&M** Unregulated international fisheries. **BV** Offshore to north and east of NZ. Regular winter visitor to eastern Northland, Hauraki Gulf and Bay of Plenty.

Laysan Albatross *Phoebastria immutabilis* VU V

PREVIOUSLY *Diomedea immutabilis*

L 79–81cm WS 1.95–2.03m Wt (M) 3.0–3.6kg (F) 1.95–2.4kg

Large black and white seabird. Body, head, neck and rump white. Upperwing, mantle and tail black, *underwing has black edges, white in middle, but very variable.* Dark patch around eye, grey on cheeks. *Bill peach coloured, yellower at base, grey tip. Legs and feet pink, in flight extend well beyond tail.* **BREEDING** 90% on Laysan and Midway in the Hawaiian Is, small populations on Oahu (Hawaii), Bonin (Japan) and Guadalupe and Revillagigedo (Mexico) islands. **FEEDING** Fish and cephalopods, may be a nocturnal feeder. **P&R** 437,000 ABP. North Pacific only, occasional individuals in NZ waters. **T&M** Unregulated industrial fishing; ingestion of plastic and other flotsam and jetsam. **BV** Offshore, but rarely observed in NZ waters.

Light-mantled Albatross *Phoebetria palpebrata* NT N

PREVIOUSLY *Diomedea fuliginosa*

L 78–90cm WS 1.8–2.20m Wt (M) 2.8–3.1kg (F) 2.6–3.7kg

Large, *elegant, all-dark seabird* with *long, slender, pointed wings.* Body and mantle light to mid-grey, wings and tail dark chocolate brown. *Head sooty black with white crescent behind eye. Bill black with blue sulcus.* **COURTSHIP** Terrestrial, not unlike mollymawks but lower key, and includes a haunting *Pee-oooo* call while sky-pointing. Aerial courtship is dramatic and graceful with pair flying in close synchronised formation. **BREEDING** Biennial, in small groups, favours cliffs and rocky ledges, sometimes inland. Nest a low mud pedestal like that of mollymawks. Single white egg laid end October, hatching early January, fledging June–July. **FEEDING** Small fish and squid, also carrion including penguins and small petrels. May dive (swim down) to as much as 12m. Not a regular scavenger around fishing vessels. **P&R** 19,000–24,000 ABP worldwide; main NZ population (5,000) in Auckland Is, Campbell Is (1,600) and a small colony on Antipodes Is. Circumpolar with breeding populations in all three oceans, from the ice to 30°S. **T&M** No information on the impact of industrial fishing, though the general overfishing of the oceans is cause for concern. **BV** Auckland, Campbell and Antipodes islands and at sea south and east of NZ.

Sooty Albatross *Phoebetria fusca* EN V

PREVIOUSLY *Diomedea fusca* | L 84–89cm WS 2.05m Wt (M) 2.2–3.25kg (F) 2.1–2.8kg

Large, *narrow-winged, all-dark seabird.* Very similar to Light-mantled Albatross but plumage a uniform dark chocolate brown, some white showing at base of primaries. White crescent behind eye. *Bill black with yellow sulcus.* **BREEDING** On islands in southern Indian and Atlantic oceans. Annual breeder, October through mid-June. **FEEDING** Very similar to Light-mantled Albatross. **P&R** 12,500–19,000 ABP. Tasmania west to South America. **T&M** Possibly at risk from industrial fishing, though does not often scavenge. **BV** At sea to the south, Antipodes, Auckland, Campbell islands. Rare in NZ waters.

Petrels and Shearwaters – Procellariidae

Petrels and shearwaters are very well represented in New Zealand. Like albatrosses, they are all members of the order Procellariformes, or tube-noses, a feature best illustrated by the giant petrel, *Macronectes* sp. Many of them are hard to tell apart at sea, and so they are arranged here by plumage coloration to help make identification easier. Sexes have similar plumage. Juveniles have generally less sharply defined markings and plumage coloration.

DARK-PLUMAGED PETRELS

B A Northern Giant Petrel *Macronectes halli* LC N

A L 87cm WS 1.9m Wt (M) 4.2–5.8kg (F) 3.1–4.5kg

Very large, heavy, dark seabird with massive bill. Sexes similar. Back, wings and tail dark, rather mottled grey-brown, *body paler especially throat and face. Bill massive, pinkish-horn coloured with darker reddish-brown tip, very prominent nostrils on top*. Iris pale. In flight has slightly humpbacked appearance and primaries often at distinct angle to rest of wing. Immature (A) near black. Adult (B) very similar to dark phase Southern Giant Petrel but plumage quite variable. Might be confused with immature Wandering Albatross but latter much larger and has white underwing with dark tip. **BREEDING** Nests in loose colonies in tussock, on Auckland, Campbell, Antipodes and Chatham islands, previously on islands off Stewart Is. Single white egg laid mid-August–mid-September, hatching October–November and fledging February. **FEEDING** Scavenger, predator and pirate, can be very aggressive. Fish, cephalopods, birds and carrion – especially of marine mammals. Males in particular predate penguins. **P&R** 17,000–21,000 ABP, NZ population *c.*2,500 ABP. Circumpolar, south to Antarctic Circle. **T&M** Some loss due to unregulated industrial fisheries. **BV** Offshore around coast, including Kaikoura, Bay of Plenty, but particularly southern NZ.

Southern Giant Petrel *Macronectes giganteus* LC RV

A L 90cm WS 1.95m Wt (M) 4.2–5.5kg (F) 3.3–4.7kg

A B Slightly larger than Northern Giant Petrel, but with *near-white head and neck*. Body browner. *Bill horn-coloured, tip greenish*, iris dark. Adult (A) plumage variable. *White phase is all white* apart from some brown barring on underparts. Albino all white with pink bill. Immature (B) is grey-brown. Juvenile as Northern but bill tip greenish. **BREEDING** Ice-free Antarctic and sub-Antarctic islands, particularly in South Atlantic. **FEEDING** As for Northern; sexes appear to feed in distinct areas. **P&R** 97,000, decreasing, circumpolar south to the ice. **T&M** As for Northern. **BV** Offshore to ~30°S. Includes Kaikoura and Bay of Plenty, especially during winter and spring, when it can be more numerous than Northern species.

Juvenile

Providence Petrel *Pterodroma solandri* VU V

L 40cm WS 1m Wt 490g

Large, dark petrel with *long wedge-shaped tail*, underwing has *prominent white patches on primaries and coverts. Face around bill and chin mottled white, bill dark and stout*. **FEEDING** Fish, cephalopods and crustaceans. **P&R** 100,000 on Lord Howe and Norfolk islands. Ranges from Tasman Sea to northwest Pacific. **BV** Rare subtropical vagrant: offshore to north and west of NZ.

White-chinned Petrel *Procellaria aequinoctialis* **VU N**

L 55cm WS 1.4m Wt 1.28–1.39kg

Large, all-dark, broad-winged petrel. Body and wings entirely dark black-brown, *small patch of white under bill* not always apparent. *Bill pale horn coloured with dark sulcus and ridge*. Feet black, *extending beyond tail in flight*. **BREEDING** Nests in burrow, in large colonies in Auckland, Campbell and Antipodes islands. Single white egg laid November–December, hatching January–February, fledging April–May. **FEEDING** Small fish, cephalopods and crustacea, by surface diving; also scavenges. **P&R** 7 million, decreasing. Colonies in sub-Antarctic zones of all three oceans. Circumpolar between 30°S and 60°S. **T&M** Has suffered significantly from unregulated industrial fishing. Predation by rats, feral cats or pigs at some breeding colonies. **BV** Sub-Antarctic islands and NZ continental shelf as far north as Cook Strait in summer and North Cape in winter.

Westland Petrel *Procellaria westlandica* **VU BE**

L 53cm WS 1.34–1.4m Wt 1.2kg

Large, all-dark, broad-winged petrel. Body, wings, tail and head entirely dark black-brown. Bill heavy, pale horn coloured with dark sulcus, ridge and noticeable black tip. **BREEDING** Nests in burrows in colonies in Paparoa Range in Westland. Single white egg laid May, hatching July, fledging November–December. **FEEDING** Fish, squid and crustacea; also scavenges after fishing vessels. **P&R** Best estimate 2,000 ABP, 20,000 individuals. Ranges to Australia and Chile. **T&M** Loss of habitat, feral cats and rats, mining operations. Pest control is helping to reduce predation. **BV** Coastal and offshore waters in winter, Cape Egmont to Fiordland in west and East Cape to Banks Peninsula in east.

Parkinson's Petrel *Procellaria parkinsoni* **VU BE**

ALTERNATIVE NAME Taiko | L 46cm WS 1.15m Wt 680–720g

Large, all-dark petrel. Plumage entirely *dark black-brown*, though underwing has *pale silvery wash on primaries and coverts. Bill pale horn coloured with dark sulcus, ridge and tip*. Significantly smaller than Westland Petrel. **BREEDING** Nests in burrow in loose colonies on Little and Great Barrier islands in the Hauraki Gulf. Single white egg laid November–December, hatching January–February, fledging late April–early July. **FEEDING** Squid, fish and crustacea; surface feeders but swim-dive to 10m. **P&R** 2,500 pairs, 10,000 individual birds. Migrates to eastern tropical Pacific. **T&M** Feral cats on Great Barrier Island, also some loss to unregulated industrial fishing. **BV** During their summer breeding season near Great and Little Barrier islands and at sea around northern half of NI.

Flesh-footed Shearwater *Puffinus carneipes* **LC N**

ALTERNATIVE NAME Toanui | L 47cm WS 1.15m Wt 530–750g

Large, all-dark shearwater. *Body, wings and head entirely dark chocolate brown, tail somewhat wedge-shaped. Bill thin, pale and slightly pinkish with dark tip. Legs and feet pink*, do not extend beyond tail. **BREEDING** Nests in burrows, on islands off the east coast of NI from Northland to East Cape, especially in Hen & Chicken and Mercury groups and Karewa in Bay of Plenty. Egg laid late November–early December, hatching mid-January–mid-February, fledging April. **FEEDING** Small fish and squid, on surface and by swim-diving, often at night; also scavenges. **P&R** 650,000 worldwide, 25,000–50,000 ABP in NZ. Migrates to North Pacific March–May. **T&M** Unregulated industrial fishing, some human predation/harvesting. Breeding colonies in NZ are on protected islands. **BV** Eastern coastal waters, especially NI during spring and summer.

Wedge-tailed Shearwater *Puffinus pacificus pacificus* **LC N**

L 46–47cm WS 97–99cm Wt 320–510g

Medium-sized, broad-winged shearwater with *long, wedge-shaped tail and languid flight*. Polymorphic, commoner form all dark brown with *faint 'M' outline* on upperwing and mantle. Underwing slightly paler on primaries and secondaries but less so than Sooty and non-reflective. Pale morph *mid-brown above, largely white underneath* with dark leading and trailing edges to wings, unlikely in NZ. Intermediate morph likewise. Bill fine and dark, legs and feet pale fleshy white with dark outer surface of tarsus and outer toe, well short of tip of tail. **BREEDING** In burrows on Kermadec Is. Adults return October but single egg laid mid–late December, hatching early February, fledging May–June. **FEEDING** Mainly fish and cephalopods. Mainly surface but can swim-dive to 60m. Solitary or in small groups. **P&R** World population 5 million. Tropical and subtropical Pacific and Indian oceans. **T&M** NZ breeding islands are all protected and feral mammals eradicated. Feral cats, pigs and Norway Rats are an issue at some other sites. **BV** Kermadecs and seas northeast of NZ.

Sooty Shearwater *Puffinus griseus* **LC N**

ALTERNATIVE NAMES Titi, Muttonbird

L 44cm Bill 42mm WS 0.94–1.05m Wt 650–950g

Large, all-dark, heavy-bodied shearwater. Plumage all dark black-brown, *long, narrow wings, light-grey/silvery area on underwing diagnostic. Bill long and slender*. Feet dark grey and extend slightly beyond tail. **BREEDING** In burrows, occasionally crevice or under dense vegetation, on islands and mainland headlands from Three Kings, to Campbell and Macquarie, including islands off Chathams, Stewart. Major colony on Snares. Adults return October, single egg laid late November, hatching mid–late January, fledging late April–mid-May. **FEEDING** Crustaceans and fish, may swim-dive to 40m; often in large, noisy flocks. **P&R** 20 million, very widespread with other populations in Australia and South America, found in all oceans. **T&M** Stoats, cats, rats, dogs and pigs, especially on mainland colonies; some control programmes in place. Some fisheries mortality and traditional harvesting around Stewart I. **BV** Widespread around entire coast, especially southern SI and Kaikoura. NZ birds migrate to North Pacific in winter.

Christmas Island Shearwater *Puffinus nativitatis* **LC V**

L 37cm WS 77cm Wt 300–400g

Medium-sized, all-dark shearwater. Plumage all dark black-brown, *underwing lighter on primaries and secondaries*. Tail rounded, wings somewhat round-tipped, *bill slender and black*. Distinctly smaller than Sooty and Short-tailed and tail proportionally longer. **BREEDING** Central Pacific islands, including Marshall, Line and Marquesas. **FEEDING** Squid and fish, on surface or by underwater pursuit. **P&R** 150,000, mainly central and eastern tropical Pacific. **T&M** None known. **BV** Offshore to the north of NZ.

Short-tailed Shearwater *Puffinus tenuirostris* **LC RV**

L 42cm WS 97cm Wt 550–670g

Medium-sized, all-dark petrel, very similar to Sooty Shearwater but with *variable dull grey underwing, and slightly rounded wing-tips*. A small number of birds have paler underwing. Legs and feet dark *and extend beyond tail. Bill short, dark and fine*. **BREEDING** Colonially in burrows on islands off southern and eastern Australia. **FEEDING** Crustaceans, fish and cephalopods; swim-dives to 20m and recorded to 70m. Often in large flocks. **P&R** 23 million, migrates north to Bering Sea in winter. **T&M** Human predation on chicks and mortality problems possibly due to climate change. **BV** September–April, west coast, Hauraki Gulf, Bay of Plenty.

Kerguelen Petrel *Lugensa brevirostris* **LC OV**

L 34cm WS 89cm Wt 360g

Medium-sized, fast-flying petrel with large head and neck. Plumage all dark slate grey with some *pale mottling on forehead and chin, underwing dark with pale silver on primaries*, especially worn plumage, bill short and dark. **BREEDING** Islands in sub-Antarctic, Atlantic and Indian oceans. **FEEDING** Cephalopods and crustaceans. **P&R** 1 million plus. Circumpolar. **T&M** No known threats. **BV** Offshore, mainly to the south.

Bulwer's Petrel *Bulweria bulwerii* **LC V**

L 27cm WS 67cm Wt 100g

Slim *all sooty-brown* petrel with *long, bluntly pointed tail and long, narrow, pointed wings*. In flight, *upperwing coverts show pale silver* forming light crescent. Tail wedge-shaped when manoeuvring. Bill short and black. Immatures as adults. Rather noddy-like appearance; *flight similar to a storm petrel*. **BREEDING** On islands in all three tropical oceans. **FEEDING** Surface feeder, mainly fish and squid with some crustaceans and sea-striders. **P&R** 0.5–1 million. **T&M** No known threats. **BV** Offshore, a rare vagrant.

Great-winged Petrel *Pterodroma macroptera* **LC OV**

L 40cm WS 97cm Wt 600–700g | TAXONOMIC NOTE Previously conspecific with Grey-faced Petrel *P. gouldi*

Large, all-dark, *long-winged* petrel. Plumage all dark black-brown but *underwing paler on primaries and secondaries. Head greyish around bill and on chin*, but very variable. *Wings long, narrow and finely pointed. Bill dark and heavy*. Legs and feet dark but not visible in flight. Smaller than Grey-faced Petrel, which is lighter around bill. **BREEDING** Offshore islands of southwest Australia and in southern Indian and Atlantic oceans. **FEEDING** Cephalopods, fish and crustaceans. Largely a surface feeder, possibly nocturnal. **P&R** 1.5 million, southern Atlantic and Indian oceans and south of Australia, 20–50°S. **T&M** Predatory mammals on breeding grounds, e.g. mice on Gough I. **BV** Offshore, south and west of NZ.

Grey-faced Petrel *Pterodroma gouldi* **NT BE**

ALTERNATIVE NAMES Oi, Northern Muttonbird | PREVIOUSLY *P. macroptera*; *P. macroptera gouldi* | L 40–43cm WS 1.02m Wt 595–740g | TAXONOMIC NOTE Previously conspecific with Great-winged Petrel *P. macroptera*

A large, all-dark, grey-brown petrel with *slender body and long, narrow wings*. Underwing *primaries and secondaries have silvery wash*, especially after moult. Bill dark but *face around bill and chin distinctly lighter. Tail wedge-shaped to pointed*. Immature has darker face. Call near nesting areas a sharp *O-hio*. **BREEDING** Winter breeder in burrows on cliffs and islands around NI from Northland to New Plymouth in the west and to Gisborne in the east, notably Three Kings, Mercury and Mokohinau groups and in Bay of Plenty on Aldermen, Whale and White islands. Mainland colonies at New Plymouth and Mt Maunganui (Bay of Plenty). Birds arrive at colonies in March, but single egg not laid until late June–July, hatching mid-August–mid-September, fledging early December–late January. **FEEDING** Squid, small fish and crustaceans, probably a night fisher. **P&R** 200,000–300,000 ABP. Tasman Sea and waters to the east of NZ. Non-migratory. **T&M** Cats, rats, Stoats and dogs, especially on mainland colonies, some human predation also. Major colonies are on protected islands, with pest-control programmes in place at several mainland locations. **BV** NI, New Plymouth, Mt Maunganui, Bay of Plenty and offshore around breeding colonies.

BLACK AND WHITE, AND WHITE PLUMAGES These have been divided into two groups: those that are generally dark on top and white underneath; and those with distinctive upperwing patterns, either a light mantle or a distinct 'M' pattern.

White-Plumaged Petrels

Lesser Snow Petrel *Pagodroma nivea* **LC V**
Greater Snow Petrel *Pagodroma confusa* **LC V**
LESSER L 33cm WS 80cm Wt 300g; GREATER L 38cm WS 90cm Wt 400g

Distinctive medium-sized, *all-white long-winged* petrels. *Bill small and black.* Two species identical apart from size, considered by some to be a single species, *P. nivea*. **FEEDING** Surface feeding and swim diving, on crustaceans, fish and cephalopods. **P&R** 4 million. Breeds circumpolar on islands around Antarctica, ranges mainly close to Antarctica but to 55°S in winter. **T&M** No known threats. **BV** Around sub-Antarctic islands, no record from main islands.

Southern Fulmar *Fulmarus glacialoides* **LC RV**
L 48cm WS 1.2m Wt 1kg

Large, very pale gull-like petrel with noticeably straight-winged flight. Upperparts: *head and neck white apart from pale grey on sides*, mantle and innerwing pale grey with darker trailing edge, *wing-tips, primaries and coverts dark with white patch, rump and tail pale grey*. Underparts almost all white, somewhat dark wing-tip and narrow dark trailing edge to wing. *Bill stout, horn coloured with black tip and bluish nasal tubes.* **FEEDING** Surface seizing, mainly fish, crustaceans and cephalopods. **P&R** 4 million. Breeds circumpolar on islands around Antarctica and South Georgia. Ranges throughout Southern Ocean, including NZ and southern Australian waters. **T&M** No known threats. **BV** Offshore, especially to the south.

Black-and-White-Plumaged Petrels

Antarctic Petrel *Thalassoica antarctica* **LC OV**
L 45cm WS 1–1.1m Wt 675g

A stocky, medium-sized black and white petrel with *long, pointed wings*. All-dark uppersides apart from *broad white wing bar and broad white band on tail*. Undersides all white apart from *dark chin and throat*, broad dark band on leading edge and narrow one on trailing edge of wing, and dark tip to tail. Bill short and dark. Often feeds in flocks, may be confused with smaller and more mottled Cape Pigeon. **FEEDING** Krill, squid and small fish; surface feeder and shallow diver. **P&R** Breeds on Antarctic continent, including coastal, inland and ice-free islands. Circumpolar, normally south of 50°S, but irregularly recorded in NZ waters mainly around August–September. **T&M** No known threats. **BV** Offshore to the south of NZ, during winter.

Cape Pigeon *Daption capense* **LC N**

ALTERNATIVE NAME Pintado Petrel | L 39cm WS 85m Wt 440g

Small to medium-sized stocky petrel. Head, nape and tip of tail black, rest of *uppersides mottled black and white with conspicuous white wing-flashes*. Undersides largely *white, black chin and throat, broad black leading edge to wing* and narrower dark band on trailing edge. Bill short and black. Flight on short, rapid wing-beats interspersed with stiff-winged glides. *Gregarious*, often follow and gather round ships. *Daption* is an anagram of 'pintado', which means painted in Spanish. **BREEDING** Nests on ledge, crevice or small cave; single white egg laid November, hatching December–January, fledging mid-February. Subspecies *D. c. australe* on Chatham, Snares, Campbell, Auckland and Bounty islands. *D. c. capsense* on Antarctic coast and sub-Antarctic islands, where breeding 2–3 weeks later. **FEEDING** Surface feeder and scavenger; crustaceans, fish and cephalopods, also offal. **P&R** 2 million, circumpolar from Tropic of Capricorn south to Antarctica. **T&M** No known threats. **BV** Chathams and sub-Antarctic islands, also common off main islands especially during winter, Kaikoura, Cook Strait, Bay of Plenty, Hauraki Gulf.

Cory's Shearwater *Calonectris diomedea* **LC V**

L 46cm WS 113cm Wt 700–970g

Large, broad-winged shearwater. Rather mottled grey-brown back, head and upperwing, tail somewhat pointed and dark. *Body and underwing white with dark wing-tip and trailing edge. Bill large and pale yellow with dark tip*. **BREEDING** Islands in the western North Atlantic and the Mediterranean. **FEEDING** Fish, cephalopods, crustaceans, on surface and by underwater pursuit. **P&R** 200,000 ABP. Mediterranean and North Atlantic, and to 30°S in Atlantic and southwest Indian oceans. **T&M** Human harvesting of chicks on Cape Verde Is. **BV** At sea. Rare in NZ region.

Pink-footed Shearwater *Puffinus creatopus* **VU RV**

L 47cm WS 1.14m Wt 900g

Large, broad-winged shearwater, very similar to Cory's but more uniform grey-brown on back and upperwing, underwing less white, *bill pale grey with dark tip. Legs and feet pink*. **BREEDING** Islands off Chile. **FEEDING** Cephalopods and crustaceans. Surface feeder, also pursues prey by plunge- and swim-diving. **P&R** At least 20,000 ABP, probably more. Breeds on islands off coast of Chile, ranges coastal and offshore waters north to Alaska. **T&M** Human harvesting of chicks, and introduced mammals. **BV** Offshore, especially Kaikoura, also Bay of Plenty.

Grey Petrel *Procellaria cinerea* **NT N**

L 50cm WS 122cm Wt 960–1,200g

Large, *heavy-bodied, long-winged* petrel. Head, back, upperwing and tail dark ashy grey. *Body, undertail coverts and chin white*, underwing uniform dark grey. Bill quite short, *greenish horn with dark ridge, tip and lower mandible*. Legs and feet pinkish grey, *extend beyond tail in flight*. **BREEDING** Winter breeder in burrows, on Antipodes, Campbell and Macquarie islands, and on islands in the South Atlantic and Indian oceans. Adults return to colonies February; single egg laid late March–early April, hatching late May, fledging late September–early December. **FEEDING** Squid, fish and crustaceans. Surface and pursuit diving, may plunge from as high as 8m, and can remain underwater for several minutes. **P&R** 400,000 individuals. Circumpolar and up both coasts of South America. **T&M** Unregulated longline fisheries. Introduced mammalian predators on some breeding islands. **BV** Off east coast including Kaikoura, East Cape and Bay of Plenty, in Cook Strait and around sub-Antarctic islands.

Tahiti Petrel *Pseudobulweria rostrata* NT V

L 39cm WS 84cm Wt 400g

Medium-sized petrel with *long, pointed wings and tail.* All dark grey-brown above, *rump lighter*. Head and neck all dark. *Lower breast, belly and undertail white with dark margin*, underwing grey-brown with *darker leading edge separated from paler primaries and secondaries by a pale band*. Bill short and dark. Rather *languid flight*. **BREEDING** Islands in central and western tropical South Pacific. **FEEDING** Surface feeder, but little information available. **P&R** 20,000. Tropical Pacific. **T&M** Probably threatened by pigs, cats and rats; little data available. **BV** Most likely to north of NZ.

Kermadec Petrel *Pterodroma neglecta* LC N

A A C
C A B

L 38cm WS 92cm Wt 500g

Medium-sized, slightly stocky petrel with long, rather broad wings and somewhat square tail. Two plumage phases, plus intermediate stage (A). Dark phase (B) all dark grey-brown with *greying around bill, white primary shafts on upperwing and light patches on underwing*. Pale phase (C), head and nape pale greyish brown, which extends to form a collar. *Chin throat and body white*, upperwing mid-grey-brown with *white primary shafts. Underwing darker with white patches, especially on primaries. Bill short and black. Flight rather leisurely*. **BREEDING** All year round, but especially summer months; colonial surface nester on Kermadec Is, also on islands in tropical and subtropical South Pacific. **FEEDING** Surface feeder on cephalopods and crustaceans. **P&R** 1,450–200,000, tropical and subtropical South Pacific, ranges into temperate North Pacific out of breeding season. **T&M** Exterminated from Raoul I. by feral cats, which have now been eradicated. No current known threats to NZ population. **BV** Kermadecs and offshore to the north of NZ.

Soft-plumaged Petrel *Pterodroma mollis* LC N

L 34cm WS 89cm Wt 300g

Medium-sized, short-bodied, long-winged petrel. Three colour phases. Pale phase, head, nape and mantle mid-grey extending out towards carpal joint, rump somewhat darker, tail mid-grey. *Distinct dark eye-line*. Wings darker grey-brown. *Forehead, throat and body white, with partial or complete grey collar*, more complete in intermediate phase. *Underwing mid-dark grey-brown with light patches* on primaries. Dark morph (rare) with variable dark streaking on underparts to almost all dark grey-brown with *whitish forehead and chin*. **BREEDING** Colonially in burrows. Egg laid December, hatching January–February, fledging May. On Antipodes Is and islands in the southern Indian and Atlantic oceans. **FEEDING** Cephalopods, crustaceans and some fish, largely by surface fishing. **P&R** 5 million worldwide, several thousand pairs on Antipodes Is and increasing. Birds range around NZ and east to Australia. Other population in southern Indian and Atlantic oceans in temperate zone. **T&M** No known threats. **BV** Offshore, especially to the south and round Antipodes Is.

Chatham Island Taiko *Pterodroma magentae* **CE E**

L 38cm WS 1.02m Wt 450g

Medium-sized, *long-winged, long-tailed* petrel. Head, neck and upper breast dark with pale throat patch, upperparts all dark grey-brown. Underparts, *lower breast, belly and undertail white with dark margin*. Underwing dark but with *lighter primaries and secondaries*. Thought to be extinct until rediscovered on Chatham Is in 1978. Very similar to Phoenix Petrel. **BREEDING** Colonial in burrows in forested southwest of main Chatham I. Egg laid late November, hatching mid-late January and fledging late April–early May. **FEEDING** Thought to be largely squid. **P&R** 120–150 only, thought to range largely to south and east of Chatham Is. **T&M** Pigs, cats, rats, possum, weka, stray dogs, habitat loss and very small population. Formerly, human predation. Currently subject to a concentrated protection and management regime, including intensive control of predators and relocation to a predator-fenced location. **BV** Chatham Is and at sea to south and east.

Phoenix Petrel *Pterodroma alba* **EN V**

L 35cm WS 83cm Wt 270g

Small petrel with long, pointed wings and a long tail. All dark grey-black above, head and neck all dark, *whitish throat*, lower *breast, belly and undertail white*. Underwing dark, especially along leading edge, *but with thin white band* in front of dark up to carpal joint, *lighter primaries and secondaries. Bill short and dark*, legs and feet dark. **BREEDING** Tropical and subtropical islands in central Pacific. **FEEDING** Largely squid, with some fish and invertebrates. **P&R** 30,000, decreasing. Confined largely to central and western tropical Pacific. **T&M** Some feral cat predation and vulnerable to rats, but no firm evidence of reason for decline. **BV** Rare vagrant, most likely around northern NI.

Fluttering Shearwater *Puffinus gavia* **LC BE**

ALTERNATIVE NAME Pakaha | L 34cm WS 75cm Wt 300–350g

Small, long-winged shearwater. Uppersides mid- to dark chocolate brown, *extending to form partial collar*. Undersides white or near white apart from *dark tips to underwings* and trailing edge, dusky grey triangular mark in armpits, *white extends up towards rump*. Tail short, *wedge-shaped with dark tip. Bill long, pale and slender with distinct hooked tip*, legs and feet flesh coloured. Flight fast on stiff wings, frequent glides. **BREEDING** Nocturnal burrow nester, near coast on islands around NI and the Marlborough Sounds. Egg laid September–mid-October, hatching November, fledging late December through January. **FEEDING** Mainly fish and some krill, on surface or by pursuit diving, to depths of several metres. Often in large flocks of up to 20,000, and with other seabirds. Often waits around fishing boats. **P&R** 100,000, mainly coastal NZ waters, especially NI, but in winter to coastal south and eastern Australia. **T&M** Vulnerable to rat predation, though most colonies are on pest-free islands. **BV** Coastal waters around NI, especially Cook Strait, Hauraki Gulf and Bay of Plenty.

Hutton's Shearwater *Puffinus huttoni* **EN BE**

L 37cm WS 75cm Wt 350g

Small, dark brown and white shearwater, very similar to but slightly *heavier and darker* than Fluttering. Upperparts entirely dark black-brown, underparts slightly dirty white with *partial darker collar*, underwing dirty white with darker leading edge, tips, trailing edge and armpits. *Bill pale, long and slender with distinct hooked tip. Flight rapid wing-beats and gliding on stiff wings.* **BREEDING** Colonially in burrows, at 1,200–1,800m in Seaward Kaikoura Range, SI. Egg laid late October–mid-November, hatching late December–January, fledging March and early April. **FEEDING** Mainly small fish and krill, surface-feeding or pursuit-diving to 2–3m. May feed in very large flocks up to 20,000 birds. **P&R** 300,000 mainly coastal NZ waters in summer, but Australian and Tasmanian waters in winter. **T&M** Late snow, erosion of steep slopes, Stoats – control measures in place in some colonies. Occasionally Kea take the young. **BV** NZ coastal waters in summer, especially east coast, Kaikoura and Cook Strait.

Manx Shearwater *Puffinus puffinus* **LC V**

L 34cm WS 82cm Wt 450g

Small, *long-winged, long-tailed*, black and white shearwater similar to Fluttering. Upperparts dark blackish grey, underparts white apart from *broad dark, sharply defined wing-tips and trailing edge. Variable dark smudging on innerwing*. Tail long, *bill pale, slender and long*. Flight stiff-winged. **BREEDING** Islands in North Atlantic. **FEEDING** Mainly fish, some cephalopods. **P&R** 1.1–1.2 million. North and South Atlantic, a rare vagrant to NZ. **BV** Chance offshore sightings only.

Little Shearwater *Puffinus assimilis* **LC BE**

L 27cm WS 63cm Wt 240g

Very small, rather short-winged shearwater. Upperparts all dark grey-black, underparts white with *dark wing-tips and narrow band on trailing edge. White on face extends up to or above the eye. Wings short, straight, rounded. Bill fine and dark, legs and feet grey-blue*. Four subspecies, 2 of which (*P. a. kermadecensis* and *P. a. haurakiensis*) breed only in NZ. **BREEDING** Colonial nester in burrow, rock crevice or in coastal scrub. *P. a. kermadecensis* breeds in the Kermadecs, eggs laid mid-June–July, hatching August–mid-September and fledging October–November. *P. a. haurakiensis* breeds on islands off north and east NI and is approximately 1 month later. **FEEDING** Surface feeder and pursuit fisher, mainly cephalopods, krill and small fish. **P&R** 900,000. 100,000 ABP of the 2 endemic subspecies. Northern NZ and across the Tasman as far as central Indian Ocean. **T&M** Cannot survive in presence of most alien pest predators. **BV** NI continental shelf waters, especially Coromandel, Mercury Is, Bay of Plenty, Hauraki Gulf, Poor Knights and further north to Kermadecs. Generally solitary or small flocks.

Sub-Antarctic Little Shearwater *Puffinus elegans* **LC N**

L 28cm WS 64cm Wt 250g

Small shearwater, very similar to Little. Dark grey-black above, white below. *Dark extends below eye*. Wings short, straight and quite rounded. Smallest of the shearwaters. **BREEDING** Colonial in burrows or rock crevices. Egg laid late August–early October, hatching late October–December and fledging mid-January–March. Colonies on Antipodes and Chatham islands. **FEEDING** Surface feeding and pursuit diving, mainly cephalopods, krill and fish. **P&R** ~100,000 breeding pairs, mainly in the Antipodes Is. Ranges widely in sub-Antarctic waters. **T&M** No known threats. **BV** Offshore to south and east of NZ, in winter, especially Kaikoura, Chathams and Antipodes Is.

Newell's Shearwater *Puffinus newelli* VU V

L 33cm WS 79cm Wt 380g

Small, straight-winged shearwater, similar to but larger than Little. *Near black above, white below with broad black wing-tips and trailing and leading edges*, tip of undertail dark, bill dark, *white thumbprint* extending up towards rump. Eye surround black but *white underside extends up behind eye*. **BREEDING** Islands in the Hawaiian Group. **FEEDING** Fish and squid caught by surface feeding and pursuit swimming. **P&R** 35,000. Tropical North Pacific around Hawaiian Is. **BV** Chance sightings offshore.

Common Diving Petrel *Pelecanoides urinatrix* LC BE

ALTERNATIVE NAME Kuaka | L 22cm WS 35cm Wt 130g

Very small, dumpy petrel with *short, rounded wings* and *noticeably short neck and tail*. All dark above apart from *white markings on scapulars*. Body white apart from *greyish neck and collar*. Underwing off-white with darker tips and trailing edge. *Bill dark and stubby*. Legs and feet blue and may extend beyond tail. Six subspecies of which 2 (*P. u. urinatrix* and *P. u. chathamensis*) breed only in NZ. Dives for long periods and appears to fly straight out of the water. At times it appears to have trouble getting airborne; rapid wing-beats, flies close to surface. **BREEDING** Colonial nesters in burrows, often densely packed, timing dependent on latitude. **Northern Diving Petrel** *P. u. urinatrix* breeds on islands around NI, eggs laid in August, hatching mid-October–November and fledging late November–December. **Southern Diving Petrel** (A) *P.u.chathamensis* breeds on Stewart, Chatham and the sub-Antarctic islands and is up to 2 months later. **Sub-Antarctic Diving Petrel** *P. u. exsul* breeds worldwide; in NZ on Auckland, Antipodes and Campbell island groups. **FEEDING** Largely crustaceans, krill, etc., caught by pursuit diving using wings to a depth of 60m. **P&R** 16 million. Circumpolar but not long-distance travellers, though found well out to sea, especially out of breeding season. **T&M** Introduced predatory mammals on some island breeding grounds. Most major NZ breeding islands now have protective status and predatory mammals removed. **BV** Widespread around coasts, especially NI, and further offshore, especially during breeding season. Cook Strait, Bay of Plenty, Hauraki Gulf.

South Georgia Diving Petrel *Pelecanoides georgicus* LC N

L 18cm WS 32cm Wt 120g

Very small, dumpy petrel, very similar but smaller than Common Diving Petrel. All dark above with *some white on scapulars*, largely white below, with distinct *white crescent extending up behind eye*. Bill stubby and dark, *legs and feet blue and extend just beyond tail*. **BREEDING** Circumpolar, breeding on sub-Antarctic islands. Colonial in burrows, in sand dunes on Codfish I. Egg laid early November, hatching late December–January, fledging February–March. **FEEDING** Small krill, fish and squid caught by pursuit diving from surface using wings underwater. **P&R** 15 million worldwide but only 100 pairs or so on Codfish I. Codfish I. population believed to forage well offshore to south of NZ near edge of continental shelf. **T&M** Colonies in Auckland and Chatham islands destroyed by human interference and introduced pests. Codfish I. population was formerly threatened by introduced predatory animals but these have now been eradicated. **BV** Around Stewart I. and further south.

White-necked Petrel *Pterodroma cervicalis* VU N

L 43cm WS 97cm Wt 450g

Medium-sized, long-tailed petrel with *long, narrow, pointed wings. White forehead, chin, throat, neck and collar with black cap extending to below eye*. Upperwing, back and tail mid-grey with *black 'M' pattern*. Undersides white, underwing white with dark tip and leading edge extending diagonally from carpal joint towards body; thin, dark trailing edge. Bill sturdy and dark. *Flight graceful with few wing-beats*. Very similar to Juan Fernandez Petrel. **BREEDING** Nocturnal summer breeder in burrow, on Macaulay Is in Kermadecs, also a few on Philip and Norfolk islands. **FEEDING** Surface feeder, possibly also catches prey in aerial pursuit; diet largely unknown but includes cephalopods. **P&R** 100,000. Bulk of population in Kermadec Is, migrates to northern Pacific in winter. Normally pelagic and solitary. **T&M** Population on Raoul I. exterminated by feral cats and Norway Rats, but no other known threats. **BV** Kermadecs and offshore to the north of NZ.

White-headed Petrel *Pterodroma lessonii* LC N

L 43cm WS 1.09m Wt 650g

Large, *long-winged*, grey and white petrel. *Head and neck white with dark patch around and below eye*. Mantle grey, becoming darker on rump. Outer upperwing dark grey-brown with primaries and secondaries rather lighter than coverts. *Innerwing grey, forming a V shape with mantle*. Overall impression is of a distinct 'M' pattern. Tail white. Body white apart from partial grey collar. *Bill dark and stubby*. **BREEDING** Nocturnal colonial burrower; egg laid mid-November–mid-December, hatching mid–late January, fledging May–June. Antipodes, Auckland and Campbell islands. **FEEDING** Surface feeder, mainly cephalopods and crustaceans. **P&R** 600,000. Circumpolar, to *c.*35°S. **T&M** Feral cats on Macquarie I.; no known threats in NZ. **BV** Offshore, especially around sub-Antarctic islands.

Juan Fernandez Petrel *Pterodroma externa* VU V

L 43cm WS 97cm Wt 430g

Slim, long-winged, long-tailed petrel. *Dark grey head darker behind the eye, forehead white*. Nape and mantle grey, rump dark, tail grey *with darker tip*, somewhat pointed. Upperwing *dark with 'M' pattern* formed by grey mantle extending onto upperwing. *Body and underwing white with grey partial collar*, black wing-tips, short black mark from carpal joint towards body, and dark, narrow trailing edge. *Bill heavy and black*. **BREEDING** Islands off coast of Chile. **FEEDING** Flying fish and squid by aerial pursuit and surface seizing. **P&R** 3 million. Ranges north from breeding area to Mexico and Hawaii. Several NZ records east of main islands, and seen ashore on South East I., Chatham Is. **T&M** No specific threats but single breeding site makes species vulnerable. **BV** Offshore, chance observation.

Mottled Petrel *Pterodroma inexpectata* **NT BE**

ALTERNATIVE NAME Korure | L 34cm WS 85cm Wt 330g

Medium-sized, grey and white petrel. *Forehead white*, head and nape dark, mottled grey with *darker area behind eye*. Upperwing dark, forming 'M' with light grey mantle, rump darker, tail long, pale grey. *Undersides white with variable mid-grey belly*. Underwing white with dark tips, very narrow trailing edge and narrow leading edge becoming *heavy and black around carpal joint and angling back across the wing* towards, but not as far as, the abdomen. *Bill black and stubby*. **BREEDING** Nocturnal colonial burrower; egg laid December, hatching late January–mid-February, fledging May. Colonies on islands around southern NZ, Fiordland, Stewart and Snares islands. **FEEDING** Fish, cephalopods and crustaceans, surface feeder and shallow plunger; may feed in large flocks. **P&R** 1.5 million; decreased in past, now stable or increasing. Pelagic and highly migratory, ranging from Antarctica to the Bering Sea. **T&M** Currently only on predator-free islands, previously widespread on mainland. **BV** Offshore, especially around southern NZ and the offshore islands.

Buller's Shearwater *Puffinus bulleri* **VU BE**

L 44cm WS 98cm Wt 400g

Medium-sized shearwater with *long, broad wings and long, somewhat pointed tail*. Head dark as far as eye, *neck and mantle almost blue-grey*, darker on rump, grey tail with dark tip. Very obvious *dark 'M' across wings and mantle*, wing-tips dark. Undersides almost *all white with dark wing-tips* and very narrow dark band on leading edge and wider one on trailing edge. White undertail with dark margin. *Bill pale, long, slender and hooked*. **BREEDING** Nocturnal and colonial in burrows and rock crevices on Poor Knights Is only. Breeding very synchronised; egg laid late November, hatching mid-January and fledging in May. **FEEDING** Surface feeder with some shallow plunge diving, mainly for crustaceans and fish. **P&R** 2.5 million. NZ breeder, but ranges across Tasman Sea and throughout Pacific apart from most western areas. **T&M** Very restricted breeding range. Previously predated by feral pigs, now removed. Vulnerable to any future introductions. **BV** Quite common in NZ coastal waters, especially east coast of NI, including Bay of Plenty, Hauraki Gulf and Bay of Islands, and to Chatham Is.

Blue Petrel *Halobaena caerulea* **LC RV**

L 29cm WS 66cm Wt 200g

Small, rather delicate prion-like petrel. *Upperparts largely blue-grey with distinct dark 'M' pattern across wings and mantle*. *Cap darker, black patch under eye, forehead white*. Tail darker with white tip. Underparts almost all white with *grey partial collar* and outertail feathers, tip white. *Bill small and black*. **FEEDING** Surface feeder but can swim-dive to 6m. Mainly crustaceans, fish and squid. **P&R** 3 million. Circumpolar, mainly Antarctic and sub-Antarctic but north to about 30°S. **T&M** No known threats. **BV** Offshore during autumn and winter months.

Cook's Petrel *Pterodroma cookii* **VU BE**

ALTERNATIVE NAME Titi | L 30cm WS 66cm Wt 200g

Small, *slim, long-winged petrel.* Upperparts all pale grey with *dark 'M' across wings and back and white forehead, tip of tail dark grey.* Undersides all white apart from dark shoulder-patch, dark wing-tips and trailing edge, *and narrow black carpal bar* extending a short way towards body, and to wing-tips along leading edge. *Bill thin and black.* Larger than Pycroft's, with longer, thinner bill and lighter grey cap. **BREEDING** Colonial forest burrower on Great and Little Barrier islands in the north and Codfish I., off Stewart I. in the south. In north, egg laid late October–early December, hatching December–January, fledging March to mid-April; one month later in south. **FEEDING** Surface feeder on cephalopods, fish and crustaceans. **P&R** 1.25 million. Round NZ during breeding season but ranges throughout northern and eastern Pacific. **T&M** Colony on Great Barrier very small but conservation measures in hand to eliminate cats and rats. **BV** Offshore and around breeding areas during breeding season.

Pycroft's Petrel *Pterodroma pycrofti* **VU BE**

L 28cm WS 53cm Wt 170g

Small, relatively *long-winged, long-tailed* petrel. Virtually indistinguishable from Cook's Petrel in the field unless both species are present. Pale to mid-grey above, *slightly darker cap, dark eye mark and white forehead, and prominent 'M' mark on wings and back.* Undersides white, dark wing-tip, very narrow trailing edge. *Narrow dark carpal band running towards body and narrowly along leading edge to tip. Bill small and black.* **BREEDING** Nocturnal burrower in native bush; egg laid late November–early December, hatching January, fledging late March–early April. Breeds only on Poor Knights, Hen & Chickens, Mercury and Ririwha islands, and recently introduced to Cuvier I., all off northeast of NI. **FEEDING** Little information; surface feeder, mainly on cephalopods. **P&R** 6,000–8,000. Little known about movement out of breeding season, but recorded from north and central Pacific. **T&M** No current threats, but clearly vulnerable to alien predators. **BV** Bay of Plenty northwards, especially during breeding season.

Gould's Petrel *Pterodroma leucoptera* **VU RV**

L 30cm WS 60cm Wt 185g

Small, rather stocky petrel with relatively *short, rounded wings and long, rounded tail. Forehead white, head and nape black extending down neck like a hood* or wig. Wings, mantle and tail mid-grey with distinct *dark 'M' pattern* and *dark tip to tail.* Undersides white apart from dark wing-tips and trailing edge, black leading edge from tip to carpal joint, then *broad and tapering black bar in towards body. Dark tip to tail. Bill short and black.* **BREEDING** Islands off Australia and New Caledonia. **FEEDING** Surface feeder; mainly cephalopods and fish; very little data. **P&R** 20,000. Ranges through Tasman Sea and across southern and central Pacific as far as Galapagos Is 90°W. **T&M** Loss of habitat and predators on Australian breeding islands have impacted population. **BV** Offshore to west and north of NZ.

Collared Petrel *Pterodroma brevipes* **NT V** L 28–30cm WS 55cm

Small, tropical, polymorphic petrel. Light phase very similar to Gould's but with longer, more pointed tail, upperwing and back lighter grey. Dark morph *underbody all dark grey* apart from throat; underwing grey-washed. Intermediate has *dark collar.* **FEEDING** As for Gould's. **P&R** To 10,000; breeds on islands in Fiji and Vanuatu; ranges into tropical eastern Pacific. **T&M** Predation at nest by mammalian predators: pigs, mongooses, rats. **BV** Chance sighting, offshore to north, Three Kings Is.

Stejneger's Petrel *Pterodroma longirostris* **VU V**

L 26–28cm WS 66cm Wt 140g

Small, *slim, long-winged, long-tailed* petrel. *Forehead white, head and eye black*, nape, wings, mantle and tail dark grey with distinct *dark 'M' shape, tip of tail dark*. Undersides white but grey on nape forms partial collar, wing-tip and trailing edge dark, thin black line from tip to carpal joint and *narrow black carpal bar extending towards body*. Bill quite short and dark in spite of species' scientific name! Smaller than Gould's Petrel. **BREEDING** Juan Fernandez Is off the coast of Chile. **FEEDING** No specific information available. **P&R** 400,000. Ranges into tropical and northern Pacific. **T&M** Feral cats are a threat. **BV** Offshore, most likely to north and east of NZ.

Black-winged Petrel *Pterodroma nigripennis* **LC N**

L 29cm WS 67cm Wt 180g

Small, *slim, long-winged, long-tailed*, grey and white petrel. *Forehead white; cap grey, becoming darker on nape; distinct black eye-patch*. Mantle mid-grey, becoming much darker on wing, with *faint 'M' pattern*, much more evident in some individuals, possibly immatures. *Rump dark, tail pale grey with dark tip*. Undersides white but with *partial grey collar and broad, dark wing-tips and trailing edge. Broad black bar either side of carpal joint extending almost to body*. Bill short and black. **BREEDING** Semi-nocturnal colonial burrower; egg laid late December–mid-January, hatching February–early March, fledging April–May; 2 weeks later in Chathams. Colonies on Three Kings and East Portland islands (off East Cape), Kermadecs and Chatham islands, as well as islands in tropical southwest Pacific. **FEEDING** Surface feeder, on cephalopods and fish; very little data. **P&R** 8–10 million, expanding. Migrates north to central and northern Pacific out of breeding season. **T&M** Colony on Raoul I. was exterminated by feral cats and Norway Rats, elsewhere, population expanding. **BV** Offshore northern and western NZ during breeding season.

Chatham Petrel *Pterodroma axillaris* **EN E**

L 30cm WS 68cm Wt 230g

Small, rather *long-winged, long-tailed* petrel with distinctive underwing markings. *Forehead white, cap and nape pale grey with dark eye-patch and ear coverts*, mantle grey, wings generally darker but with *indistinct 'M' pattern. Rump dark, tail mid-grey with darker tip*. Undersides largely white but *partial grey collar* and dark wing-tips and trailing edge; *very broad carpal bar extends to the body and the trailing edge, widening to include most of the axillaries*. Bill small and black. **BREEDING** Nocturnal burrow breeder in native bush. Egg laid late December, hatching February–March and fledging May–mid-June. Single colony on South East I. in Chathams. **FEEDING** Probably surface feeder on cephalopods and fish; no data available. **P&R** 500. No information on range; probably to east of Chathams, but possibly also to north. **T&M** Competition for burrows with prions and diving petrels. **BV** Chatham Is and to south of them.

PRIONS Prions are small, rather broad-winged petrels with generally pale blue-grey plumage and pale, often very large bills. All six species are found in New Zealand waters.

Slender-billed Prion *Pachyptila belcheri* LC RV

L 26cm WS 56cm Wt 150g

One of the *smallest and palest* of prions. Upperparts: *forehead and cap light grey with large white eyebrow and modest dark eye-stripe*. Wings, back and tail pale blue-grey with *indistinct 'M' markings*. Very tip of tail dark. Underparts white apart from slightly darker tip to wing, *partial grey collar* and *small dark tip to tail*. Bill pale blue-grey and slender (11mm) compared to other prions. **BREEDING** Chile, Falkland Is, Crozet and Kerguelen islands. **FEEDING** Crustaceans, fish and cephalopods, surface-seizing and pursuit-diving to 7.5m. **P&R** 7 million. Ranges mainly South Atlantic and south Indian Oceans; regular visitor to NZ waters, especially during winter. **T&M** No known threats, though previously considered a pest in Falklands. **BV** Offshore, especially west coast, in winter.

Salvin's Prion *Pachyptila salvini* LC RV

L 28cm WS 56cm Wt 160g

Typical prion, with pale, fairly broad bill. Upperparts, forehead and head mid-grey with *distinct white eyebrow and dark eye-stripe*. Otherwise mid-blue-grey with *distinct 'M' pattern across wings. Dark tip to tail quite broad*. Underparts white or pale grey with *light grey partial collar*, a hint of dark on the wing-tip and dark tip to tail. Bill pale blue-grey and *broad (17mm)*. Very similar to, but slightly smaller than, Broad-billed and with narrower pale bill. **BREEDING** Islands in southern Indian Ocean. **FEEDING** Surface feeder, especially filtering, as with Broad-billed. Mainly crustaceans, also fish and cephalopods. **P&R** 12 million. Ranges to temperate and sub-Antarctic waters from southern Africa to NZ. **T&M** Mammalian predators on some islands, but not a significant threat. **BV** Offshore, especially to south and west, mainly during winter months.

Antarctic Prion *Pachyptila desolata* LC N

L 27cm WS 56cm Wt 150g

Typical prion, very similar to Salvin's and Broad-billed but pale bill smaller and narrower. Forehead and cap mid-grey, *white eyebrow and dark eye-stripe*; upperparts otherwise mid-blue-grey with *pronounced 'M' pattern on wings and back. Narrow black tip to tail*. Underparts white or pale grey with grey partial collar, slightly darker wing-tips and trailing edge and dark tip to tail. *Bill pale and relatively narrow (14mm)*. Very similar to Salvin's but with narrower bill, present during summer. **BREEDING** Largely nocturnal, densely colonial in burrows or crevices. Egg laid December, hatching late January–February, fledging mid-March–April, possibly earlier in NZ colonies. Breeds on Auckland and possibly Campbell islands, on islands in southern Indian and South Atlantic oceans, and off Antarctica. **FEEDING** Surface feeding and filtering, mainly crustaceans but also fish and cephalopods. **P&R** 50 million. Virtually circumpolar and up both coasts of South America. **T&M** Some predation by introduced mammalian predators, also habitat loss on South Georgia due to fur seals. **BV** Offshore, especially to south around breeding grounds.

Fairy Prion *Pachyptila turtur* **LC N**

ALTERNATIVE NAME Titi Wainui | L 25cm WS 56cm Wt 125g

Smallest of the prions. Upperparts, crown and forehead grey, *dark around eye and ear coverts, white bar above eye*. Otherwise mid-blue-grey with *dark 'M' pattern on upperwing and broad dark tip to tail*. Undersides mainly very pale grey to white, somewhat darker on side of neck and dark tip to tail. *Bill light grey, wide (11mm) and stubby,* smaller than that of similar Fulmar Prion. **BREEDING** Nocturnal colonial burrower. Breeding time varies with latitude. In north, egg laid mid-October, hatching late November, fledging early January. Colonies on many islands around NZ, as well as in Chatham, Snares and Antipodes islands. Also on islands off Australia, and in south Indian and South Atlantic oceans. **FEEDING** Surface feeding and dipping mainly for crustaceans, with some fish and occasional cephalopods. **P&R** 5 million. Ranges around NZ and across Tasman Sea. **T&M** No known threats. **BV** Offshore around coast, especially near breeding colonies, Cook Strait and Kaikoura.

Fulmar Prion *Pachyptila crassirostris* **LC N**

L 28cm WS 60cm Wt 140g

Small prion, very similar to but slightly larger than Fairy Prion. Upperparts mid-blue-grey with distinct *dark 'M' across wings*, and *broad dark tip to tail*; forehead and cap grey, *dark eye-patch and ear coverts, white stripe above eye*. Underparts all pale grey, fading to whiter apart from dark tip to tail. Bill pale grey and *wide (13mm)*. Distinguished from Fairy Prion by larger bill, and from other prions by broad black band on tail. **BREEDING** Colonies on Auckland, Snares, Bounty and Chatham islands, also Heard I. in Indian Ocean. Diurnal, at least on Bounty I.; colonial, under rocks and in crevices. Egg laid late October–November, fledging probably mid–late February. No specific information available. **FEEDING** Surface feeding and shallow pursuit-diving, including juvenile goose barnacles, amphipods and pteropod molluscs. **P&R** 200,000. Two subspecies: *P. c. crassirostris* (endemic subspecies) on Chathams, Snares and Bounty islands; *P. c. flemingi* on Auckland Is and Heard I. in Indian Ocean. Thought to remain relatively close to breeding grounds. **T&M** No known threats. **BV** Offshore and around Chatham Is and other breeding grounds.

Broad-billed Prion *Pachyptila vittata* **LC N**

ALTERNATIVE NAME Parara | L 28cm WS 60cm Wt 200g

Largest prion, with distinctive *dark, duck-like bill*. Upperparts, forehead and crown dark grey, *dark eye-stripe with white eyebrow*. Otherwise blue-grey with *strongly marked dark 'M' pattern across wings*. Narrow dark tip to tail. Undersides almost entirely white or greyish white with *grey partial collar*, slightly darker wing-tip and dark tip to tail. *Bill very large, broad (21mm) and steely grey*. **BREEDING** Nocturnal and colonial in burrows or rock crevices, under buildings. Egg laid late August–mid-September, hatching late October, fledging mid-December. Varies with location. Colonies on Snares, Chathams and islands around Stewart I. and SI. Also South Atlantic. **FEEDING** Surface feeding with shallow dives; filters water through lamellae in very broad bill similar to baleen whales. Feeds on crustaceans, especially copepods, and cephalopods. **P&R** 15 million. NZ population remains relatively close to breeding area, possibly into Tasman Sea. Larger population on Tristan and Gough islands in South Atlantic. **T&M** Predated by cats, rats and skuas, but apparently not in significant decline. **BV** Offshore around NZ, especially during breeding season close to breeding grounds.

STORM PETRELS Storm petrels are the smallest of all pelagic seabirds, and are largely dark in colour. Also known as 'sea swallows', they are graceful and often feed hovering just above the surface, or even 'walk on the water' using their webbed feet. Of the 23 species, seven are found in NZ waters with six species breeding and one, the recently rediscovered New Zealand Storm Petrel, being endemic.

Wilson's Storm Petrel *Oceanites oceanicus* LC RV

L 17cm WS 40cm Wt 35g

Small, dark storm petrel with *long legs*. Plumage all sooty black apart from conspicuous *white rump and indistinct pale carpal bar on upperwing coverts*. Tail square or slightly indented. *Legs are long and often protrude beyond tail*; feet and legs black with yellow webs. **BREEDING** Islands around Antarctica including Ross Sea sector, Falklands and Tierra del Fuego. **FEEDING** Surface feeder, often using feet to patter or 'walk on water'. Feeds on cephalopods, gastropods, crustaceans and carrion, varying with location. **P&R** 20 million. Migrates to northern hemisphere in all three oceans. Three subspecies, but not distinguishable in the field. **T&M** No known threats. **BV** Offshore during spring and autumn migrations, when occasionally seen passing through NZ waters, especially to south and off east coast, Kaikoura and Bay of Plenty.

New Zealand Storm Petrel *Oceanites maorianus* CE E

L 17cm WS 38cm Wt 30–36g

Small, black and white storm petrel. Upperparts, head and chest dark chocolate brown apart from *white rump and inconspicuous pale crescent carpal bar. Underparts white and uniquely patterned with variable dark, blotchy linear streaks on lower breast, flanks and thighs, and barring on undertail.* Underwing dark with large white patches on underwing coverts. *Tail square*, legs and feet extend beyond tail, feet black. **BREEDING** No information, but possibly on islands in Hauraki Gulf. **FEEDING** Known to be attracted to 'chum' but otherwise no information. **P&R** Unknown but likely very small. Range unknown, but observed since 2003 in Hauraki Gulf and recently in coastal waters off eastern Australia. **T&M** Likely threatened by alien predators at breeding grounds. **BV** Hauraki Gulf.

Leach's Storm Petrel *Oceanodroma leucorhoa* LC V

L 20cm WS 46cm Wt 45g

Medium-sized, long-winged storm petrel with *deeply forked long tail*. Plumage all dark sooty brown apart from *lighter head, nape and mantle, with curved whitish wing bar from carpal joint to rump. Rump white divided by a dark central line*. Legs do not protrude. Bill small and black. Subspecies *O. l. chapmani* lacks white rump. Distinguished from Wilson's – the only other dark storm petrel with white rump in region – by dark central line dividing white rump and long forked tail. **BREEDING** Islands in North Atlantic and North Pacific. **FEEDING** Surface feeder, sometimes patters. Crustacea, small fish and cephalopods. **P&R** 20 million. Migrates to tropical and subtropical zones. Vagrant to NZ waters. **T&M** Alien mammal predation at some breeding sites, also possible susceptibility to organochlorine pollution. **BV** Subtropical waters around northern NI during summer months.

Grey-backed Storm Petrel *Garrodia nereis* LC N

L 17cm WS 39cm Wt 34g

Very small, black and white storm petrel. *Head and neck dark grey-black giving hooded appearance, grey on mantle extending onto primary and secondary coverts*. Primaries and secondaries dark grey-black, *rump barred grey-black, tail square with black tip*. Underparts, *chin and throat grey-black, breast and belly white becoming barred under tail*. Rounded wings, *underwing largely white with dark tip and trailing and leading edges*. Legs

and feet black, extending beyond tail. Flight direct with *shallow bat-like wing-beats.* **BREEDING** Nocturnal in burrows in dense vegetation, rather than underground. Some activity year round, but mainly August–April with considerable variation between locations. Colonies on Chatham, Antipodes, Auckland and Campbell islands as well as in South Atlantic and south Indian oceans. **FEEDING** Surface feeding by pattering, with occasional underwater plunges. Crustacea, especially immature stalked barnacles, and some fish. **P&R** 200,000. Circumpolar in sub-Antarctic; ranges relatively close to breeding colonies. **T&M** No specific threats but breeding restricted/absent where mammalian predators present. **BV** Offshore, especially to south and east of NZ. Kaikoura, but rarely seen near mainland coast.

White-faced Storm Petrel *Pelagadroma marina* **LC N**

L 20cm WS 42cm Wt 50g

Large, slender, long-legged, rather pale storm petrel. Upperparts, *head and neck mid-grey with dark patch through eye and prominent white eyebrow*. Mantle and primary and secondary coverts light brownish grey; flight feathers grey-black, extending as a band across mantle. *Rump grey, tail grey-black and slightly forked*. Underparts largely white but with *broad, dark collar, sometimes partial, and dark flight feathers and undertail*. Legs and feet long, dark grey, *extending well beyond tail*. **BREEDING** Nocturnal colonial burrower. Eggs laid late October to mid-December, hatching in December–January and fledging in February–March. Colonies on many islands off all 3 main islands from Three Kings to Stewart, plus Kermadec, Chatham and Auckland islands. Also breeds on islands off southern and western Australia and in the sub-Antarctic to subtropical South and North Atlantic and southwest Pacific oceans. **FEEDING** Surface feeder, sometimes using foot pattering, on wide variety of krill, amphipods and other planktonic crustacea, and small fish. **P&R** 4 million. Temperate and subtropical Pacific, Atlantic and Indian oceans. Six subspecies; *P. m. albiclunis* breeds in the Kermadecs and is the most likely to be seen in mainland coastal waters. **T&M** No known threats. **BV** Offshore and around breeding islands, Hauraki Gulf, Bay of Plenty, New Plymouth during summer months.

White-bellied Storm Petrel *Fregetta grallaria* **LC N**

L 20cm WS 46cm Wt 55g

Medium-sized, broad-winged, black and white storm petrel. Upperparts, including *head and neck, dark chocolate brown* with mottled mantle and diffuse, crescent-shaped carpal wing bar; *rump small and white*. Underparts: dark 'hood' contrasts at breast with *all-white belly. Variable white underwing coverts with broad, dark margin*. Tail square and black with some barring on undertail coverts; feet dark and do not protrude beyond tail. Plumage very variable, with dark and intermediate morphs (uncommon in New Zealand waters) lacking white rump. **BREEDING** Largely nocturnal, loosely colonial in shallow burrow or rock crevice; breeds late summer elsewhere, but little detailed information on NZ population on Kermadecs. **FEEDING** Surface feeder, dipping and pattering, sometimes on one foot, mainly on cephalopods and planktonic crustacea. **P&R** 300,000. Largely tropical and subtropical waters in all 3 southern oceans. NZ population probably disperses to north and east after autumn breeding. Four subspecies; NZ birds are *F. g. grallaria*, found also on Lord Howe I. Other subspecies breed on islands in south Indian, South Atlantic and eastern South Pacific. **T&M** Introduced mammalian predators at nesting sites. **BV** Vagrant to NZ coastal waters. Offshore to north of NZ, Kermadecs.

Black-bellied Storm Petrel *Fregetta tropica* **LC N**

L 20cm WS 45cm Wt 56g

Medium-sized, black and white storm petrel. Upperparts grey-black apart from *broad white rump*, and slightly paler *crescent-shaped bar on coverts*. Underparts dark apart from *white chin and belly extending up to rump*. Variable irregular dark central line on belly, which is sometimes absent and is often difficult to see. Underwing dark apart from *white underwing coverts*. Feet black and normally *protrude well beyond square tail*. Extent of white on undersides varies considerably. **BREEDING** Nocturnal, nesting colonially in holes or rock crevices. Eggs laid late December, hatching February, fledging mid-April, possibly earlier in NZ colonies. Circumpolar sub-Antarctic and Antarctic. In NZ region, colonies on Auckland,

Antipodes and possibly Campbell islands. **FEEDING** Surface feeder, dipping and pattering, mainly on planktonic crustacea and fish. **P&R** 500,000. Found throughout the southern oceans as far south as Antarctic Circle. In non-breeding season it ranges north as far as the Equator in all three oceans. **T&M** No known threats. **BV** At sea, to the east of NZ and near Chatham Is during migration in May–June and October–November.

Penguins – Spheniscidae

There are 18 species of penguin worldwide, 13 of which have been recorded in New Zealand. Of these, only six breed here: three species on the main islands, and a further three species on the sub-Antarctic islands, although these are regularly recorded on the main islands. Four of the breeding species are endemic to NZ. Sexes have identical plumage and all species have webbed feet, though they use their flippers for propulsion.

Penguin weights vary widely depending on time of year and food availability.

Emperor Penguin *Aptenodytes forsteri* LC V

L 120cm Wt 20–41kg

Very large, heavy penguin. Head and nape black, *bill dark, long and downcurved* with dull orange coloration on inner lower mandible. *Dull orange collar becoming large ear-patch.* Back and top of flippers dark steely grey. *Upper breast dull yellow, fading to white on lower breast and belly.* Undersides of flipper white. Feet dark on short, stout legs. Immatures lack yellow coloration and have shorter bill. **BREEDING** Coastal Antarctica, often on sea ice. **FEEDING** Fish, cephalopods and crustaceans; pursuit diving typically to 50m, frequently to 150m and on occasion to 500m. Dives may last 20 minutes. **P&R** 300,000. Circumpolar to 60°S. **T&M** No known threats, though climate change may present a challenge. **BV** Chance sighting, sub-Antarctic islands most likely.

King Penguin *Aptenodytes patagonicus* LC V

L 90cm Bill 13cm Wt 9–17kg

Large, long-billed, grey and white penguin. Head, nape and throat black *with bright orange to orange-yellow* collar extending into large ear-patches. *Bill, long and slightly down-curved; upper mandible dark, lower is orange with dark tip. Back, tail and top of flipper dark blue-grey* with dark margins. *Upper breast diffused orange-yellow from collar*, lower breast and belly white. Underside of flipper white with dark tip. Feet black on very stout, short legs. Immature duller and has yellow rather than orange coloration. **BREEDING** Circumpolar on sub-Antarctic islands: in NZ biogeographic region, breeds only on Macquarie I. **FEEDING** Small fish and some cephalopods. Pursuit diver to 25m, exceptionally to 300m. Dives last *c.*10 minutes. **P&R** 2 million. Circumpolar between 45°S and 55°S, apart from Pacific section. NZ birds likely from Macquarie I. Regular visitor to NZ sub-Antarctic islands. **T&M** No known threats; population increasing. **BV** Rare vagrant to NZ mainland. Chance sightings, most likely on sub-Antarctic islands.

Gentoo Penguin *Pygoscelis papua* NT V

L 85cm Wt 4.5–8.5kg

Medium-sized, black and white penguin with *large, red-orange bill*. Head, throat and neck black with *broad white blaze running up from eye to eye* over top of head, narrowing somewhat on crown. *Bill large, stout and bright orange-red* with dark tip. Back and top of flippers black, undersides white. *Feet large and orange-pink*, legs short and stocky. Immature duller with smaller white eye-blaze. The fastest underwater swimmer of all penguins. **BREEDING** Circumpolar on cool temperate and sub-Antarctic islands. **FEEDING** Crustaceans and fish, pursuit diving to 100m. **P&R** 500,000. Circumpolar to about 50°S. **T&M** No known threats. **BV** Chance observation, sub-Antarctic islands most likely.

Adelie Penguin *Pygoscelis adeliae* **LC V**

L 70cm Wt 4–8kg

Medium-sized penguin with rather *angular head* and small bill. Head, throat, neck, back and top of flippers black. *White ring around eye*. Undersides all white. *Bill short and stout, dark with reddish tinge*. Feet and legs pink. Immature similar but with white chin. **BREEDING** Colonial on Antarctica and islands around the continent. **FEEDING** Crustaceans with some fish and cephalopods, by pursuit diving normally to 40m, but at times to 175m. **P&R** 4–5 million. Circumpolar, south of the Antarctic Convergence. **T&M** No known threats. **BV** Chance observation, sub-Antarctic islands best.

Chinstrap Penguin *Pygoscelis antarctica* **NT V**

L 75cm Wt 3–5kg

Medium-sized penguin with distinctive facial pattern. Forehead, cap and upperparts black. Face, chin and throat white with thin black line running from ear to ear across throat. Eye red. Undersides all white, legs and feet dull pale pink. **BREEDING** Islands within Antarctic Convergence. **FEEDING** Crustaceans and fish, pursuit diving quite close to surface, exceptionally to 70m. **P&R** 8 million. Circumpolar south of Antarctic Convergence. **T&M** No known threats. **BV** Chance sighting, most likely in sub-Antarctic islands.

Magellanic Penguin *Spheniscus magellanicus* **NT V**

A ALTERNATIVE NAME Jackass Penguin | L 70cm Wt 3–7kg

Medium-sized penguin with distinctive facial markings. Face, head and upperparts black with *prominent broad white crescent running from forehead, over eye, around ear and across throat*. Undersides white apart from *broad irregular black band running up flanks and across upper breast. Bill large, black and very strongly built, with white mark on both mandibles close to tip. Pink patch at base of bill* extending to and around eye. Immature (A – right-hand bird) has less distinct facial markings. Feet and legs a rather dull dirty pink. **VOICE** A distinctive donkey-like bray, hence its alternative name. **BREEDING** Southern South America, Falkland Is. **FEEDING** Crustaceans, fish and cephalopods by pursuit diving. **P&R** 5–10 million. Coastal southern South America, Falkland Is. **T&M** Oil pollution, commercial fisheries, human predation. **BV** Chance sighting, east coast most likely.

Macaroni Penguin *Eudyptes chrysolophus* **VU V**

L 71cm Wt 3–6kg

Medium-sized, plumed penguin. Head, *chin, throat and upperparts black*. Underparts white. *Golden-yellow plumes from central forehead to behind eye*. Bill very large, stout, brown-orange with patch of pink skin at base. Feet and legs dull pink. Face colour distinguishes it from Royal. **FEEDING** Crustaceans with some fish and cephalopods by pursuit diving to 20m, but exceptionally to over 100m. **P&R** 18 million. Mainly South Atlantic and south Indian oceans, but small numbers to Australia and NZ. **T&M** No known threats. **BV** Chance sightings, sub-Antarctic islands best.

Royal Penguin *Eudyptes schlegeli* **VU V**

L 75cm Wt 3–8kg

Medium-sized, orange-crested penguin. Crown, back and top of flippers black, undersides white. *Face, chin and throat white or off-white. Bright red-orange and black plumes from central forehead to behind eye. Bill red-brown and massive* with bright pink skin at base. Feet and legs flesh-coloured. Juvenile greyer, lacks long plumes, bill duller. **BREEDING** Macquarie I. **FEEDING** Fish, cephalopods and crustaceans by pursuit diving. **P&R** 1.75 million. Vicinity of Macquarie I. **T&M** No specific threats. **BV** Chance sightings, on south and east coasts, and sub-Antarctic islands.

Yellow-eyed Penguin *Megadyptes antipodes* **EN EG**

ALTERNATIVE NAME Hoiho | L 65cm Wt 4–8kg

Medium-sized, pale-headed penguin. Head and neck rather pale grizzled yellow with *distinct yellow band from eye round back of head; eye yellow*. Back and top of flippers dark slate grey. Undersides: throat rather brownish, otherwise all white. Legs and feet flesh pink. *Bill long and flesh pink-coloured with darker red-brown tip*. Immature (A) has rather greyer head and lacks yellow eye and head band. **BREEDING** Loosely colonial, with open nest beside bank, flax or tussock close to water. In Otago, 1 or 2 eggs laid September–October, hatching November–December, fledging February–March. Small colonies found from Banks Peninsula to Bluff, islands in Foveaux Strait and around Stewart I. Also Campbell and Auckland islands, where breeding *c.*2 weeks later than further north. **FEEDING** Mainly fish with some cephalopods and crustaceans, by pursuit diving. **P&R** 5,000–6,000. Remains fairly close to breeding areas, with some dispersal to the north, as far as Bay of Plenty during winter. **T&M** Habitat loss, mammalian predators and net fishing. **BV** Coastal areas, from Banks Peninsula to Bluff. Occasionally seen further north in winter, including Marlborough and southern NI.

Fiordland Crested Penguin *Eudyptes pachyrhynchus* **VU E**

ALTERNATIVE NAME Pokotiwha | L 55cm Wt 4kg

Small, crested penguin with short, very stout bill. Head and throat black with *distinctive yellow eyebrow extending back to become a short yellow plume*; lighter *cheek patch may appear as white lines*, no skin visible at base of bill. Back, tail and top of flippers dark charcoal grey to black. Undersides all white apart from small black tip to flipper. *Bill stout, dark orange, feet and legs pink*. Immature has yellow eyebrow but lacks plumes, chin and throat pale greyish brown. **BREEDING** In small colonies under roots, in crevice or rockfalls, in native bush close to the water. Eggs laid July–August, second egg is larger and normally hatches first in September, fledging November–early December. Only one chick survives. Colonies around south and southwest coasts of SI, and on islands in Foveaux Strait and around Stewart I. **FEEDING** Mainly cephalopods, as well as crustaceans and fish, by pursuit diving. **P&R** 5,000–6,000. Close to breeding colonies during season, dispersing to north and west during summer and autumn; vagrants to Australia and sub-Antarctic islands. **T&M** Loss of habitat, human disturbance, dogs and introduced mammals, especially mustelids. Wekas may take some chicks. **BV** Close to breeding colonies during season, otherwise inshore waters around NZ during late summer and autumn.

Snares Crested Penguin *Eudyptes robustus* **VU E**

L 60cm Wt 2.5–4kg

Small, large-billed penguin. Head, throat, back, top of flippers and tail black with *bright yellow-gold eyebrow turning to long plumes*. Underparts all white apart from *black tip to flipper*. *Bill orange-brown, very large and stout with pink facial skin at base*. Legs and feet pink. Immature rather greyer, especially chin and throat, and lacking long plumes. **BREEDING** In small dense colonies, under shrubs or in open. Eggs laid September–October, hatching November and fledging January–February. 2 eggs, second is larger, hatches first and is normally only survivor. Colonies on several islands in Snares Group, those on Western Chain breeding 3–6 weeks later than the majority on main Snares. **FEEDING** Cephalopods, fish and crustaceans by pursuit diving to 20–80m. **P&R** 60,000. Around colonies during breeding season, some dispersal in autumn and winter, mainly SI and vagrants to Australia. **T&M** No known threats. **BV** Snares Is during breeding season, otherwise south and east coasts of SI and sub-Antarctic islands.

Erect-crested Penguin *Eudyptes sclateri* **EN E**

L 60cm Wt 3.5–7kg

Small, crested penguin. Head, throat, back, top of flippers and tail black. *Prominent bright yellow eyebrows becoming longer plumes and tending to stay erect*, almost brush-like. Undersides all white apart from *black tip to under-flipper*, which extends along leading edge. Bill large, orange-brown and with *white facial skin at base*. Feet and legs pink. **BREEDING** In large, noisy colonies, often with mollymawks, in open on rocky coastal slopes. Eggs laid October–November, hatching December and fledging January–February. Two eggs laid, 1 chick survives, smaller deliberately starved to death. Large colonies on Antipodes and Bounty islands with some also in Auckland Is. **FEEDING** Crustaceans, cephalopods and small fish, by pursuit diving. **P&R** 150,000. Remain at breeding site for annual moult then disperse widely to both sides of Tasman Sea. **T&M** No known threats. **BV** Around breeding colonies, or around east coasts of NI, SI and Stewart I. during autumn and winter.

Southern Rockhopper Penguin *Eudyptes chrysocome* **VU N**

L 50cm Wt 2–4kg

Smallest of the crested penguins. Head, neck, throat, back, top of flipper and tail all black. *Bright yellow eyebrow becoming long, drooping plumes* behind the eye. Undersides all white apart from *small black tip to flipper*. Bill red-brown, short and stout. Feet and legs pink. Immature (A) rather greyer and lacking plumes. **BREEDING** In large, noisy colonies, often shared with mollymawks or other crested penguins on open rocky slopes. Two eggs, only 1 survives, laid October–November, hatching December and fledging February–March. Breeds on Antipodes, Bounty, Auckland and Campbell islands, later in last 2. **FEEDING** Fish as well as crustaceans and cephalopods, pursuit diving to 100m. **P&R** 0.5–1 million. Circumpolar with colonies in southern South America, Falkland Is and islands in South Atlantic and south Indian oceans. Colonies disperse to sea during autumn and winter. **T&M** No identified threats, but recent significant population declines may be due to global warming. **BV** Sub-Antarctic islands and around southern and eastern coasts of main islands during autumn and winter. The **Northern Rockhopper Penguin** *E. moseleyi* is now considered a separate species.

Little Blue Penguin *Eudyptula minor* **LC E** (ssp.)

ALTERNATIVE NAME Korora | L 45cm Wt 1–2kg

The *smallest penguin. Head, face to below eye, back, top of flippers and tail dark blue-grey*, flippers darker with *narrow white trailing edge*. Underparts all white. Feet and legs yellowish. *Bill dark and quite short*. Immatures slightly bluer on back. Can be very noisy at night: selection of screams, growls and trumpeting. In Canterbury there is a variety with rather more white on the upper surface of the flippers. **BREEDING** Widespread, in loose colonies, around coast of all three islands, in burrow, rock cavity or driftwood, sometimes several hundred metres inland. 1–2 eggs laid July–December and fledging from October to March. Only penguin known to lay and rear 2 clutches. **FEEDING** Cephalopods and fish by pursuit diving to 5m, but occasionally to 60m. **P&R** 1 million. No accurate statistics due to nature of 'colonies'. Remains largely within coastal waters year round. **T&M** Predation by dogs, cats and other introduced predators; also at risk from cars when crossing roads. **BV** Widespread around coasts, including Tauranga, Wellington, Akaroa and Otago harbours.

Tropic Birds – Phaethontidae

Red-tailed Tropic Bird *Phaethon rubricauda* **LC N** (RV to main islands)
L 46cm Tail 40cm WS 1.12m Wt 800g

Elegant, largely white diving seabird with impressively long red tail streamers. *Head and upperparts all white* or occasionally light pink, apart from *black crescent before and above eye*, black shafts to the primaries, some black may also show on tertiaries, flanks and tail. Underparts all white or light pink. *Very long red tail* streamers are lost in moult. *Bill coral red, long, strong and pointed.* Immature lacks tail streamers, has dark bill, becoming yellow, then orange, and barred black and white upperparts. Flight more leisurely than other tropic birds. **VOICE/CALL** Harsh scream, sometimes more of a rattle, hence common name of Bosun Bird after bosun's whistle. **BREEDING** Kermadecs on ledge or cliff face. Single egg laid December–January, hatching February, fledging April–May. **FEEDING** Fish and squid, by plunge-diving, often from considerable height. **P&R** 32,000. Tropical Indian and Pacific oceans, very pelagic. **T&M** No known threats, though vulnerable to introduced pest predators. **BV** Kermadecs, but small numbers in northeastern waters as far south as Bay of Plenty.

White-tailed Tropic Bird *Phaethon lepturus* **LC V**
L 38cm Tail 40cm WS 92cm Wt 300g

Elegant, black and white diving seabird with immensely long tail streamers. Similar to Red-tailed but has *black wing-tips, diagonal black bar on innerwing, chrome-yellow bill and white tail streamers*. Immature lacks streamers and black barring on back. **VOICE/CALL** Similar to Red-tailed. **FEEDING** As with Red-tailed. **P&R** 50,000. Tropical and subtropical zones, all 3 oceans, occasional sightings in NZ waters. **T&M** No known threats. **BV** Chance viewing, most likely northeast coast.

Frigatebirds – Fregatidae

Lesser Frigatebird *Fregata ariel* **LC V**
L 80cm WS 2.3m Wt 1.0kg

Very large, long-winged, long-tailed, acrobatic seabird. Male (A) plumage all black, often with purple metallic sheen on back, apart from *pale whitish patches on flanks* under the wings. Female (B) similar but with *broad white band across breast and upper belly*. Male has *red gular pouch*, especially in breeding season. *Tail very long and deeply forked.* Bill long, dark and *distinctly hooked.* Feet reddish brown. Immature (C) as female but with *buff head* and neck. In flight 'W' shape of wings and long, deeply forked tail are diagnostic. **FEEDING** Flying fish and squid taken on the wing, also kleptoparasitises other seabirds, especially boobies and tropic birds, forcing them to disgorge catch. **P&R** 200,000. Pan-tropical, occasional sightings in northern waters. **T&M** No known threats. **BV** Chance sightings, Kermadecs, NE of NZ after cyclone.

Greater Frigatebird *Fregata minor* **LC V**
L 1.1m WS 2.3m Wt 1.5kg

Very large, black seabird with long, deeply forked tail. Very similar to Lesser but larger, *male (A) all black* apart from gular pouch and *green rather than purple sheen* to back feathers. Female (B) with *black with white chest and throat and red ring around eye*. Both sexes have brownish band across secondaries, visible in flight. Bill long and hooked, male's dark, female's reddish. Feet reddish. Immature as female but with *buff head.* **FEEDING** As for Lesser. **P&R** 350,000–1 million. Pan-tropical. **T&M** No known threats. **BV** As for Lesser.

Gannets and Boobies – Sulidae

A family of large, tropical and subtropical plunge-diving seabirds. Of the 11 species, two breed in NZ and its surrounding islands and one species is an occasional visitor.

B A **Australasian Gannet** *Morus serrator* **LC N**

ALTERNATIVE NAME Takapu | L 90cm WS 1.7m Wt 2.3kg

Large, long-winged, black and white seabird (A). *Head creamy gold*, rest of plumage white apart from *black primaries, secondaries and central tail feathers*. Dark facial patch around eye, *bill long, dagger-shaped* and bluish grey with dark line either side of culmen. Legs and feet slate grey with bright green lines along top of toes. Immatures (B) largely mottled brown and white, obtaining adult plumage over 4–5-year period. **VOICE/CALL** Not very vocal at sea, harsh squawk. Noisy at colonies, slightly throaty ululating call. **BREEDING** Colonial breeder, nests sited with remarkable geometric regularity, on rock stacks or ledges on coast. Breeding varies between colonies and yearly. In north, single egg generally laid late July–mid-October, hatching 6 weeks later and fledging in December–January. Further south, sequence may be 6–8 weeks later. **FEEDING** Mainly fish, but some squid, by plunge-diving from as much as 30m. **P&R** 110,000, probably increasing. During breeding season, close to colonies; coastal waters, especially NI and across Tasman to Australian waters. **T&M** No known threats. **BV** At least 28 colonies around coasts, especially NI, mainly on islands but 3 mainland colonies: Muriwai near Auckland, Cape Kidnappers in Hawke's Bay and Farewell Spit on SI.

Cape Gannet *Morus capensis* **VU V**

L 85–94cm WS 1.71–1.85m Wt 2.3–3.3kg

Virtually identical to Australasian Gannet but with *all-black tail, rather than just central feathers*. **P&R** 300,000. Confined largely to the coast of southern Africa, but disperses during winter. **T&M** Decimation of fish stocks, predation by fur seals and pelicans. **BV** Chance viewing, most likely off NI.

Masked Booby *Sula dactylatra* **LC N**

A

B B L 85cm WS 1.52m Wt 1.7kg

Large, black and white, *plunge-diving* seabird (A). All-white plumage apart from *black primaries and secondaries. Bill pale yellow, long and dagger-like with dark skin or mask around base*. Feet and legs dull slate grey. Immature (B) has largely brown wings and brown head. Smaller than a gannet. **BREEDING** Colonial on open ground. 2 eggs laid almost year-round with peak in August–November. Cycle takes 5–6 months. Breeds in Kermadecs and elsewhere. **FEEDING** Fish and squid by plunge-diving. **P&R** Unknown, but breeds pan-tropically. **T&M** No known threats. **BV** Infrequent visitor to northern NI.

Brown Booby *Sula leucogaster* **LC V**

L 72cm WS 145cm Wt 1.2kg

B A Very large, brown and white, *plunge-diving* seabird (A). Head, neck, back and tail dark chocolate brown. Underparts, *body and undertail white*; *underwing with dark brown edges, white in the middle. Bill yellowish*, more so in female, *long and dagger-like*, bluish facial skin at base. Legs and feet yellowish. Juvenile (B) underparts pale brown, feet and legs pinkish grey. **FEEDING** Fish by plunge-diving. **P&R** 200,000. Pan-tropical, vagrant to NZ. **T&M** No known threats. **BV** Chance sightings, most likely Hauraki Gulf and northern NI.

Shags or Cormorants – Phalacrocoracidae

Shags, often called cormorants in other parts of the world, are medium to large, long-necked, long-tailed, heavy-bodied seabirds that are often found well inland. They have long, hooked bills and short legs with large webbed feet, which they use for underwater pursuit of fish and occasionally crustaceans or molluscs. Some species dive to depths of up to 30m and can stay submerged for over a minute. They often make several dives in succession with only a short break in between. When swimming they sit very low in the water. Their feathers are not fully waterproofed, and so you will often see them hanging their wings out to dry. There are 34 species worldwide with 12 recorded in NZ, of which eight are endemic, many with very small ranges. Sexes have similar plumage, though females are generally slightly smaller.

Black Shag *Phalacrocorax carbo* **LC N**

ALTERNATIVE NAME Kawau | L 90cm WS 1.52m Wt 2.5kg

Large, all-dark shag (A). *Head, neck and body black with white patch on cheeks and throat.* Wings and tail dark black-brown. Breeding adult has small crest, *white filoplumes on head and neck and white patch on thigh. Bill grey with yellow lores and facial skin at base.* Eye green, feet and legs black. Immature (B) generally brown with rather paler underparts. **VOICE** Hoarse croak and a wheezy whistle. **BREEDING** Nests in colonies, in trees overhanging water, or on cliff ledges, both coastal and riverine. Large untidy platform of sticks and leaves. Season variable but 2–5 eggs laid June–October, hatching 4–5 weeks later, fledging at 7 weeks. **FEEDING** Mainly fish in water up to 12m deep. Dives last 20–30 seconds with *c.*6 seconds between dives. **P&R** 1.4–2.9 million. Worldwide range. Widespread in NZ; found all around coast and on inland lakes and rivers. **T&M** No known threats. Insignificant loss due to commercial fishing. **BV** Coastal waters, especially estuaries and harbours. Inland lakes.

Little Black Shag *Phalacrocorax sulcirostris* **LC V**

L 62cm WS 82cm Wt 800g

Small, all-black shag. Adult plumage (A) *all black with a dull, dark green gloss.* Wing coverts are slightly grey with dark edges resulting in a scalloped appearance. *White filoplumes on head and neck in breeding season*, but not easily seen. *Bill markedly hooked, lead grey*, facial skin dark, eye emerald green. Immature (B) similar but dark brown rather than black. Makes short, shallow dives. **VOICE** Variety of hoarse croaks and whistles. **BREEDING** Colonial nester in trees, sometimes on ground, close to water; nest is a platform of sticks and leaves, 2–5 eggs laid mainly November–December but some rather earlier. **FEEDING** Fish and some crustaceans, regularly fishes in flocks. Fairly short, shallow dives, 10 seconds or so with 2–3 seconds between dives. **P&R** 25,000–100,000. Mainly NI and northwest of SI. Also Australasia, east of Borneo and Java. **T&M** No known threats. **BV** Coastal waters, mainly harbours and estuaries, also inland lakes. Disperse quite widely in winter, particularly southwards.

B A **Pied Shag** *Phalacrocorax varius* **LC N**

ALTERNATIVE NAME Karuhiruhi | L 81cm WS 1.06–1.37m Wt 2kg

Large, black and white shag (A). *Upperparts are all dark black with a glossy green sheen*, upperwing more bronzed. *Underparts including face are white apart from black thighs*. Eye green, *patch of yellow skin in front of eye*. *Bill dull horn* coloured, darker upper mandible, skin around base pinkish. Legs and feet black. Immature (B) brown rather than black and with less white on face and neck. **VOICE/CALL** Deep croak, or repetitive wheeze. **BREEDING** Colonial in trees on cliffs overhanging the sea, occasionally around harbours and estuaries. Sometimes on navigational structures. Nest a platform of sticks and seaweed. Year-round breeder with peak laying of 2–5 eggs in July–October and January–March. Eggs hatch at 4 weeks, chicks fledge at 8 weeks and fed by parents for up to a further 11 weeks. **FEEDING** Fish caught by pursuit diving up to 10m; dives last to 30 seconds, with up to 10-second rests. **P&R** Up to 1 million. Coastal area, especially northern NI, from Gisborne round to Raglan and on SI in the northeast and southwest quadrants. Also found in Australian coastal waters. **T&M** No known threats. **BV** Coastal waters and harbours, northern NI especially Kaipara and Hokianga harbours.

Little Shag *Phalacrocorax melanoleucos* **LC N**

A B **B C** L 56cm WS 84–91cm Wt 700g

Smallest shag, with 2 distinct plumage phases. Dark (A) or white-throated phase is *all black apart from white throat and face*. Pied (B) phase has *upperparts all black, underparts including face and sides of neck, all white*. Tail rather long. *Bill yellow, stubby with hooked tip*. Legs and feet black. Intermediate phases also observed, which have *variable white on breast and abdomen*. Immature (C) largely brown with yellow bill. *Head profile is rather angular*. Pied phase commoner further north, especially Northland. **VOICE/CALL** Not very vocal; soft coughing and cooing during courtship. **BREEDING** Widespread throughout all 3 main islands, in large colonies in trees, overhanging or close to water, sometimes on cliff ledges, in fresh water, estuaries and coastal. Long breeding season, starting July, 2–5 eggs laid August–February, hatching after 4 weeks and fledging 6 weeks later. Nest a rough platform of sticks and leaves. **FEEDING** Mainly fish with some crustaceans (freshwater crayfish), frogs and tadpoles. Pursuit diving, mainly in shallow coastal waters to 3m, occasionally to 10m. Dives last up to 15 seconds in shallow or 40 seconds in deep water with *c*.6 seconds between dives. **P&R** Up to 1 million. Throughout 3 main islands, coastal and inland lakes and waterways, small colony in Campbell I. Also in Australia, Indonesia and PNG. **T&M** No known threats. **BV** Sheltered coastal waters, lakes, ponds and rivers throughout NZ.

Spotted Shag *Phalacrocorax punctatus* **LC E**

ALTERNATIVE NAME Parekareka | L 70cm Wt 1.2kg

Medium-sized, rather slender, grey shag. Distinctive breeding plumage (A): *head and back of neck black* with black, forward-curled, double crest and some white feathers; *broad white band running from above eye to shoulder. Upperwing and mantle light grey-brown with dark spots.* Rump and tail dark. Undersides of throat and neck dark, *breast and body slightly pinkish grey, black thighs and undertail* with some white feathers. *Feet and legs bright yellow. Bill long, yellowish brown with green facial skin.* Non-breeding (B) lacks crest and white line on head, and neck much narrower. Breast paler grey and facial skin dull yellow. Immature (C) generally brown, paler below, no white line on neck, dull-yellow bill and facial skin. **VOICE/CALL** Hoarse croak. **BREEDING** Ground nesting, colonial, mainly on cliffs or isolated rocks. Breeding season varies with year and location, but generally year-round. Nest of seaweed and vegetation, 1–4 eggs hatch after 4–5 weeks, fledging 8–9 weeks later. **FEEDING** Mainly fish with some invertebrates. Pursuit diving mainly in deeper water up to 15km from shore, but also in estuaries and harbours. Dives last 30 seconds, exceptionally 70 seconds, with 1–15 seconds between dives. **P&R** 50,000–150,000. Coastal, 2 subspecies. *P. p. punctatus* in NI Hauraki Gulf, Waikato coast, Coromandel, Kapiti I. and Wellington Harbour. SI north and east coasts south to Catlins. **Blue Shag** *P. p. steadi* in Westland and on Stewart I. and islands in Foveaux Strait. **T&M** No known threats. **BV** Coastal areas, Auckland region, Coromandel, Hawke's Bay, Wellington, Marlborough Sounds, Kaikoura coast to Catlins and Stewart I.

Pitt Island Shag *Phalacrocorax featherstonii* **EN E**

L 63cm Wt 1.2kg

Very similar to Spotted Shag but *lacks white head and neck stripe*; head and neck much darker than immature Spotted. **BREEDING** Similar to Spotted, but August–March, Chatham Is only. **FEEDING** Similar to Spotted. **P&R** 1,100, decreasing. Found only in Chatham Is. **T&M** Some human predation still likely, also mammalian predators. **BV** Chatham Is coastal waters.

King Shag *Phalacrocorax carunculatus* **VU E**

L 68-76cm Wt 2.5kg

Medium-sized shag, *head and upperparts all black* with rather dull blue-green metallic sheen, apart from *broad white wing bar.* Underparts white with black thighs. Bill dull-horn coloured with blue-grey facial skin and gular pouch, which become reddish in breeding season. *Bright yellow-orange caruncles at base of bill. Legs and feet pink.* Immature brown rather than black, and lacks caruncles. **VOICE/CALL** Hoarse croak. **BREEDING** Ground nesting in colonies, very long breeding season with 1–3 eggs laid mainly in May–June. No information on hatching or fledging but likely to be similar to other shag species. Now found in Marlborough Sounds only. **FEEDING** Mainly fish, especially bottom dwellers and some crustaceans, by pursuit diving to depths of 40m. Dives last from *c.*45 up to 90 seconds. **P&R** 600+. Found only in the Marlborough Sounds on SI. **T&M** Illegal human predation, nesting disturbance and fishing set nets a serious threat. **BV** Marlborough Sounds.

The following 5 species are all very similar and closely related to the King Shag (*see* p86). All have very restricted ranges.

Stewart Island Shag *Phalacrocorax chalconotus* **VU E**
L 65–70cm WS 1.05m Wt 2.3kg
Medium-sized shag with pink feet. Two phases. Pied phase (A) very similar to King Shag but with small forward-curled crest on forehead. *Lacks caruncles and facial skin somewhat purplish.* Bronze phase (B) is uniform bronze-brown. **BREEDING** Colonial ground nester on cliffs, often close to high-water mark. Long variable breeding season, 1–3 eggs laid mainly September–November, no specific information on hatching and fledging. **FEEDING** Mainly bottom fish with some crustaceans and cephalopods, by pursuit diving to 30m and up to 15km from land. Dives last 30–40 seconds, but up to 3 minutes, with 20–40 seconds between dives. **P&R** 5,000–8,000. Southeast coast of SI, Stewart I. and islands in Foveaux Strait. **T&M** Illegal human predation as well as fishing set nets. **BV** Coastal waters in SE of SI and around Stewart I.

Similar Species

Campbell Island Shag *Phalacrocorax campbelli* **VU E**
POPULATION 8,000
Smaller than Stewart I. pied phase, with white chin and throat but all-black neck. Breeds May–November; found only in the Campbell Is.

Auckland Island Shag *Phalacrocorax colensoi* **VU E**
POPULATION 2,000
Smaller than but very similar to Stewart I. pied phase. Breeds November–May; found only in waters around the Auckland Is.

Bounty Island Shag *Phalacrocorax ranfurlyi* **VU E**
POPULATION 600+
Very similar to Stewart I. pied phase. Breeds October–March but found only in vicinity of the Bounty Is.

Chatham Island Shag *Phalacrocorax onslowi* **CR E**
POPULATION 500+
Slightly smaller than Stewart I. pied phase, but with prominent orange caruncles. Breeds August–March. Found only in the Chatham Is and surrounding waters.

Darters – Anhingidae

Australian Darter *Anhinga novaehollandiae* **LC V**
L 90cm Wt 1.75kg
Large, slim, *very long-necked, long-tailed* waterbird. Male largely rich dark brown with cream-coloured feathers on wing and mantle. Reddish patch on front of neck. Prominent *white flash from below eye down upper neck. Bill yellow, long and dagger-like*. Female and immature much lighter, especially on underparts, and lack reddish throat patch. Legs and feet dull yellow-brown. *In flight, neck kinked.* **FEEDING** Mainly fish, by 'spear fishing' underwater using sharp bill. Dives last up to 30 seconds, with 5 seconds between dives. **P&R** 25,000–100,000. Africa, Asia and Australasia. **T&M** No known threats. **BV** Chance sighting, harbours, freshwater lakes and slow-moving rivers.

Skuas, Gulls and Terns

SKUAS – STERCORARIIDAE Skuas, also known as jaegers, are large, aggressive predatory oceanic seabirds, many of which migrate long distances. There are eight species, one of which breeds in NZ; three others are regular migratory visitors and in non-breeding plumage are often difficult to identify.

Arctic Skua *Stercorarius parasiticus* **LC NBM**

L 43cm + 6–10cm central tail feathers WS 1.0–1.11m Wt 400g

Medium-sized, *slim, almost falcon-like* skua, with 2 phases. Dark phase (A), *all dark chocolate brown with darker cap* and white underwing on primary shafts. *Tail wedge-shaped, pointed central feathers can be up to 10cm long*. Bill and feet black. Light phase (B) is similar but with white chin and throat, buff nape and ear coverts, broad, dark neck band and white abdomen. Immature (C) all lighter brown with somewhat barred underparts and lacking central tail feathers. Flight strong and purposeful. *Kleptoparasite, often chases gulls or terns to force them to disgorge food*. On water, very upright position with *tail cocked up*. **FEEDING** Predatory, young of other birds; piratical, fish and cephalopods by aerial pursuit of other species. **P&R** To 10 million. Worldwide, breeds Arctic, winters in tropical and southern temperate waters. **T&M** No known threats. **BV** At sea around coast, but occasionally inshore or in harbours, November–May.

Pomarine Skua *Stercorarius pomarinus* **LC NBM**

L 48cm + 6–8cm central tail feathers WS 1.11–1.22m Wt 600g

Large, broad-winged skua, *bulkier and less falcon-like* than Arctic Skua but with similar plumage. Dark phase virtually identical but *double white flash on underwing tips and central tail feathers blunt-ended and twisted*. Light phase similar to Arctic apart from central tail feathers. Immature largely mid-brown, paler and barred underneath, lacks central tail feathers, gradually attaining adult plumage, resulting in many intermediate stages. Sexes similar, but male larger and heavier than female. **FEEDING** Rodents (in breeding grounds), fish, other birds; kleptoparasite, piratical in pursuit and harassment of other species for their prey. **P&R** Up to 3 million. Breeds in Arctic and migrates south to the tropics and warmer temperate waters in northern winter. **T&M** No known threats. **BV** More likely viewed offshore than Arctic, but occasionally in more sheltered waters, December–April.

Long-tailed Skua *Stercorarius longicaudus* **LC OV**

L 35cm + 20cm central tail feathers WS 92–1.05m Wt 220–440g

Slim, rather greyish skua with *very long tail*. In breeding plumage has *black cap, yellow-buff neck, white throat and breast, and grey body and wings with dark primaries and secondaries*. Tail wedge-shaped with *very long central feathers*. Non-breeding *cap becomes less distinct and neck whiter*, tail feathers likely to be shorter. Bill brown with dark tip, legs and feet bluish grey. Immatures more barred with indistinct white collar and lacking central tail feathers. Flight rather *tern-like*. **FEEDING** Fish and cephalopods; kleptoparasitic on other species. **P&R** Up to 5 million. Arctic breeder, migrating south during winter; very pelagic and solitary. **T&M** No known threats. **BV** Well offshore around the coasts.

Brown Skua *Catharacta lonnbergi* **LC N**

ALTERNATIVE NAME Hakoakoa | L 52–64cm WS 126–160cm Wt 1.25–2.5kg

Large, heavy-bodied, broad-winged skua. All-brown plumage, darker on back and wings, lighter underparts; some fine bronze-yellow feathers visible on head and neck. *White flashes at base of primaries on underwing. Bill large and with hooked tip*, legs and feet black. Immature similar but lacks yellow flecking on head and neck. Females generally larger. Darker than immature Black-backed Gull. **VOICE/CALL** Noisy at nest site; loud, raucous display call. **BREEDING** Territorial, ground-nesting in open grassy area; 1–3 eggs laid mid-September–December, varies with latitude, hatching after 4 weeks, fledging 9 weeks later. Breeds in southern Fiordland, Stewart I., Chathams, Snares and the sub-Antarctic islands. Very aggressive when nesting. **FEEDING** Breeding diet includes penguin eggs, chicks and other seabirds. Also scavenges and kleptoparasitic, especially on terns, gulls and even gannets or shags. **P&R** To 20,000. Circumpolar sub-Antarctic islands, in NZ, Fiordland, Stewart, Snares and Chatham islands. **T&M** Human predation in Chatham Is. **BV** Stewart I., Chathams and sub-Antarctic islands. Around coasts of main islands during winter.

South Polar Skua *Catharacta maccormicki* **LC OV**

L 50–55cm WS 1.2–1.6m Wt 1.0–1.65kg

Medium to large, heavy-bodied, broad-winged skua. Two plumage phases: dark very similar to Brown Skua but *yellower on nape and with much shorter, very stout bill.* Light phase much *lighter on head, neck and body, yellow nape more prominent*, with darker wings. Both phases have white flashes on underwing at base of primaries. Legs and feet black. Female generally larger. **BREEDING** Antarctic mainland and islands. **FEEDING** Fish and crustaceans; scavenger and kleptoparasite. **P&R** Up to 20,000. Migrates to northern hemisphere in winter; not often observed in NZ waters. **T&M** No known threats. **BV** Offshore around coasts, autumn and spring.

GULLS – LARIDAE Part of a worldwide family of coastal birds, but may be found well inland, especially on lakes and rivers. They are largely scavengers, but are also predatory and kleptoparasitic. Some species are very long-lived, to 40 years. Nesting is generally colonial, often very loose. Sexes are similar.

Southern Black-backed Gull *Larus dominicanus* **LC N**

ALTERNATIVE NAME Karoro | L 55–65cm WS 125–140cm Wt 950–1,500g

A Large, black and white gull. Head, neck and body and tail all white. *Upperwing and mantle all black with narrow white trailing edge.* Eye yellow with red ring, *bill chrome-yellow with red spot near tip of lower mandible. Feet and legs dull yellow.* Immature (A) all mid-brown, somewhat flecked, gradually develops adult plumage over 4 years. Flight slow and languid. **VOICE/CALL** Quite vocal, especially when disturbed near nest; loud piping, or raucous scream. **BREEDING** Loosely colonial, on ground, 2 or 3 eggs laid mid-October–December, hatching after 4 weeks, fledging after 7 weeks, but remain semi-dependent on parents for further 2 months. Breeds around coast of all 3 main islands, plus Chathams and sub-Antarctic islands, also inland on lakes and rivers. **FEEDING** Scavenger and predator, consuming young birds, lizards, invertebrates, but also offal, rubbish, etc. **P&R** 3–4 million. Circumpolar, temperate and sub-Antarctic islands. In NZ found throughout the country, both on the coast and inland. **T&M** No known threats. Potential pest when preying upon native species. **BV** Coastal areas, lakes, rivers, rubbish dumps.

Red-billed Gull *Larus scopulinus* **LC E**

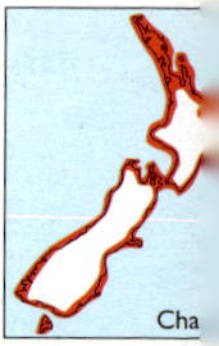

L 37cm WS 92cm Wt 250–360g

Medium-sized, grey and white gull. Head, neck, body and tail white, upperwing and mantle light grey, *wing-tips black with white mirrors*. Eye yellow with *red eye-ring, bill rather stout and bright red. Legs and feet bright red*. Immature (A) browner on back and mantle, bill brownish, legs and feet flesh-coloured, and lacks white wing mirrors. **VOICE/CALL** Strident scream, very noisy at nesting colony.

BREEDING On ground close to sea, in large colonies, whose location may vary from year to year. Mostly 2 eggs laid October–December, hatching after 25 days, fledging 5 weeks later. Southern colonies can be a month later. Colonies throughout country and in Chathams and sub-Antarctic islands. **FEEDING** Surface feeder on plankton: crustaceans, small fish and invertebrates, also scavenges and steals from other birds. **P&R** Up to 1 million. Found in coastal areas throughout the country, well adapted to human populations and good at scavenging picnic scraps. **T&M** No known threats. **BV** Widespread around coasts, especially outside breeding season.

Black-billed Gull *Larus bulleri* **EN E**

L 37cm WS 93cm Wt 300g

Medium-sized, rather fine, grey and white gull. Very similar in general appearance to Red-billed Gull, largely white but *with soft-pearl grey on upperwing, wing-tips white with black tip*. Eye yellow but *lacks red ring. Bill black and fine*, feet and legs dark reddish black. Immature (A) has horn-coloured bill, legs and feet, which become red before turning black. **VOICE/CALL** Typical gull scream. **BREEDING** On ground in large, dense colonies on shingle banks or margins of braided rivers. 1–4 eggs laid late September–December, hatching in 3–4 weeks, fledging after 4 weeks. Chicks leave nest after 1–2 days, and form crèches after 2 weeks. Breeds mainly in the braided rivers in Southland, also Otago and Canterbury. Some small colonies in NI, where it is gradually increasing in numbers, whilst declining in SI. **FEEDING** Fish and small invertebrates, aquatic and terrestrial; often feeds in freshly ploughed farmland. **P&R** 96,000. A largely inland gull, found in NI and SI only. **T&M** No specific information on reason for decline in population; likely causes are loss of habitat, mammalian predators and human disturbance. **BV** Braided rivers of SI. Also Wellington region, Hawke's Bay, Rotorua and Bay of Plenty and Auckland harbours.

Franklin's Gull *Larus pipixcan* **LC V**

L 35cm WS 89cm Wt M 281g, F 250–325g

Small, lightly built gull. *Head and throat black, white rim above and below eye*. Rest of body all white apart from mid-grey upperwing. *First 5 primaries black with white tips*. Bill dark blackish red, legs red. Winter plumage (photo) loses most of black on head and has *white forehead*, immatures much browner with black band on tail. **P&R** 1–1.5 million. A North American species, vagrant to Australasia. **T&M** No known threats. **BV** Chance sighting in coastal waters, especially NI.

TERNS AND NODDIES – LARIDAE A worldwide group of generally small, finely built seabirds with often deeply forked tails and rather buoyant flight, giving rise to their common name of sea swallows. They feed almost entirely on small fish caught by shallow plunge-diving or surface dipping while on the wing.

Caspian Tern *Hydoprogne caspia* **LC N**

ALTERNATIVE NAME Taranui | L 51cm WS 1.4m Wt 700g

The *largest tern*, with a prominent large red bill. Breeding plumage (A), *forehead, cap and nape black*, upperwing and mantle pale grey, rest of body, tail and underwing white apart from dark tips to the underwing. Tail slightly forked and quite short. *Bill massive, pointed, bright red with dark end and yellow tip*. Out of breeding season adult (B) loses most of black on head, feet and legs dark. Immature has greyish cap and duller yellow-orange bill. Upperwing rather mottled grey. Strong direct flight; when fishing, often hovers with head down. **VOICE/CALL** A rather crow-like *kaar* and a gruff *cuk cuk*; also *yakety-yak* is very distinctive. **BREEDING** Ground nester in small colonies in sand or shingle on estuarine shell banks or sandspits. 1–3 eggs laid late September–early December, hatching after 4 weeks, fledging 5 weeks later. **FEEDING** Small fish, some invertebrates and worms, hovering and plunge-diving; immatures may fish standing in shallow water. **P&R** 250,000–400,000. A worldwide species, found in small numbers throughout NZ, especially around harbours, estuaries and sandspits of NI. Birds from far south tend to migrate north during winter, otherwise fairly sedentary. **T&M** No known threats though potentially liable to predation from introduced mustelids, and to human disturbance at breeding colonies. **BV** Estuaries, harbours and coastal waters throughout the country.

Crested Tern *Sterna bergii* **LC V**

L 47cm WS 1.25m Wt 350g

Large, rather dark-winged, *yellow-billed tern*. Breeding plumage *cap and nape black with distinct crest on nape*. Upperwing and mantle mid-grey, tail and rump pale grey, rest of body and forehead white. *Bill long, finely pointed and yellow. Legs and feet black*. Non-breeding cap much greyer and crest less obvious. Immature similar but rather browner head and upperwings. **FEEDING** Fish in shallow coastal waters and estuaries. **P&R** Up to 1 million. Tropical Indian Ocean and southwest Pacific. **T&M** No known threats. **BV** Chance sighting, most likely NI harbours and estuaries.

Gull-billed Tern *Sterna nilotica* **LC V**

L 43cm WS 1.03m Wt 230g

Medium-sized, rather pale tern with short, heavy black bill. *Forehead, cap and nape black, upperparts all pale grey*, underparts white apart from outer primaries, which are greyish. Tail only *slightly forked, bill heavy, gull-like and black*. Legs, which are rather long, and feet black. Non-breeder (A) loses most of black cap and forehead and has a black patch behind eye. Immature similar but somewhat grey on head and mottled brownish on upperparts. **FEEDING** Fish, largely found over fresh water and even flooded grasslands. **P&R** 200,000–400,000. Widespread tropical and subtropical species. **T&M** No known threats. **BV** Chance sighting, coastal lagoons and estuaries.

Adult breeding

White-fronted Tern *Sterna striata* **LC BE**

ALTERNATIVE NAME Tara | L 42cm WS 79–82cm Wt 60g

Medium-sized, largely white tern with *long, deeply forked tail*. In breeding (A), *forehead white, cap and nape black*. Wings long, narrow and pointed, pale grey above, white below. Forehead, body and tail all white apart from pale grey mantle. *Bill long, black, sharply pointed. Legs short, and feet dull dark red*. Non-breeder (B) black cap recedes and becomes less intense. Immature (C) has streaked cap and barring and mottling on upperparts, including tail. **VOICE/CALL** High-pitched *zeet or sssiit* when fishing, rather harsh *kaaark* or *keeek* when disturbed. **BREEDING** Colonies, often large, on sandbanks and beaches in coastal harbours and on sandspits, offshore rocks and islands. 1 or 2 eggs laid mid-October–January, hatching 3–4 weeks, chicks form crèche after 1 week, fledge after 4–5 weeks. Colonies all around coasts, often together with Red-billed Gulls. **FEEDING** Small surface-shoaling fish; often feeds in large flocks, by shallow plunge-diving or hovering and dipping. **P&R** 1.5 million. All of coastal NZ including Chatham and Auckland islands. Many migrate to southwest Australia during winter. **T&M** No specific threats, but considerable loss during breeding season to cats, rats and mustelids. **BV** Widespread around coasts, inshore waters and harbours, rarely inland.

Adult breeding

Common Tern *Sterna hirundo* **LC OV**

L 36cm WS 79cm Wt 120g

Small, rather grey tern with long, deeply forked tail. In breeding plumage, *forehead, cap and nape black*. Wings mid-grey above with darker primaries. *Rest of body pale grey*, underwing white apart from greying on primaries, *tail long, deeply forked and pale grey. Bill long, sharply pointed, deep red with black tip, legs and feet red*. Non-breeding black cap recedes, breast and abdomen white, bill largely black, feet duller red. Immatures white forehead and streaked cap, wings and mantle somewhat mottled brown, body white, bill yellowish, legs flesh-coloured. Flight rather buoyant. **VOICE/CALL** A short *keek* and rather grating *keeer*. **FEEDING** Similar to White-fronted Tern. **P&R** 2–4 million. A worldwide species, breeds in temperate northern hemisphere, migrates south in northern winter. **T&M** No known threats. **BV** Occasional visitor, NI most likely; Bay of Plenty, Kapiti Coast have most records.

Arctic Tern *Sterna paradisaea* **LC OV**

L 35cm WS 79cm Wt 110g

A rather small, pale tern with *long, deeply forked tail*. All plumages very similar to Common Tern, but *lacks dark wing-tips* and in breeding plumage has *bright red bill, legs very short and feet coral red*. Flight as for Common Tern, hard to differentiate at sea. **VOICE/CALL** Very similar to Common Tern. **FEEDING** As for Common and White-fronted. **P&R** 2 million. Worldwide, breeds in Arctic and migrates to southern oceans during northern winter. **T&M** No known threats. **BV** Chance sightings, coastal waters and harbours during summer.

Antarctic Tern *Sterna vittata* **LC N**

L 36cm WS 79cm Wt 140g

Medium-sized, rather grey tern with *deeply forked tail*. Breeding (A) plumage largely soft grey with white rump and undertail. Black cap down to bill and below eye, cheeks white, underwing white, outermost primaries have black edge. *Bill long and bright red, feet and legs also red.* Non-breeding (B) loses black forehead and bill is dark horn colour. Immature (C) rather brown and mottled with dark bill and dull pink legs. Flight undulating. Larger and greyer than Arctic Tern. **VOICE/CALL** Shrill, high-pitched scream. **BREEDING** Colonial on ground, sometimes cliff ledges, sometimes in bush, on offshore islands, especially sub-Antarctic. Breeding varies according to island group. On Snares, 1 or 2 eggs laid September–March, later further south. Hatching after 4 weeks, with fledging 4–5 weeks later. **FEEDING** Fish and crustaceans, also some molluscs and invertebrates, mainly by dipping and shallow plunge-diving. **P&R** 130,000–140,000. Circumpolar, in NZ on islands around Stewart I. and on all sub-Antarctic islands. **T&M** Vulnerable to introduced pest predator species. **BV** Stewart I., otherwise around breeding grounds further south.

Adult breeding

Black-fronted Tern *Chlidonias albostriata* **EN E**

ALTERNATIVE NAME Tarapiroe | L 30cm WS 65–72cm Wt 80g

Small, rather grey tern with fairly short, forked tail. In breeding (A), *forehead, cap and nape black, cheeks white, throat, breast and abdomen blue-grey, undertail and rump white*. Upperwing, mantle and tail blue-grey but darker than breast. *Bill, which is quite short, and legs and feet bright orange*. Non-breeding (B) loses black cap and forehead, nape black streaked with white, dark eye-patch, bill orange with darker tip. Immature (C) similar to non-breeding, crown and nape streaked brown, back brownish grey, bill yellowish brown. **VOICE/CALL** High staccato whistle, but also short *kit*, and *kee-kee-kee* when disturbed or a harsh *yark*. **BREEDING** Colonially on ground inland, on shingle banks in braided rivers of eastern and northern SI. 1–4 eggs laid early October–late November, hatching after 3–4 weeks, fledging 4–5 weeks later. **FEEDING** Very varied diet: insect larvae, crustaceans and small fish from rivers by dipping, also small lizards, invertebrates on farmland, and during winter mainly crustaceans and invertebrates on coast. **P&R** 7,000–10,000, declining. Breeds only inland on SI, migrates to coast in winter, small number to NI, east coast as far as Bay of Plenty, and southwest coast. **T&M** Seriously threatened by introduced pest predators, including Australian Magpie, also dogs and sheep, human recreational activities, loss of water in rivers due to farming and hydroelectricity projects, alien weed species and alien tree planting, which reduce invertebrate populations. **BV** SI, inland on braided rivers in spring and summer, coastal areas in winter. NI east coast in autumn and winter.

White-winged Black Tern *Chlidonias leucopterus* **LC NBM**

L 23cm WS 66cm Wt 65g

Small, distinctive, *black and white tern* with *short, only slightly forked tail.* Breeding (A) *head, body and mantle black*, tail and undertail white. Upperwing white with mid-grey primaries. Underwing coverts all black, primaries and secondaries greyish white. *Bill quite small and reddish black, legs and feet light orange.* Non-breeding black becomes grey apart from *band from eye to eye across nape.* Immatures (B) similar to non-breeding but darker grey on upperwing and mantle. Flight swift, agile and buoyant. **FEEDING** Mainly insects by surface dipping, some fish and tadpoles. **P&R** 2.5–4.5 million. Breeds from eastern Europe to China, migrating south in winter. Predominantly a freshwater species. **T&M** Habitat loss and avian influenza. **BV** Widespread but in very small numbers, coastal lagoons and rivers, especially Auckland and Canterbury.

Whiskered Tern *Chlidonias hybrida* **LC V**

L 26cm Ws 69cm Wt 90g

Small grey tern, with short, modestly forked tail. In breeding plumage (A), *forehead, cap and nape black, cheeks white*, upperparts all mid-grey, underparts grey apart from undertail. *Bill bright red, legs and feet duller red.* Non-breeding (B) is white below with *dark band from eye to eye across nape.* Immature similar but with brownish borders on upperwing and pale rump. Flight buoyant and purposeful. **FEEDING** Largely insects, taken by surface dipping. **P&R** To 1.5 million. Africa and Australia, vagrant to NZ. **T&M** Habitat loss. **BV** Chance sighting on coastal lakes, wetlands and sewage ponds.

Fairy Tern *Sterna nereis* **VU** (NZ ssp. CE) **N**

L 25cm WS 15cm Wt 70g

Very small tern with *short, forked tail.* In breeding (A), *cap and nape black*, upperwing and mantle pale grey. Rest of body and tail white. *Bill finely pointed and orange-yellow. Legs and feet orange.* Non-breeding (B) cap less black, *bill dull yellow with dark tip.* Immature (C) similar but bill largely black, hint of yellow at base, faint dark leading edge to wing, legs brown. **VOICE/CALL** Harsh *zwit* or *zewit.* **BREEDING** Solitary ground nesters, on sand-spits or shingle banks close to high-tide mark. 1 or 2 eggs laid mid-November–early December, hatching after 3–4 weeks, fledging after a further 3+ weeks. **FEEDING** Mainly small fish by shallow plunge-diving, in harbours and estuaries or close inshore. **P&R** 5,000–6,000, declining. In NZ, *S. n. davisae* numbers 80–100 birds, confined to Northland. Also, in Australia *S. n. nereis* and New Caledonia *S. n. exulsa.* **T&M** Critically endangered in NZ through loss of habitat and disturbance, predation by pest species and extreme weather events affecting exposed nesting locations. Under intensive management, numbers have increased recently. **BV** Northland harbours; ventures south to Bay of Plenty and Kaipara Harbour in winter.

Little Tern *Sterna albifrons* **LC RV**

L 25cm WS 51cm Wt 50g

Very small, delicate tern with *short, forked tail*, like a dark Fairy Tern. In breeding (A), *forehead white, cap and nape and lores black*. Upperwing and mantle mid-grey with dark edge to outer primaries, rest of plumage white. *Bill long and sharply pointed, yellow with black tip, feet and legs dull yellow*. Non-breeding (B), *crown streaked white, bill dull yellow with larger black tip*. Immature similar but upperparts somewhat mottled and dark band along leading edge of upperwing, bill all black, legs brown. Flight erratic with long wing-beats. **VOICE/CALL** Chittering *chee-chee-chee* or *peep-peep-eep* and sometimes a rasping *zweek*. **FEEDING** Mainly small fish by hovering and splash diving. **P&R** 200,000–400,000. Widespread, North America, Europe, Africa, Australasia; migrates south during northern winter. **T&M** No known threats. **BV** Northland harbours south to Auckland, occasionally further south.

Sooty Tern *Sterna fuscata* **LC N**

L 45cm WS 86cm Wt 210g

Large, elegant, black and white tern with long, deeply forked tail (A). Cap, nape and lores black, upperwing and tail black apart from white band on leading edge. Rest of plumage white, including *long outer tail feathers. Bill long, sharply pointed and black*. Immature (B) is largely browny black with pale belly and undertail, light brown feather edges on upperwing give scalloped appearance, tail shorter. Darker than Bridled Tern. **VOICE/CALL** Distinctive *wideawake* call. **BREEDING** Colonial ground nester, NZ colonies in the Kermadecs, single egg laid October–December, hatching after 4 weeks and fledging after 4+ weeks. Young form crèches. **FEEDING** Squid and small fish, mainly nocturnal well out to sea, by surface dipping. **P&R** Worldwide 21–22 million, NZ 50,000+. Worldwide, tropical and subtropical, very pelagic out of breeding season. **T&M** Introduced predator species: rats, cats. Human disturbance: egg harvesting. **BV** Kermadecs and occasionally off NI, especially in autumn.

Bridled Tern *Sterna anaethetus* **LC V**

L 41cm WS 76cm Wt 120g

Medium to large, elegant, *dark-brown and white* tern with *very long, deeply forked tail*. Looks very like a small, brown Sooty Tern. *Cap, nape and lores black. Upperparts all dark brown with white leading edge to wing*. Underparts and long, outer tail feathers all white. *Bill long, black and finely pointed*. Legs and feet black. Immature cap less distinct and browner, feathers on wings and mantle tipped buff, giving scalloped or mottled appearance. **FEEDING** Small fish by splash diving, rarely hovers. **P&R** 600,000–1.5 million. Pan-tropical. **T&M** No known threats. **BV** Chance observation, most likely northern NI.

Noddies Unlike terns, noddies have a more upright posture, longer legs and neck and a long, fine bill; unlike most, they frequently settle on water.

Common Noddy *Anous stolidus* **LC N**

L 39cm WS 84cm Wt 200g

Medium-sized, *all-dark tern with very long, bluntly forked tail. Head mid-grey with paler forehead, lores black.* Rest of plumage all dark chocolate brown apart from greyish patches on underwing coverts. *Bill long, black and finely pointed,* legs and feet black. Immatures similar with darker head. Flight buoyant and undulating. **VOICE/CALL** Rather crow-like *kaaark.* **BREEDING** Loosely colonial on ground, on cliff ledge or in trees. In NZ a few pairs breed in Kermadecs. Single egg laid September–November, hatching after 4–5 weeks, fledging 4–5 weeks later. **FEEDING** Small fish taken from surface of ocean by dipping; very pelagic out of breeding season. **P&R** 0.5–1.5 million. Worldwide in tropical, subtropical and warm temperate waters. **T&M** No known threats. **BV** Chance sighting, most likely northern NI.

Black Noddy *Anous tenuirostris* **LC N**

PREVIOUSLY White-capped Noddy | L 37cm WS 71cm Wt 100g

Medium-sized, *very dark* noddy. Plumage *entirely dark black-brown* apart from *white forehead and cap,* blending gradually into black. Tail long and forked. Legs and feet dark brown. Bill long, black and finely pointed. Lacks pale underwing of Common Noddy. **BREEDING** In NZ in Kermadecs only. Single egg laid August–January, in rather untidy nest in small tree or shrub, hatching after 5 weeks, fledging after 7–8 weeks. **FEEDING** Fish and plankton, by hovering and dipping. **P&R** 1.2 million. Tropical Atlantic and Pacific oceans. Remain around breeding areas year-round. **T&M** Some human predation in past. **BV** Kermadecs, vagrant to northern NI.

White Tern *Gygis alba* **LC N**

L 28–33cm WS 66–78cm Wt 110g

Delicate, all-white noddy. Plumage *all white apart from small black feathered eye-ring* and slightly grey shafts to primaries and tail feathers. Tail long and forked. Bill long (4cm), finely pointed and black. *Legs and feet black with yellowish webs.* Immature has dark patch behind eye, darker primary and tail feather quills and rusty tinge to mantle. *Flight swift and erratic.* The only all-white tern or noddy. **BREEDING** Kermadecs only. No nest; single egg laid in depression on horizontal branch, hatching after 4 weeks, fledging after 9–10 weeks. Chick remains in tree for the whole period. **FEEDING** Fish caught by hovering close to the surface and dipping. **P&R** 0.2–1.15 million. Pan-tropical, becoming pelagic out of the breeding season. **T&M** No known threats. **BV** Kermadecs, rare vagrant to northern NI.

Grey Ternlet *Procelsterna cerulea* **LC N**

L 28cm WS 61cm Wt 110g

Small, delicate, all-grey noddy. Head and body pale grey, upperwing mid-grey, somewhat darker on primaries and with thin white trailing edge. Underwing near white. *Tail long and modestly forked.* Eye-ring is dark in front, *white behind,* making eye appear larger. *Legs and feet black with yellow webs.* Bill short (3cm) and black. **VOICE/CALL** A high-pitched scream when on the wing. Softer purr-like *crorrr* when perching. **BREEDING** Kermadecs and occasionally northern NZ, Three Kings, Poor Knights. On bare rock ledge or cavity, single egg laid August–December, hatching after 4–5 weeks, fledging 5 weeks later. **FEEDING** Plankton and some small fish, hovering and dipping, often in flocks. **P&R** 30,000–120,000. Central and southern Pacific. **T&M** No known threats. **BV** Coastal waters of northeast NI, Three Kings, Poor Knights, down to Coromandel, Bay of Plenty and White I.

Waterside and Wetland Birds

Coastal and inland wetlands are an important feature of the New Zealand ecosystem, but what remains is only around 10% of the original, most having been drained to create farmland, often quite marginal. This has resulted in a significant reduction in range and numbers of several bird species. What remains is still impressive, and there is increasing evidence that the tide has turned and the appreciation of the value and importance of wetlands is growing with a number of wetland restoration and creation projects underway throughout the country.

This section is ordered as a logical extension from seabirds, starting with waders, most of which are found on the coast, followed by herons and other long-legged wetland birds, next come rails and swamp hens, which are also 'waders' in a general sense, and finally swans, geese and ducks.

Waders and Shorebirds

With such a large coastline and many intricate and extensive harbours, New Zealand is an excellent place to find waders. Apart from the 16 native species or subspecies, there are a dozen or so regular migrants that spend the summer here, often in very large numbers, and a further 36 or more occasional visitors or vagrants.

Migrant species are generally found in winter plumage, which is often very much plainer than their breeding plumage. This makes identification difficult or at times impossible. To complicate matters, many species retain some elements of their breeding plumage on arrival in New Zealand, while others start to develop breeding plumage before they leave. Because of this you may see a very large variety of plumages. As a result of this, legs, bill and jizz become very important factors in identifying species.

A	
C	B
B	B

Variable Oystercatcher *Haematopus unicolor* **LC E**

FAMILY Haematopodidae | ALTERNATIVE NAME Toreapango

L 48cm WS 88cm Bill (M) 8.3cm (F) 9.2cm Wt 725g

Large, *all-black or nearly all-black wader with massive bright red-orange bill and red eye-ring*. Two phases: dark (A) is all black; *pied phase (B) has white belly* and lower breast, but no partial collar. *Short white bar on secondaries and grey-whitish rump*. Amount of white varies greatly. *Legs long, sturdy and coral pink*. Immature (C) browner, duller bill and legs. **VOICE/CALL** Similar to but hoarser than South Island Pied Oystercatcher. **BREEDING** Ground nester, territorial, on sandy beach; occasionally shingle or rock ledge, close to high-tide mark. 1–5 eggs laid September–February, hatching after 4 weeks; chicks leave nest after 1–2 days, fledging after 6–7 weeks. **FEEDING** Mainly molluscs, especially bivalves, small crabs and invertebrates, and occasionally small fish. **P&R** 4,500, increasing. Very much a coastal bird, occasionally inland lakes. Generally remains in same area year round. **T&M** Habitat loss, introduced mammalian predators. **BV** Widespread around coast of all 3 main islands, rarely inland.

South Island Pied Oystercatcher *Haematopus finschi* **LC E**

FAMILY Haematopodidae | ALTERNATIVE NAME Torea

L 46cm WS 80–86cm Bill 7.3–9.8cm Wt 420–617g

Large, strikingly coloured, *black and white wader with massive bright orange-red bill and orange eye-ring*. Head, neck, upper-breast and tail black. Upperwing and mantle black with *broad white wing bar on secondaries* visible in flight. Underbody *white, extending up to form partial collar*. Underwing white with dark tip and trailing edge. White rump extends into mantle. *Legs long, sturdy and coral pink*. Immature browner, duller bill and legs. **VOICE/CALL** Loud, piping *kleep*. **BREEDING** Ground nester. 2–3 blotched eggs laid August–December, in scrape in shingle bank in river, or on farmland. Hatching after 4 weeks, leave nest after 1–2 days, fledging after 5 weeks. **FEEDING** Largely bivalve molluscs, marine worms and invertebrates, earthworms and terrestrial invertebrates. **P&R** 130,000, increasing. Most breed in SI, inland in river beds and farmland, but since 1980 a few pairs have bred in Hawke's Bay and Wairarapa. Most winter in NI and northern SI coasts, especially harbours and estuaries. **T&M** Habitat loss, introduced mammalian predators. **BV** Inland on braided rivers and farmland in SI during spring and summer. Coastal harbours and mudflats in NI and SI during autumn and winter, especially Miranda, Kaipara and Manukau harbours and the Bay of Plenty.

Chatham Island Oystercatcher *Haematopus chathamensis* **EN E**

FAMILY Haematopodidae | L 48cm Bill (M) 6.8cm (F) 7.7cm Wt 600g

Distinctive large *black and white wader with very large red-orange bill*. Similar to pied phase of Variable Oystercatcher, but black/white margin on breast more distinct and has small white patch ahead of folded wing as South Island Pied Oystercatcher. Bill somewhat smaller than previous 2 species. *Legs rather sturdy, and coral pink. Only large black and white shorebird in Chatham Is*. **VOICE/CALL** Similar to South Island Pied Oystercatcher. **BREEDING** Similar to Variable Oystercatcher, but nest may be under small shrub for protection from skuas and gulls. **FEEDING** Bivalve molluscs, limpets and chitons, and marine invertebrates. **P&R** 320+. Found only in Chatham Is. **T&M** Habitat loss, stock on beaches and introduced alien predators. **BV** Chatham Is.

Pied Stilt *Himantopus himantopus leucocephalus* **LC N**

FAMILY Recurvirostridae | ALTERNATIVE NAME Poaka

L 35cm WS 67cm Bill 6.3cm Wt 190g

Elegant, black and white wader with *extremely long (to 18cm) pink legs, and long, thin, black bill*. Plumage (A) *largely white but with variable black on nape and shoulder, and all-black wings with white patch in armpit*. Immature (B) lacks black on nape and shoulder but has greyish crown. Legs extend 10–12cm beyond tail in flight. **BREEDING** Loosely colonial, ground nester in pastures near water or pond edges or coastal harbours. 4 eggs laid August–October, 1–2 months later further inland. Hatch after 3–4 weeks; chicks leave nest soon after hatching, fledging after 5 weeks. **FEEDING** Aquatic and terrestrial invertebrates. **P&R** 450,000–780,000. NZ subspecies of global species. Found throughout NZ apart from alpine and forested areas. Internal migration to northern NI during winter. **T&M** Introduced alien predators. **BV** Coastal mudflats and inland rivers, ponds and lakes.

Black Stilt *Himantopus novaezelandiae* **CE E**

FAMILY Recurvirostridae | ALTERNATIVE NAME Kaki

L 40cm WS 58cm Bill 6.3cm Wt 220g

Elegant, *all-black wader (A) with extremely long (to 90mm) bright pink legs and long, black, very thin, pointed bill*. Plumage all black. Immatures have some white on face, neck and breast; juveniles (B) have white head, neck and breast. Often hybridises (C) with Pied Stilt with very variable results. **VOICE/CALL** High-pitched yapping alarm call. **BREEDING** Solitary ground nester, in wetlands, by ponds or in braided rivers. 4 eggs laid September–December, hatching after 3.5 weeks and fledging after 5–8 weeks. **FEEDING** Aquatic invertebrates, also some fish and molluscs. **P&R** *c*.200. Breeds only in Mackenzie Basin in central SI. Out of breeding season birds disperse locally but some migrate north to coastal mudflats and harbours in NI. **T&M** Loss of habitat and predation by introduced alien mammals. Subject to an intensive management and captive breeding programme. **BV** Mackenzie Basin, also mudflats along east and north coasts of SI and Tauranga, Manukau and Kaipara harbours in NI.

Red-necked Avocet *Recurvirostra novaehollandiae* **LC V**

FAMILY Recurvirostridae | L 44cm WS 75cm Bill 9cm Wt 310g

Unmistakable *long-legged, long-necked wader with long, fine, upcurved bill. Head and neck dark chestnut, body and wings white* apart from black-brown primaries, secondary coverts and stripes either side of mantle. Underwing white with black tips visible in flight. *Legs very long (to 12.5cm) and blue-grey*. Immature paler and duller. **VOICE/CALL** Short barking call, also flute-like *tuut*. **FEEDING** Invertebrates, crustaceans, occasionally seeds and foliage. **P&R** 110,000. Australian endemic, from 1859 to 1892 reported widely in NZ and attempted to breed, last reported in NZ during 1968–70. **T&M** Loss of breeding habitat. **BV** Wetlands, lakes and estuaries.

Banded Dotterel *Charadrius bicinctus bicinctus* **LC N**

FAMILY Charadriidae | ALTERNATIVE NAME Tuturiwhatu | L 20cm WS 40cm Wt 70g

Small, rather *plump* wader with *upright stance*. Breeding male (A) has mid-brown nape, upperwing, mantle and tail. *Narrow white wing bar and white indents either side of rump. White on forehead extends back into pale eyebrow*. Undersides all white apart from *broad black throat band and broader chestnut breast band*. Bill short, stout and black. Legs quite long and grey. Female breeding similar but markings less distinct. Non-breeders lose chestnut breast band and throat band less distinct. Immature (B) has diffuse throat band only. **VOICE/CALL** Repeated '*chip*' or longer '*tweep*'. **BREEDING** Solitary ground nester, on sand or gravel spits, coastal and inland areas, especially river beds. 3 eggs laid July–November in lowland areas, but as late as November–December in upland areas of SI. Hatching after 3.5 weeks, and fledging after 5–6 weeks. **FEEDING** Invertebrates, terrestrial and aquatic, and some berries. **P&R** 50,000. Widespread in NZ, including Chatham Is. More common in coastal areas in NI, but breeds inland in SI and Stewart I., these populations migrating to NI or Australia during winter, but coastal breeders are mainly sedentary. **T&M** Habitat loss, introduced mammalian pests. **BV** Sandy spits and river beds, widespread in small numbers. NI from Coromandel northwards and Hawke's Bay southwards. SI inland braided rivers, especially North Canterbury. **SUBSPECIES** **Auckland Island Banded Dotterel** *C. b. exilis* (C) is very similar but found only in the Auckland Is.

New Zealand Dotterel *Charadrius obscurus* **VU E**

FAMILY Charadriidae | ALTERNATIVE NAME Tuturiwhatu
L 27cm WS 48cm Wt 150g

Medium-sized, *approachable*, rather *dumpy wader with stout black bill* and quite short grey legs. Upperparts largely greyish brown with *narrow white wing bar and white indentations on sides of rump*. Adult breeding (A) has *warm cinnamon colouring on breast and belly*, sometimes almost chestnut on males. Forehead and throat white, faint white eyebrow. Non-breeding (B) loses cinnamon colouring and is generally greyer. Immature similar but browner with slightly dirty underparts; head has 'capped' look. **VOICE/CALL** Short, repeated trill, *trrrt* or *chrrp*. **BREEDING** Northern ssp. nests individually or in small groups, a ground nester on sand spits and beaches, especially near stream mouths. Southern ssp. nests on open subalpine mountain and ridge tops. 2–3 eggs laid August–January, starting later in Stewart I., hatching after 4–4.5 weeks, fledging after 6–7 weeks. **FEEDING** Mainly invertebrates, terrestrial and aquatic, also small fish and molluscs. **P&R** 2,000. Northern ssp. in NI from North Cape south to Napier in the east and Kawhia Harbour in the west, mainly sandy beaches. Southern ssp. breeds on subalpine tops on Stewart I., winters mainly on southern coasts of SI with a few as far north as Farewell Spit. **T&M** Loss of habitat, human disturbance on beaches. Introduced mammalian pests, especially Hedgehogs, rats, Stoats and possums in north, and cats on Stewart I. Both subspecies subject to intensive protection measures, which has seen numbers gradually increase. **BV** Northern ssp. on sandy beaches and spits on east coast from Bay of Plenty northwards. Southern ssp. on Southland beaches in autumn–winter. **SUBSPECIES** **Southern New Zealand Dotterel** *C. o. obscurus* (C) is larger (160g) and more brightly coloured than **Northern New Zealand Dotterel** *C. o. aquilonius*.

Black-fronted Dotterel *Elseyornis melanops* **LC N**

FAMILY Charadriidae | L 17cm WS 34cm Wt 33g

Small, slim dotterel with striking head plumage. Adult (A) *has black forehead, brown cap, a white band above eye and a broad black eye-stripe*; cheeks and throat white. Upperwing brown with *large black tips and diffuse white wing bar*. Tail black with *white outer tail feathers*. Underside white apart from *broad black chest band*. Underwing white with black wing-tips and trailing edge and dark patch outward of carpal joint. Bill stout, pointed, *red with black tip, legs dull orange*. Immature (B) similar but paler, lacks black forehead and chest band, bill dull orange, legs dull yellow. **VOICE/CALL** Sharp, high-pitched *dip-dip* or softer *tink-tink,* not very vocal. **BREEDING** Solitary ground nester, on shingle banks in river beds. 2–3 eggs laid August–February, starting later in some areas. Hatching after 3–3.5 weeks, fledging 4–6 weeks later. **FEEDING** Mainly molluscs, crustaceans, insects and earthworms. **P&R** NZ population ~1,700. Mainly southern NI and east and northeast of SI. Widespread in Australia. **T&M** Alien mammalian predators. **BV** Southern Hawke's Bay and south to Wellington. In SI mainly Marlborough and South Canterbury.

Lesser Sand Plover *Charadrius mongolus* **LC OV**

FAMILY Charadriidae | L 20cm WS 52cm Wt 64g | TAXONOMIC NOTE 4 or 5 races or populations, sometimes viewed as two species, Mongolian Dotterel *C. mongolus* and Lesser Sand Plover *C. atrifrons*.

Small, long-legged dotterel. Breeding adult (A) has grey-brown upperparts and white underparts with *broad rufous collar and nape*. *White forehead, large black eye-patch* extending forward to *short dark bill*, in male this may extend around throat on top of rufous band. Throat and chin white. Narrow *white wing bar visible in flight*. Non-breeding (B) lacks black and rufous colouring, largely grey-brown and white with partial breast band. Immature similar. **VOICE/CALL** Short ,hard *chitik*. **FEEDING** Molluscs, worms, crustaceans and insects. **P&R** 350,000. Breeds central and northeast Asia, migrates south; a very small number reach NZ each summer. **T&M** Loss and degradation of habitat. **BV** Firth of Thames, Manukau, Kaipara and Maketu harbours.

Non-breeding

Greater Sand Plover *Charadrius leschenaultii* **LC OV**

FAMILY Charadriidae | L 24cm WS 57cm Wt 90g

Breeding adult (A) very similar to, but larger than, Lesser Sand Plover, and with *significantly longer bill. Black eye-patch does not extend around throat*. Non-breeding (B) similar to non-breeding New Zealand Dotterel, but smaller, slimmer and longer-legged. **VOICE/CALL** Short, trill-like *treep*. **FEEDING** Molluscs, crustaceans, worms, insects, occasional lizard. **P&R** 200,000–300,000. Breeds central Asia, migrates south; small numbers reach NZ most summers. **T&M** Loss of habitat, both in breeding and overwintering areas. **BV** Firth of Thames, Manukau, Parengarenga, Kaipara and Maketu harbours.

Red-capped Dotterel *Charadrius ruficapillus* **LC V**

FAMILY Charadriidae | L 15cm WS 30cm Wt 38g

Very *small, active* dotterel. White underparts and forehead, pale to mid-brown back, with *white wing bar visible in flight. Male has distinctive chestnut cap and partial collar and a black line on forehead between cap and white forehead,* also dark loral line running through eye to bill. Female has less rufous cap and lacks black line on forehead. Immature similar but duller. Legs dark, bill short and dark. **VOICE/CALL** A rather soft *wit-wit-wit* or *plink-plink*. **FEEDING** Small invertebrates, molluscs, crustaceans and worms. **P&R** 95,000. Breeds in Australia, occasional visitor to NZ. **T&M** Habitat loss a potential problem. **BV** Estuaries, harbours and braided rivers, NI and SI.

Oriental Dotterel *Charadrius veredus* **LC RV**

FAMILY Charadriidae | L 24cm WS 50cm Wt 95g

Medium-sized, *slim, upright, long-legged, short-billed* wader. Breeding adult white belly and undertail, greyish-brown back, tail and wings, rather darker at tips. Head pale brown with *white face and throat. Rich chestnut-red band on breast with blackish line between it and white belly.* Non-breeding (photo) largely pale brown on breast and neck with diffuse *white line above eye.* Underwing grey-pale brown. Bill dark and quite fine, legs long and dull yellow, extending beyond tail in flight. Immature similar but duller. **VOICE/CALL** A rather high-pitched, piping *klink* in flight, long undulating trill on ground. **FEEDING** Invertebrates, especially insects. **P&R** 70,000. Breeds in northern China, migrates south to Indonesia and Australia, rare stragglers reach NZ. **T&M** Habitat loss a potential problem. **BV** Harbours and estuaries.

Semipalmated Plover *Charadrius semipalmatus* **LC V**

FAMILY Charadriidae | L 19cm WS 50cm Wt 60g

Small, dumpy, strikingly plumaged plover. Breeding adult head grey-brown and black with *white forehead and eye-stripe, complete white collar followed by broad black breast-band,* underparts white, back, tail and wings greyish brown; in flight, darker at tips with white wing bar. *Bill short, orange-red with black tip,* legs dull orange. Non-breeding (photo) and immature lack black on head, and breast band browner, bill dark brown, legs duller. **VOICE/CALL** Liquid, piping *queeep*. **FEEDING** Small crustaceans, molluscs, worms, isopods, amphipods and insects. **P&R** Up to 1 million. Breeds in Arctic, migrates south mainly to Africa. Vagrant to NZ. **T&M** No known threats. **BV** Estuaries and harbours, especially NI.

Red-kneed Dotterel *Erythrogonys cinctus* **LC V**

FAMILY Charadriidae | L 18cm WS 35cm Wt 50g

Small, *dumpy, long-legged dotterel* with distinctive *black cap*. Head to below eye and nape black, mantle and wings grey-brown, rump and tail brown with *white edges*. Underparts white with *broad black band across chest, turning rufous on abdomen*. In flight, wings have dark primaries and secondaries have broad white trailing edge. *Bill dull red with black tip*. *Legs pink to below knee, then grey*. Immature has grey-brown instead of black on head and breast, bill and legs duller. **VOICE/CALL** Rapid *wit-wit*, in flight a series of staccato notes. **FEEDING** Seeds, molluscs and invertebrates. **P&R** Breeds in Australia, rare vagrant to NZ. **T&M** Loss of breeding habitat a cause for concern. **BV** NI estuaries and harbours.

Shore Plover *Thinornis novaeseelandiae* **EN E**

FAMILY Charadriidae | ALTERNATIVE NAME Tuturuatu | L 20cm Wt 60g

Small, *very short-legged*, long-billed plover. Male (A) *head and throat black, cap has white ring with brown on top like a skullcap*, underparts and underwing white, back, wings and tail grey-brown with *black tip to tail*; black patches on primary coverts and *white wing bar* visible in flight. Red eye-ring. *Bill bright red-orange with dark tip*, legs dull orange-yellow. Female (B) similar but somewhat duller. Immature (C) grey-brown and white, bill dark, legs dull brown. **VOICE/CALL** High-pitched *peep peeep*. **BREEDING** Individually, 2 or 3 buff eggs spotted darker brown laid October–January in a nest set under dense vegetation, beach rack or boulders, either on the shore or further inland; incubation 4 weeks, fledging after 5–8 weeks. **FEEDING** Feeds on small crustaceans, molluscs and other invertebrates. **P&R** 300. Previously widespread but seriously preyed upon by cats and rats, and was restricted to Rangatira/South East I. (Chathams). Successfully reintroduced to Mangere I. (Chathams), and several NI locations. Population increasing. **T&M** Subject to an intensive protection programme, captive breeding, and release at predator-free or pest-controlled sites. **BV** Mana I. (Wellington), Rangatira/South East I. (Chathams), Portland I. (Hawke's Bay) and Hauraki Gulf.

Spur-winged Plover *Vanellus miles novaehollandiae* **LC N**

FAMILY Charadriidae | ALTERNATIVE NAME Masked Lapwing

L 34cm WS 80cm Wt 360g

Medium-large, *upright, long-legged* wader. *Head above eye is black, extending down nape, and forming broad partial collar*. Very distinctive *yellow wattles* on either side of head, extending above and below *bill, which is also yellow*. Undersides, breast, neck and lower face white. Upperwing and mantle mid-brown with dark primaries and secondaries visible only in flight. Underwing white with dark primaries and secondaries. *Spur on wing joint* often visible, especially in flight. *Legs long, dull to deep red*. Immature (A) similar but frontal shield and wattles not fully developed, back and upperwings rather mottled, legs grey. *Broad, very rounded wings and very distinctive undulating flight*. Subspecies *V. m. miles* has smaller black cap, no black on nape and lacks partial black collar. **VOICE/CALL** Loud, raucous *ker-rik -ker-rik* or staccato *ki-ki-ki*. **BREEDING** Ground nester, in open ground, June–November; up to 4 dark brown mottled eggs, hatching after 4–5 weeks, fledging after 7–8 weeks. Very noisy and aggressive while breeding. First recorded nesting in NZ in 1932. **FEEDING** Invertebrates, especially worms and insects, also some molluscs and crustaceans when near shore. **P&R** Up to 2 million. Recent arrival in NZ but now widespread, clear beneficiary of agricultural development. **T&M** No known threats; known to predate some native species, especially during breeding season. **BV** Widespread throughout country; open farmland and coastal wetlands.

Pacific Golden Plover *Pluvialis fulva* **LC NBM**

FAMILY Charadriidae | L 25cm WS 66cm Wt 150g

Medium-sized, *upright, long-legged, short-billed* wader. Breeding (A – left-hand bird) plumage very dramatic. *Black undersides, breast, throat and chin extending to behind eye. Crown, back and tail flecked black, white and gold.* White on forehead extends as a dividing line between 2 contrasting plumages. Non-breeding (B) is generally light speckled brown all over, but retains some *yellow on back and head; chin pale and pale line above eye.* Bill quite *short and dark*, legs dark. Immature similar to non-breeding, slightly darker. In NZ often seen with some breeding plumage, especially in autumn. In flight, primaries and secondaries show darker and feet extend beyond tail. **VOICE/CALL** Clear double whistle *too-il too-il* or a clear *keeey - yee*. **FEEDING** Feeds in saltmarsh, mudflats and pastures around estuaries and harbours. Predominantly insects, molluscs, worms, crustaceans and spiders. **P&R** To 250,000. Breeds in Arctic and migrates south to NZ in September–October. Leaves March–April. **T&M** No known threats. **BV** Widespread during spring and summer in and near estuaries and harbours; few if any overwinter.

American Golden Plover *Pluvialis dominica* **LC V**

FAMILY Charadriidae | L 26cm WS 60–70cm Wt 165g

Very similar but rather *bulkier and longer-winged* than Pacific Golden Plover. In breeding plumage it is *less golden on back and white dividing plumage stops on breast.* Non-breeding plumage (photo) almost identical but greyer than Pacific. **VOICE/CALL** Similar to Pacific. **FEEDING** Similar to Pacific. **P&R** 200,000, decreasing. Breeds in Arctic, migrates to inland South America; 1 confirmed NZ record. **T&M** No known threats. **BV** Harbours and wetlands, NI most likely.

Grey Plover *Pluvialis squatarola* **LC NBM**

FAMILY Charadriidae | L 29cm WS 77cm Wt 250g

Medium-sized, stout, *heavy-billed* plover, with shorter legs than the golden plovers. Breeding plumage has *lower half of face, breast and belly black, black and silver-white flecked back and upperwing.* Broad white band separates upper- and underparts but not on flanks. *Bill heavy and black, legs dark.* Non-breeding (photo) flecked grey and white all over, paler underneath, faint white line above eye and base of bill. In flight, *black armpits* visible. Immature similar but darker and some yellow on back. **VOICE/CALL** Trisyllabic *hee-ooo-eee*. **FEEDING** Invertebrates, small molluscs and crustaceans. **P&R** 360,000. Breeds in Arctic, migrates south in winter, with small numbers reaching NZ each spring–autumn. **T&M** No known threats; some indication that removal of *Spartina* from mudflats is beneficial. **BV** Harbours and estuaries throughout the country; occasionally overwinters.

Chatham Island Snipe *Coenocorypha pusilla* **VU E**

FAMILY Scolopacidae | L 20cm WS 28–30cm Bill 4.0–4.5cm Wt (M) 75g (F) 85g

Very small, dumpy, brown, variegated snipe. *Top of head striped black, brown/reddish brown.* Rest of body mottled black, brown/reddish brown except for pale lower breast and belly. *Bill long and legs short.* Only long-billed, short-legged wader in Chatham Is. **VOICE/CALL** Male call a low *trerk, trerk, trerk* and *queeyoo, queeyoo, queeyoo*. **BREEDING** Ground nester, 2–3 eggs laid September–January. **FEEDING** Insects, earthworms and other invertebrates. **P&R** 2,000. Confined to 4 small islands in the Chatham Is; main population is on Rangatira/South East I., also on Mangere I. Occasional on other islands in the group. **T&M** Confined to predator-free islands, very susceptible to rats and other mammalian predators. Population increasing but attempts at captive breeding have not been successful. **BV** Chatham Is.

New Zealand Snipe *Coenocorypha* spp. **NT E**

FAMILY Scolopacidae | ALTERNATIVE NAMES Hakawai, Hokioi

A L 23cm WS 30–35cm Bill 4.5–5.0cm Wt 90–120g

Small, plump brown wader. Bill long, brown, slightly down-curved; top of head *striped black and brown/reddish brown*; rest of body mottled black and brown/reddish brown; female larger than male. **VOICE/CALL** Very similar to Chatham Island Snipe, low *trerk, trerk, trerk* and *queeyoo, queeyoo, queeyoo*, mainly by male. **BREEDING** Ground nester, 2 eggs laid August–January, hatching after 3 weeks, each parent looking after 1 chick for up to 9 weeks. **FEEDING** Wide range of insects and other invertebrates. **P&R** Restricted to their respective island groups. *C. huegeli* less than 1,000 individuals, *C. aucklandica aucklandica* in thousands, with no reliable estimate and *C. a. meinertzhagenae* ~8,000 birds in 1995. **T&M** Very susceptible to alien mammalian predators. Its existing range is largely on sanctuary islands. In April 2005, 30 Snares Is subspecies were transferred to Putauhinu I. off Stewart I. **BV** Snares, Auckland or Antipodes islands.

Until recently, it was considered that there were 5 subspecies of the New Zealand Snipe, all similar but geographically isolated. Recent research has indicated that there were in fact 5 distinct species, 1 of which had 2 subspecies. Three of the species, the **North Island Snipe** *C. barrierensis*, the **South Island Snipe** *C. iredalei* and **Forbes' Snipe** *C. chathamica* are extinct. The remaining species and subspecies are: **Snares Island Snipe** *C. huegeli*, which is found only in the Snares Is; and **Sub-Antarctic Snipe** *C. aucklandica*, which has 2 distinct populations, the **Auckland Island Snipe** *C. a. aucklandica* and the **Antipodes Island Snipe** (A) *C. a. meinertzhagenae*; these are found only in their respective island groups.

Snare's Island Snipe

Australian Painted Snipe *Rostratula australis* **EN V**

PREVIOUSLY *R.benghalensis australis* | FAMILY Rostratulidae
L 25cm WS 52cm Bill 4.0–4.8cm Wt 120g

Medium-sized, *long-billed*, snipe-like, skulking wader with very distinctive plumage. *Female has dark chestnut head, neck and upper breast with prominent white eye-stripe and buff-coloured median line from base of bill to crown.* Belly white, undertail cinnamon, broad white harness at front of wings. *Upperwing dark ashy grey with greenish gloss and vermiculations.* In flight, underwing shows white with broad dark band on leading and training edges. Male (photo) similar, but smaller and less colourful. *Bill long and dull yellow*, legs long for a snipe and dull yellow. **VOICE/CALL** Occasional loud *kek*, otherwise only during courtship. **FEEDING** Feeds on insects, crustaceans and molluscs in fresh- and brackish-water wetlands and margins. **P&R** 2,500. Breeds in Australia; 1 record for NZ. **T&M** Loss of wetland habitat and also grazing by cattle in and around wetlands. Management looking to protect breeding and wintering sites. **BV** Chance sighting, most likely near harbours, estuaries and shallow freshwater wetlands.

Japanese Snipe *Gallinago hardwickii* **LC OV**

FAMILY Scolopacidae | L 29–30cm WS 50–54cm Bill 6.6–7.7cm Wt 150–230g

Distinctive, heavy-bodied snipe with *very long, straight bill.* Plumage all brown, *barred and vermiculated*, darker on back and paler underneath. Head has series of *dark and pale stripes*. Legs rather short and greyish yellow. Rufous end to tail visible in flight, which is *typical zig-zagging snipe* flight. **VOICE/CALL** Short *zak* or *chrak*. **FEEDING** Insects, molluscs and crustaceans. **P&R** To 100,000, declining. Breeds in Japan, migrates south to Australia, occasionally to NZ. **T&M** Habitat destruction and degradation. **BV** Chance sighting mainly in long grass, rushes near freshwater wetlands.

Upland Sandpiper *Bartramia longicauda* **LC V**

FAMILY Scolopacidae | L 28cm Wt 140g

Medium-sized, unusual-looking, *long-legged* wader with an *upright stance, long neck and short, fine bill.* Plumage generally pale to mid-brown, *heavily streaked and barred*, darker on back, paler underneath, belly white. *Legs yellow, bill dull yellow, darker at tip, faint eye-stripe*. Often holds wings up after landing, revealing *dark barring on underwing*. **VOICE/CALL** A rather slow *kwip-ip-ip-ip*. **FEEDING** Invertebrates; feeds mainly in pastures away from water. **P&R** 350,000. Breeds on inland grasslands in USA and Canada; migrates south in winter; 1 record for NZ. **T&M** No known threats, population appears to be increasing. **BV** Chance sighting.

Red Knot *Calidris canutus* LC NBM

FAMILY Scolopacidae | L 24cm WS 45–54cm Bill 3.2cm Wt 120g

Small to medium-sized, *stocky*, slightly rounded wader. Breeding (A) plumage *face, breast and belly rich rust red*, back, mid- to dark brown with black and rust-red flecking. Non-breeding (B) plumage generally grey, undersides near white, back and head flecked brown and black. *Bill long, pointed and black*, legs short and grey. In NZ often seen with some breeding plumage colour, especially in autumn. In flight, *white wing bar and barred rump* visible. Immature similar to non-breeding. **VOICE/CALL** Not very vocal, occasionally low *k-nut*. **FEEDING** In NZ mainly intertidal invertebrates such as bivalve and gastropod molluscs, annelid worms and insects, rarely also fish and seeds. **P&R** 1.1 million. Breeds in Arctic and migrates south to Australasia. **T&M** Loss of habitat, feeding areas, pollution and human disturbance, especially on migratory routes. **BV** Second commonest summer visitor, widespread in main estuaries and harbours throughout the country. Many overwinter.

Great Knot *Calidris tenuirostris* LC NBM

FAMILY Scolopacidae | L 27cm WS 58cm Bill 4–4.5cm Wt 150–160g

Medium-sized, stocky, rather short-legged wader with large, heavy bill. Non-breeding plumage (A) *head and neck slightly brownish grey, streaked*, back and upperwing brownish grey with darker streaking, *narrow white wing bar* visible in flight. *Rump white*, tail dark. Undersides largely white with some streaking and flecking on flanks. *Bill long and black, legs dull yellow*. Breeding adult (B) much *darker upperparts with some reddish brown on wings, breast and flanks* black-spotted and flecked. Immature similar to non-breeding but greyer. **VOICE/CALL** Not very vocal, occasional *nye-ut nye-ut*. **FEEDING** Very similar to Red Knot. **P&R** *c.*380,000. Breeds in Siberia, migrates south in northern winter. **T&M** Loss of habitat, feeding areas, pollution and human disturbance, especially on migratory routes. **BV** Coastal lagoons and harbours, often seen with Red Knot and other migratory waders. Not common.

Curlew Sandpiper *Calidris ferruginea* LC NBM

FAMILY Scolopacidae | L 18–23cm WS 38–41cm Bill 3.2–4.3cm Wt 55–60g

Small, *dumpy*, rather *short-legged* wader with *long, fine, dark, distinctly down-curved bill*. Non-breeding (A) plumage is largely pale brownish grey above and white beneath. Some streaking and flecking on breast, *faint white eye-stripe, white wing bar visible in flight. Rump white, tail dark*, legs dark. Breeding (B) plumage is a *rich rusty red with dark and light flecking and white undertail*. Immature similar to non-breeding but browner with pale buff breast. **VOICE/CALL** Rather soft *chirrup*. **FEEDING** Small aquatic crustaceans, molluscs and worms; characteristic pecking and probing feeding behaviour, on mud or in belly-deep water. **P&R** 1.8 million. Breeds in central Siberia, migrates south to Australasia. **T&M** Loss of habitat, feeding areas, pollution and human disturbance, especially on migratory routes. **BV** Main coastal lagoons and estuaries, especially northern NI. Moderate numbers, up to 150 recorded each year with up to 50 overwintering.

Dunlin *Calidris alpina* **LC NBM**

FAMILY Scolopacidae | L 16–22cm WS 33–40cm Bill 2.5–4.0cm Wt 50–60g

Small, *short-legged* wader with *long, dark, slightly down-curved bill.* Non-breeding (A) generally pale grey-brown above and white below with pale wash and flecking on breast. *Rump white with broad dark central line.* Breeding male (B) has *rufous crown and back, flecked and mottled grey head and breast, black belly and white undertail,* faint white eyebrow. Breeding female similar but more muted. Legs dark. Immature much browner, like dull breeding but with pale buff breast and lacks black belly. Bill length quite variable, female's generally longer, down-curve is close to the tip. **VOICE/CALL** In flight, a high, reedy *kreee* or *treeeep*. **FEEDING** Largely molluscs, worms and crustaceans, typically by deep probing in mud, with short runs after several probes. **P&R** *c.*5 million. Breeds in the Arctic and migrates south in winter. There are 11 subspecies, which vary significantly in size and plumage. There is no information on which one(s) have been recorded in NZ. **T&M** Loss of breeding and winter feeding habitat are a concern. **BV** Coastal lagoons and harbours, very rare vagrant to NZ.

Sanderling *Calidris alba* **LC NBM**

FAMILY Scolopacidae | L 20–21cm WS 35–39cm Bill 2.1–2.8cm Wt 50–70g

Small, compact, energetic shorebird. Non-breeding (photo) is very pale grey above and white below, with *dark patch on shoulder, white on forehead and white eyebrow*. Bill *short and black, legs black*. Breeding has *rufous head, neck and breast* and rather mottled rufous, black and white on back, undersides white. Immature is darker than non-breeding but lacks rufous coloration of breeder. In flight, broad white wing bar is visible with pale grey on either side of rump. **VOICE/CALL** Short, sharp *twik* or *tik* in flight, sometimes repeated. **FEEDING** Small crustaceans and invertebrates; very busy style, typically close to tideline, following waves in and out; generally prefer sand to mud. **P&R** 600,000–700,000. Breeds in high Arctic, migrates south during winter. **T&M** Loss of habitat on migration routes, especially China, Korea and Southeast Asia. **BV** Coastal areas, especially near harbours and estuaries, in very small numbers.

White-rumped Sandpiper *Calidris fuscicollis* **LC V**

FAMILY Scolopacidae | L 15–17cm WS 36–38cm Bill 2.1–2.6cm Wt 30–45g

Very small, slender, short-legged wader. Non-breeding (photo) largely brownish grey above and white beneath with slightly coloured and flecked breast. Distinct *white eyebrow, rump white, central tail feathers darker than outer ones. Bill short and dark with tip slightly drooped* and pale base to lower mandible. Legs mid- to dark grey, sometimes with slight greenish tinge. Breeding much browner on head and upperparts with distinct flecking on breast and flanks. Wings long, with *narrow white wing bar, and extending well beyond tail when at rest*. **VOICE/CALL** Short *prrrt* or *chirrrp*; also sharp *tik-tik-tik*. **FEEDING** Small molluscs, crustaceans and worms, with rapid pecking action; sometimes probes. **P&R** *c.*1 million. Breeds in Arctic North America, migrates south in winter. **T&M** No known threats. **BV** Coastal lagoons and harbours, a rare vagrant to NZ.

Common Sandpiper *Actitis hypoleucos* **LC NBM**

FAMILY Scolopacidae | L 19–21cm WS 32–35cm Bill 2.3–2.7cm Wt 40–80g

Small, rather slim, nondescript, *short-legged* shorebird. Non-breeding head and upperparts largely greyish brown, with *dark eye-stripe and pale eyebrow*. Undersides white with white extending onto shoulder. *Bill short and brown*, legs pale greenish grey. Breeding (photo) has rather greenish tinge to head and back. Immature similar to non-breeding. In flight, *broad white wing bar and white outer tail feathers* visible, underwing white with dark tip, trailing edge and pattern around carpal joint. Frequently bobs head and flies short distances on *fluttering down-curved wings, teeters on landing*. **VOICE/CALL** High-pitched *twee-wee-wee-wee* in flight. **FEEDING** Small crustaceans, invertebrates and fish. Feeding action slow and deliberate. **P&R** 2.5–3 million. Breeds in northern and central Europe, migrates south in winter. **T&M** No known threats, but population declining. **BV** Coastal wetlands, especially in NI; a rare vagrant.

Sharp-tailed Sandpiper *Calidris acuminata* **LC NBM**

A B

FAMILY Scolopacidae | L 17–22cm WS 36–43cm Bill 2.2–2.8cm Wt 60–90g

Medium to small, *upright, speckled* wader. Non-breeding (A) upperparts mid-brown with *rufous crown and white eyebrow*. Underparts white apart from buff on upper breast. Bill dark brown, slightly yellow towards base, appears *slightly down-curved. Legs dull yellow*. Breeding (B) *crown and back richer chestnut colour*, neck and breast heavily streaked brown. Lower breast and flanks flecked with dark chevrons. *White eyebrow more prominent*. Immature quite similar to breeding with buff breast. In flight, thin white wing bar visible and white on either side of rump. Tail not noticeably sharp. **VOICE/CALL** A rather soft *wheeep, pleep* or *trrt*. **FEEDING** Crustaceans and invertebrates, in fresh and brackish lagoons and low saltmarsh vegetation and mudflats. Gregarious, often in small flocks. **P&R** 160,000. Breeds in northern Siberia, migrates south in winter. **T&M** Loss of habitat on migration routes. **BV** Lagoons and coastal wetlands, especially NI. Small numbers every year, a few may overwinter.

Pectoral Sandpiper *Calidris melanotos* **LC NBM**

FAMILY Scolopacidae | L 19–24cm WS 37–45cm Bill 2.4–3.2cm Wt (M) 85g (F) 60g

Medium to small, *upright* wader, very similar to Sharp-tailed, but with *longer bill* and breast more coloured and streaked. Non-breeding (photo) largely pale brown, heavily streaked with darker brown. Very faint white eyebrow, white belly, undertail and underwing. Breeding rather *more coloured, especially on back and head* but *crown less rufous* than Sharp-tailed. In flight, *faint white wing bar and white either side of rump*, more prominent than Sharp-tailed. *Bill dark, sometimes yellowish towards the base*, and very *slightly decurved, legs dull yellow or greenish yellow*. Immature similar to non-breeding with pale cinnamon wash on breast. **VOICE/CALL** Loud, rather harsh *churk* or *trrrit*. **FEEDING** Invertebrates, small crustaceans and molluscs. Often feeds away from water's edge in grassy areas, and amid low vegetation. **P&R** 25,000–100,000. Breeds in northern Siberia and North America, migrates south in winter. Small numbers arrive in NZ. **T&M** No known threats. **BV** Sheltered harbours and estuaries on east coast, NI and SI.

Baird's Sandpiper *Calidris bairdii* **LC V**

FAMILY Scolopacidae | L 14–16cm WS 36–40cm Bill 2.1–2.6cm Wt 40g

Small, rather nondescript, long-winged, short-legged wader. Non-breeding (photo) head, breast and upperparts greyish brown; chin, belly and undertail white; *faint white eyebrow. Wings extend well beyond tail* when folded. In *flight, faint white wing bar, white underwing and white on either side of rump* visible. *Legs dark, bill dark and finely pointed.* Breeding has browner head, upperparts and breast with heavy streaking. Immature similar to non-breeding (photo) but with a *cinnamon wash on breast.* **VOICE/CALL** Normally low, trill-like *preeeet*; also a harsh *krrrt* or sharp *tsick.* **FEEDING** Small crustaceans, molluscs and invertebrates; prefers margins and even inland areas. **P&R** 300,000. Breeds in Arctic Siberia, North America and Greenland, migrates south in winter. **T&M** No known threats. **BV** Coastal estuaries and harbours, a rare vagrant to NZ.

Red-necked Stint *Calidris ruficollis* **LC NBM**

FAMILY Scolopacidae | L 13–16cm WS 29–33cm Bill 1.6–2.2cm Wt 22–33g

Very small, rather short-legged wader. Non-breeding (A) head, neck and back pale grey with some streaking on breast. Undersides white, *faint white eyebrow. Legs black, bill black, short and quite stout.* In flight, *white wing bar and white on either side of rump* visible. Breeding (B) develops rich chestnut coloration on head, neck, upper-breast and back. Immature rather darker than non-breeding with a *hint of a collar.* **VOICE/CALL** Short, rather high-pitched *chit* or *prit*, quite similar to other stints. **FEEDING** Small crustaceans, molluscs and invertebrates. Feeds with a busy, quick 'pecking' action, often probes. **P&R** 300,000. Breeds in northern Siberia, migrates south in northern winter. 100–250 visit NZ each year. **T&M** No known threats. **BV** Tidal mudflats in estuaries and harbours, also coastal lagoons. Summer visitor with a few overwintering.

Little Stint *Calidris minuta* **LC V**

FAMILY Scolopacidae | L 12–14cm WS 28–31cm Bill 1.7–2.0cm Wt 25g

Tiny grey and white wader with very *slightly down-curved bill*, slightly smaller than Red-necked Stint. Non-breeding (photo) head and upperparts mid-brownish grey, *whitish forehead and white eyebrow.* Undersides white with *some greying across breast.* Breeding has chestnut tint to previously grey-brown areas, and cinnamon breast with dark flecks, lacks the white forehead and eyebrow. Bill *dark and quite short, very slightly down-curved at tip, legs black.* Immature half-way between breeding and non-breeding but with white eyebrow. In flight, shows clear, but narrow, *white wing bar and white on either side of rump.* **VOICE/CALL** A sharp, high-pitched *stit* or *chit.* **FEEDING** Small crustaceans, molluscs and invertebrates, occasional vegetation; feeds with a rapid pecking action, but sometimes probes. **P&R** *c.*1.5 million. Breeds in Arctic Europe and Asia, migrates south during northern winter. A rare vagrant to NZ. **T&M** Loss of habitat on migration routes. **BV** Coastal harbours and estuaries, mudflats, occasionally inland.

Long-toed Stint *Calidris subminuta* **LC V**

FAMILY Scolopacidae | L 13–16cm WS 26–30cm Bill 1.6–2.0cm Tarsus 1.9–2.4cm Wt 25g

Tiny, upright wader with pale legs. Non-breeding (photo) head, neck and upperparts mid-grey, *white eye-stripe and chin*, breast pale grey streaked with grey. Belly and undertail white. *Bill short, dark*, sometimes brownish at base and slightly *down-curved at tip, legs pale yellow*. Breeder has *rufous cap and ear coverts*, back darker with chestnut and black flecking, breast somewhat creamy coloured. In flight, *white wing bar and white sides to rump visible*. Long toes difficult to observe. Immature similar to breeder but somewhat browner. **VOICE/CALL** A short, soft *prrrrt* or *chrrrp*. **FEEDING** Small crustaceans, molluscs and invertebrates. **P&R** 25,000. Breeds in northern Asia, migrates south in the winter. **T&M** Loss of habitat on migration routes. **BV** Mudflats in harbours and estuaries. Two NZ records.

Least Sandpiper *Calidris minutilla* **LC V**

FAMILY Scolopacidae | L 13–15cm Bill 1.6–2.1cm Wt 25g

Tiny, grey and white wader with very *slightly down-curved bill* and pale legs. Non-breeding (photo) head, neck and upperparts grey with a hint of brown. Chin and underparts white, underwing white with dark primaries and trailing edge. Bill dark with *brownish base to lower mandible, legs dull yellow*. Breeding has *chestnut tinge to back and breast and distinctly streaked head and neck*. Immature rather browner than breeding and with rufous crown. The *smallest* of the waders but almost impossible to distinguish from Long-toed Stint in the field. **VOICE/CALL** Shrill, rising *trrreee* or *prrrtt*. **FEEDING** Small molluscs, crustaceans and invertebrates. **P&R** 700,000. Breeds in Alaska, northern Canada and northeast USA, migrates south in winter. **T&M** Loss of habitat on migration routes. **BV** Coastal harbours and estuaries, mudflats. A vagrant to NZ.

Western Sandpiper *Calidris mauri* **LC V**

FAMILY Scolopacidae

L 14–17cm WS 28–31cm Bill 2.2–2.8cm Tarsus 2.0–2.5cm Wt 20–35g

Tiny, grey and white wader with few distinguishing features. Non-breeding (photo) head, neck and upperparts mid-grey, *faint white eyebrow*, white chin, throat and belly. Breast white with pale grey and a few dark streaks. Bill *black and distinctly down-curved at very tip*, legs black. Breeding darker grey, breast flecked with dark chevrons, *rufous coloration on wings, back and head, eye-stripe and eyebrow* more prominent. *White wing bar and white sides to rump visible in flight.* Immature similar to breeding but less brown on head and wings and lacks breast markings. **VOICE/CALL** Thin, high-pitched *cheet* or *jeeet*. **FEEDING** Small crustaceans, molluscs and invertebrates. **P&R** 3.5 million. Breeds in northern Alaska and eastern Siberia, migrates south in winter. **T&M** Loss of habitat on migration routes. **BV** Mudflats in harbours and estuaries; rare vagrant.

Stilt Sandpiper *Calidris himantopus* **LC V**

FAMILY Scolopacidae

L 18–23cm WS 38–41cm Bill 3.7–4.4cm Tarsus 3.5–4.6cm Wt 47–68g

Medium-sized, long-winged wader with a long bill and very long legs. Non-breeding (photo) generally grey with a *white eyebrow* and a hint of brown on back, *breast heavily streaked, belly and undertail white*. Bill long and *slightly down-curved at tip, legs very long and yellow*. Breeding has *chestnut lores, ear coverts and nape, back and wings dark brown with rufous tinge. Neck and breast streaked brown, belly and undertail heavily barred*. Immature intermediate with *pale buff breast* but lacks barring and head coloration of breeding. In flight, non-breeding *shows broad white rump and very faint white wing bar*, while breeder has barred rump. **VOICE/CALL** In flight, a soft *kirrr* or *grrrt* or a clear *whoo*. **FEEDING** Small crustaceans, molluscs and invertebrates. Rapid sewing machine-like, probing action, often in belly-deep water. **P&R** 800,000. Breeds in northern Alaska, migrates south in winter; 1 record for NZ. **T&M** Loss of habitat on migration routes. **BV** Mudflats in harbours and estuaries, Lake Ellesmere most likely.

Broad-billed Sandpiper *Limicola falcinellus* **LC NBM**

FAMILY Scolopacidae | L 16–18cm WS 34–37cm Bill 2.7–3.6cm Wt 35–40g

Small, long-billed, short-legged, rather nondescript wader. Non-breeding (photos) head and upperparts slightly brownish grey, and some streaking and flecking on breast. Distinctive *double white eyebrow*. Underparts white, tail dark. *Bill dark, sometimes tinged yellow at base, long, laterally flattened and noticeably down-curved near tip. Legs short, dark*, sometimes tinged green, yellow or brown. Breeding much darker, upperparts and breast streaked black and chestnut, belly white, eyebrows more pronounced. In flight, *white wing bar and white on either side of rump visible*. Immature similar to breeding but paler and with buff wash on breast and streaking at sides only. **VOICE/CALL** Buzz-like, trill *chreeet*, also short, sharp *tzit*. **FEEDING** Small crustaceans, molluscs and invertebrates, sometimes seeds; prods and sometimes probes deeply and rather deliberately. **P&R** 70,000–160,000. Breeds in northern Scandinavia, Russia and Siberia, migrates south in winter. **T&M** Loss of habitat on migration routes. **BV** Mudflats in harbours and estuaries, especially Firth of Thames, in very small numbers.

Ruff (Reeve, female) *Philomachus pugnax* **LC V**

FAMILY Scolopacidae | L (M) 26–32cm (F) 20–25cm WS 46–59cm Bill (M) 3.3–3.7cm

A B (F) 2.6–3.4cm Wt (M) 180g (F) 110g

Medium-sized, *long-legged upright* wader with *shortish, decurved bill*. Male significantly larger than female. Non-breeding generally grey-brown with *dark-centred feathers on wings. Chin and throat white*, breast greyish, belly and undertail white. *Legs dull yellow-orange, bill dark*, rather yellowish at base. Breeding adult male (A) develops striking *head tufts and ruff around neck*, varying from black to white. Back and breast rich brownish yellow flecked with black, forehead yellowish orange. Female (B) lacks ruff and tufts but head darkish brown. Immature similar to non-breeding but with pale cinnamon wash, white eyebrow, legs greenish. In flight, *white underwing and wing bar and white on either side of rump visible, feet extend beyond tail*. **VOICE/CALL** Not very vocal, occasionally a low grunt-like *kurr* or *kook*. **FEEDING** Small crustaceans, molluscs and invertebrates. Often feeds with head submerged and may swim. **P&R** 2–2.5 million. Northern Europe and northern Siberia, migrates south in winter. A very rare, irregular visitor to NZ. **T&M** Industrial and commercial use of breeding and feeding grounds. Susceptible to avian diseases. **BV** Mainly at margins of freshwater or brackish lakes. Present in very small numbers.

Terek Sandpiper *Tringa cinerea* **LC NBM**

FAMILY Scolopacidae | L 22–24cm WS 36–45cm Bill 4.0–5.5cm Wt 60–90g

Small, *short-legged wader with long, upcurved bill*. Non-breeding (A) head, neck and back ash grey, *white chin, throat and eye-stripe*, breast streaked pale grey, undersides all white. *Legs dull orange, bill dull orange at base, darker at tip*. Breeding (B) is brown rather than grey with streaked buff upper breast and white chin. Juvenile generally browner than adult. In flight, *wing shows broad white trailing edge and white outer tail feathers*. **VOICE/CALL** Typically a short *twit-wit'wit'wit* in flight. **FEEDING** Small crustaceans, and invertebrates, especially in shallow water and near mangroves. **P&R** Up to 1.2 million. Breeds northern Europe and Asia, migrates south in winter. **T&M** Potential threat from loss of feeding areas on migration route in China, Korea and Southeast Asia. **BV** Coastal lagoons, harbours and estuaries, especially in north of NI; not common, but small numbers seen every year.

Wrybill *Anarhynchus frontalis* **VU E**

ALTERNATIVE NAME Ngutuparore | FAMILY Charadriidae

L 20–21cm WS 36cm Bill 2.6–3cm Wt 50–70g

Small, grey and white, short-legged wader with unique *bent bill*. Breeding male (A) has ashy-grey head, nape and back with *white forehead, eye-stripe*, throat and belly, and distinctive *black throat band*. Female similar but browner and with *narrower throat band*. Non-breeding (B) has no throat band. Immature similar to non-breeding but back feathers white-edged. *Bill black and sharply curved to right near tip*. In flight, *white wing bar* shows, especially on inner primaries, and underwing shows white apart from broad dark smudge near carpal joint. **VOICE/CALL** High-pitched *wheeet* or *peeep*; in courtship, a long, bubbling trill. **BREEDING** Breeds on shingle bank in braided rivers of central SI. 2 eggs laid August–January; incubation takes 4–5 weeks, fledging after 5–6 weeks. **FEEDING** Aquatic insects and other invertebrates; uses bent bill to forage under stones in rivers; in winter forages for crustaceans and invertebrates. **P&R** 4,500–5,000. Migrates to estuaries and harbours on the east coast of SI and all of NI in winter; some remain year-round. **T&M** Loss and degradation of braided river habitat due to industrial farming, water extraction, encroachment of alien vegetation, recreational activities and damming of rivers. Also introduced mammalian predators and increased populations of Black-backed Gull and Swamp Harrier. Protected but no active management plan. **BV** Harbours and estuaries; nesting areas should be avoided.

Ruddy Turnstone *Arenaria interpres* **LC NBM**

FAMILY Scolopacidae | L 22–24cm WS 50–57cm Bill 2.0–2.5cm Wt 90–120g

Distinctive, *long-bodied, short-legged* shorebird with colourful variegated plumage. Non-breeding (A) largely *brown and black on head and back*, often with a hint of chestnut. *Broad dark bib*, and pale eyebrow, white chin and forehead. Undersides white, *legs bright orange*, bill, short, stout and black. *Breeding male (B) has dramatic tortoiseshell coloration over back and wings with striking black and white pattern on head and breast*. Female similar but less dramatic. Immature variegated dark brown and black on head and back, white underneath. In flight, distinctive white double wing bar, broad white stripe on mantle, white rump, tail black with thin white band at tip. Underwing white apart from dark tip and trailing edge. **VOICE/CALL** Clear staccato *trik-tuk-tuk-tuk*. **FEEDING** Small crustaceans, molluscs and invertebrates along shelly and stony shore and tideline. **P&R** 500,000–800,000. Breeds circumpolar in sub-Arctic, migrates south in winter. Two subspecies, *A. i. interpres* and *A. i. morinella*, known to visit NZ, but not visually distinct. **T&M** Some predation from alien pests. **BV** Widespread along coasts and around harbours and estuaries, especially NI, also Chatham and Auckland islands.

Far Eastern Curlew *Numenius madagascariensis* **LC NBM**

FAMILY Scolopacidae

L 60–66cm WS 110cm Bill 12.8–20.1cm Tarsus 8.3–10.0cm Wt 900g

Very large, *long-legged*, brown wader with an *immensely long, down-curved bill*. Non-breeding (photo) is all brown with much streaking and flecking, and a *pale undertail*, somewhat grey-brown on back, *faint pale eyebrow*. Bill dark brown, pinkish towards base of lower mandible, legs dull grey. Breeding largely *cinnamon brown with dark streaking on head and breast and flecking on wings and back*. In flight, *feet extend beyond tail*. Immature similar to breeding but buff-white edges to feathers on upperparts. **VOICE/CALL** Clear and pipe-like *ker-leeeuw*; sometimes flatter *kuu-reee*. **FEEDING** Mainly crustaceans and polychaete worms; probes deep into mud. **P&R** 40,000. Breeds in Northeast Asia, Kamchatka and Manchuria, migrates south in winter. **T&M** Loss of habitat, hunting and pollution. **BV** Mudflats and mangrove areas in harbours and estuaries; a regular visitor but in small numbers (5–10), especially Auckland area, Firth of Thames and Bay of Plenty.

Whimbrel *Numenius phaeopus variegatus* **LC NBM**

FAMILY Scolopacidae

L 40–45cm WS 76–89cm Bill 7.0–9.3cm Tarsus 5.2–6.8cm Wt 450g

Large, brown, long-legged, long-billed wader. Adult overall slightly grey-brown, darker on back. Breast *streaked dark brown, flanks somewhat barred*, belly pale and unbarred. *Crown is striped dark and pale brown Bill dark*, often flesh-coloured near base, *long and down-curved; legs very long*, dull bluish grey. In flight, *rump whitish with brown barring*. Immature browner with less barring on flanks and belly, lacks whitish rump. **VOICE/CALL** Diagnostic piping whistle repeated up to 7 times *pi-pi-pi*, etc. **FEEDING** Mainly crabs and marine worms by probing into mud. **P&R** 1–2.3 million. Breeds in northern Europe, Asia and America. Migrates south in winter. **T&M** Loss of habitat on migration routes. **BV** Mudflats in harbours and estuaries, especially Auckland, Firth of Thames, Bay of Plenty.

American Whimbrel *Numenius phaeopus hudsonicus* **LC V** (N.Am)

FAMILY Scolopacidae | L 40–46cm WS 75–85cm Bill 60–90cm Tarsus 5.5–6.5cm Wt 450g

Almost identical to *N. p. variegatus*, but slightly browner and lacks whitish rump. Bill long, heavy and decurved. **P&R** Breeds in northern and Arctic North America, migrates south in winter. **T&M** Loss of habitat on migration routes. **BV** Harbours and estuaries; regular visitor in very small numbers; most whimbrel are the Asiatic race.

Bristle-thighed Curlew *Numenius tahitiensis* **VU V**

FAMILY Scolopacidae | L 40–44cm Bill 7.0–9.5cm Tarsus 5.1–6.2cm Wt 380–600g

Large, all-brown wader with *long, down-curved bill*. Adult very similar to Whimbrel but shorter-legged and more cinnamon. All-over cinnamon-brown, darker on back, breast heavily streaked, *crown has pale centre line with 2 dark brown lines either side and whitish eyebrow*. Bill pale flesh-coloured at base, dark brown at tip; *legs bluish grey, shorter than Whimbrel and rather heavy*. In flight, *cinnamon rump* and *barred tail* visible. Immature more spotted on back, lacks striations on breast and head pattern more subdued. **VOICE/CALL** Quite varied: short *chee-oo-it*, or a longer whistling *whe-whe-whe-whe* and a clear *wheee-wheeeoo*. **FEEDING** Small crustaceans, molluscs and invertebrates, occasionally seabird eggs. **P&R** 7,000. Breeds in Alaska, migrates south to Pacific islands as far south as Kermadecs in winter. **T&M** Predation by feral mammals on wintering grounds on Pacific islands, including some human predation. Protection on some wintering grounds has helped reduce losses. **BV** Coastal areas of Pacific islands, especially Kermadecs.

Little Whimbrel *Numenius minutus* **LC NBM**

FAMILY Scolopacidae

L 29–32cm WS 68–71cm Bill 3.8–4.8cm Tarsus 4.4–5.4cm Wt 175g

Medium-sized, *long-legged* wader with *slender, down-curved bill.* Adult all brown, darker above, heavily streaked on breast, belly pale buff. Head pattern similar to Whimbrel with 2 *dark brown stripes above pale eyebrow*. Bill dark brown but pinkish brown at base of lower mandible, initially *straight but significantly decurved towards tip*. Immature similar but less marked on breast and flanks. **VOICE/CALL** A rising *te-te-te*, sometimes a harsh *tchew-tchew-tchew* or *kweek-ek*. **FEEDING** Mainly insects and other invertebrates, with some seeds. **P&R** 180,000. Breeds in central and northeastern Siberia, migrates south in the winter. **T&M** Some habitats and stopover sites threatened by alien plants and predators. **BV** Wide range of habitats, from dry grasslands to mudflats, coastal and inland. Regular visitor in small numbers.

Bar-tailed Godwit *Limosa lapponica baueri* **LC NBM**

FAMILY Scolopacidae | ALTERNATIVE NAME Kuaka | L 37–41cm WS 62–75cm

Bill (M) 6.1–8.5cm (F) 7.5–10.8cm Tarsus 4.6–6.3cm Wt (M) 300g (F) 350g

Medium-large, *long-legged* wader with *very long, slightly upturned bill.* Non-breeding (A) greyish brown on head, neck and back, *darker on crown, and white eyebrow,* light brown streaked darker on throat and breast, underparts white with some *barring on flanks. Bill finely pointed, yellowish or pinkish at base becoming dark brown at tip, legs dark slate grey*. Breeding (B)male *head, neck and underparts become rich chestnut red*, upperparts chestnut flecked with black and brown. Female upperparts similar but paler, and *head and underparts pale cinnamon*. In flight, shows pale rump and *brown and white barred tail, underwing heavily barred*. Male significantly smaller than female and starts developing breeding plumage from February onwards. Immature similar to non-breeding but darker on back and lacks streaking on breast. **VOICE/CALL** Not very vocal; sharp bark-like *kak-kak* and a deeper *kirruc*. **FEEDING** Worms, molluscs and small crustaceans, probing deep into mud, often with head underwater, staying close to tide-line. Often in very large flocks. **P&R** 1.1–1.2 million, decreasing. Breeds in Arctic, eastern Siberia and western Alaska, migrates south in winter. NZ visitors are from Alaska. On southward journey, when weather permits, most fly non-stop for 8–9 days from Alaska to NZ, a world record for non-stop flight. Western race is *L. l. lapponica*. **T&M** Loss of habitat at wintering and migratory staging posts, from changed land use, especially in China and North Korea. Mangrove invasion caused by increased sedimentation and global warming is a problem in NZ. **BV** Coastal harbours and estuaries throughout the country but especially Auckland, Firth of Thames, Bay of Plenty, Farewell Spit, Tasman Bay, Christchurch, and Southland lagoons. High tide always best. Significant number (5,000–10,000) overwinter in NZ. Commonest Arctic migratory wader in NZ, with around 100,000 counted each summer.

Hudsonian Godwit *Limosa haemastica* **LC NBM**

FAMILY Scolopacidae

L 37–42cm Bill 6.4–9.3cm (F longer than M) Tarsus 4.7–6.0cm Wt (M) 222g (F) 290g

Medium-sized, *very long-legged* wader. Non-breeding (photo) generally greyish brown with white belly and undertail, pale throat and *white eyebrow. Bill long, finely pointed and upturned, yellowish brown at base becoming dark at tip, legs dark grey*. Breeding male *head and neck finely barred black and white*, upperparts brown flecked buff and black, breast and underparts rich chestnut red. Female generally paler especially on breast and belly. In flight, shows *narrow white wing bar, black armpits* and extensive black on underwing and *white rump*, tail *with broad black tip* and *feet extending well beyond tail*. Immature as non-breeding but underparts buff, upperparts brown tinged buff. **VOICE/CALL** Not very vocal; clear *toe-whit* or *whit*. **FEEDING** Small crustaceans, molluscs and invertebrates, probes deep into mud. **P&R** 70,000, decreasing. Breeds in northern Canada and Alaska, migrates south in winter. **T&M** Loss of habitat on migration routes. **BV** Mudflats in coastal harbours and estuaries; small numbers arrive in NZ each year and a few overwinter.

Black-tailed Godwit *Limosa limosa melanuroides* **NT NBM**

B FAMILY Scolopacidae

A L 36–44cm WS 63–75cm Bill 6.7–9.3cm Tarsus 5.9–7.3cm Wt 200–350g

Medium-sized, elegant, very long-legged wader. Non-breeding (A) head and upperparts greyish brown, with white eyebrow. *Chin and throat very pale brown, breast pale grey-brown*, belly white with some coloration on flanks. *Bill very long, straight and finely pointed, orange-pink near base, becoming dark brown at tip, legs very long* and dark blue-grey. Breeding (B) male has *rich red-cinnamon head, neck and breast*, blending into barred black and white belly and white undertail. Upperparts rather mottled reddish, black and brown, eyebrow less prominent. Breeding female similar to male but *red on upper breast only and barring on lower breast*, head greyer. In flight, shows *large white wing bar and white rump*, tail black with *feet extending well beyond it*. Immature as male breeding but cinnamon rather than red and browner on back and white on belly. **VOICE/CALL** Not at all vocal out of breeding season but in flocks a soft *kip-kip* or *chut-chut*. **FEEDING** Small crustaceans, molluscs and invertebrates, by picking and probing; also feeds on berries and seeds. **P&R** 600,000–800,000, decreasing. Breeds in northern Asia. Migrates south in winter. **T&M** Habitat loss, hunting (European subspecies). **BV** Mudflats in harbours and estuaries, especially Manukau, Firth of Thames and Christchurch.

Asiatic Dowitcher *Limnodromus semipalmatus* **NT V**

FAMILY Scolopacidae | L 34–36cm WS 59cm Bill (M) 7.5–8.2cm (F) 7.8–8.7cm
Tarsus (M) 4.6–5.3cm (F) 4.8–5.4cm Wt 146–235g

Medium-sized, *short-legged* wader. Non-breeding (photo) head, neck and upperparts dark brownish grey, *prominent white eyebrow and dark eye-stripe*, chin white, breast streaked and flecked with grey, belly white, some flecking on flanks. *Bill very long and straight, dark but pinkish on lower mandible near base*, laterally flattened near tip, legs dark grey. In flight, underwing almost all white, indistinct white wing bar, *rump and tail barred brown and white, feet extend* well beyond tail. Male breeding has *head, neck and underparts chestnut red, flanks barred*, upperparts mottled brown, black and chestnut. Loses white eyebrow. Female breeding similar but more subdued and with more white on breast and flanks. Immature as non-breeding but with pale buff wash on upperparts and breast, more barring on flanks. **VOICE/CALL** A sharp *yep-yep* or *chowp*, and a rather softer *kiaow*. **FEEDING** Molluscs, invertebrates and insect larvae. **P&R** 23,000, decreasing. Breeds central Asia, migrates south in winter. **T&M** Loss of habitat due to wetland drainage. **BV** Estuaries and harbours.

Marsh Sandpiper *Tringa stagnatilis* **LC NBM**

FAMILY Scolopacidae

L 22–26cm WS 40–45cm Bill 3.6–4.2cm Tarsus 4.7–5.5cm Wt 70g

Small, *elegant, very long-legged wader*. Non-breeding (A) has grey-brown head, neck and upperparts with *faint white eyebrow*; underparts all white. *Bill dark*, sometimes greenish grey near base, *long, fine and sharply pointed*. Legs *very long* and *greyish green to dull yellow*. In flight, *white rump extends in 'V' shape well up mantle, tail barred and feet extend well beyond it*. Breeding (B) has head and upperparts *streaked and spotted dark brownish grey, breast and flanks heavily streaked dark brown*. Immature similar to non-breeding but head and neck browner. Significantly smaller than Greenshank. Non-breeding and immature look rather like a small juvenile Pied Stilt. **VOICE/CALL** A rather high-pitched *yip* or *plew*. **FEEDING** Small fish, crustaceans, molluscs and invertebrates. Feeds in shallow water with head down–tail up stance. **P&R** 260,000–1.2 million. Breeds from central Europe to Mongolia, migrates south in winter. **T&M** Breeding areas reduced by agricultural intensification, some egg predation and industrial pollution. Loss of habitat on migratory route due to change of land use, declining river flows. Loss of wintering habitat in Africa, India and Southeast Asia. **BV** Harbours and estuaries; small numbers each year, a few may overwinter.

Greenshank *Tringa nebularia* **LC NBM**

FAMILY Scolopacidae

L 30–35cm WS 55–65cm Bill 4.7–6.6cm Tarsus 5.2–6.6cm Wt 170g

Medium-sized, long-legged wader with slightly upcurved bill. Non-breeding (photo) upperparts slightly brownish grey and *streaked darker, especially on head and neck. Bill long, broad and greyish at base, becoming darker and tapering to fine point, slightly upcurved toward tip, legs pale greyish green*, sometimes yellowish. In flight, shows *large white rump extending as 'V' shape up mantle and barred tail*, feet extend beyond tail. Breeding much browner with *strong streaking on breast and flanks*. Immature similar to non-breeding but with *brownish tinge to upperparts*. **VOICE/CALL** Clear ringing *teu-teu-teu* or sharp *tchuk* or *chip*. **FEEDING** Small fish, crustaceans and molluscs. On mudflats, margins of pools and lagoons, walks quickly, probing frequently, often up to belly in water. **P&R** 440,000–1.5 million. Breeds from northern Europe through to Kamchatka. Migrates south in winter. **T&M** Some loss of habitat, especially in east Asia. **BV** Harbours and estuaries, brackish ponds and lagoons. Small numbers each year with some overwintering.

Lesser Yellowlegs *Tringa flavipes* **LC V**

FAMILY Scolopacidae

L 23–25cm WS 59–64cm Bill 3.4–3.9cm Tarsus 4.7–5.7cm Wt 75g

Small, *elegant, long-legged* wader. Non-breeding (photo) pale brownish grey on head, neck and upperparts, crown somewhat darker and *white eyebrow* mainly in front of eye. Throat white, *breast heavily streaked mid-grey*, belly and undertail white with *some barring on flanks. Bill short, straight and finely pointed. Legs long and bright yellow*. In flight, shows *white rump and feet extend well beyond end of tail*, which is somewhat barred. Breeding is *strongly streaked brown* on head, breast and neck. Upperparts blackish with brown and white flecking. Immature similar to non-breeding but upperparts browner with buff flecking, breast has pale buff wash. **VOICE/CALL** A rather flat *tew-tew* or *tew*. **FEEDING** Small fish and invertebrates. Often picks food from surface of water. **P&R** 400,000. Breeds in Alaska and northern Canada; migrates south in winter. **T&M** Loss of habitat on migration routes. **BV** Harbours and estuaries and freshwater lakes and ponds. An occasional visitor.

Wandering Tattler *Tringa incana* **LC NBM**

FAMILY Scolopacidae

L 26–29cm WS 54cm Bill 3.5–4.5cm Tarsus 3.0–3.8cm Wt 110–130g

Small, distinctive, *solitary grey* wader with *quite short yellow legs* found mainly on rocky shores. Non-breeding (photos) has slate-grey upperparts with *faint white eyebrow*, mainly in front of eye. Breast and flanks mid-grey, belly and undertail white. *Bill near black but yellowish at base, quite long and heavy, legs short and yellow*. In flight, shows all-dark upperwing and mid-grey underwing. Breeding is similar but *breast and belly heavily barred slate grey and white*. Immature similar to non-breeding but whiter on lower breast and eyebrow more prominent. **VOICE/CALL** Clear whistling trill, 6–10 notes, *pew-tu-tu-tu*. **FEEDING** Crustaceans, molluscs and invertebrates. Characteristic bobbing and teetering movement; feeds mainly on rocky shores when away from breeding grounds. **P&R** 10,000–25,000. Breeds in eastern Siberia, Alaska and British Columbia. Migrates south during winter. **T&M** Loss of habitat on migration route. **BV** Rocky shores, especially on the east coast of Northland to Canterbury. Small numbers reach NZ each summer.

Siberian Tattler *Tringa brevipes* **LC NBM**

B A

FAMILY Scolopacidae | L 24–27cm WS 51cm Bill 3.5–4.0cm Tarsus 2.9–3.4cm Wt 100g

Small, solitary, short-legged, grey wader. Non-breeding (A) very similar to Wandering Tattler but *rather paler with more distinct white eyebrow, basal half of bill distinctly yellow,* and nasal groove extends half-way down bill compared with 70% for Wandering Tattler. In flight, upperwing lighter than Wandering but underwing similar. Breeding (B) has *distinct barring on breast and flanks, but belly remains white*. Immature similar to non-breeding but with white spotting on upperwing. **VOICE/CALL** Fairly short, rising *tu-wheep* and a strident *klee-klee* or *weet-weet*. Calls distinguish it from Wandering Tattler. **FEEDING** Crustaceans and invertebrates. Has similar bobbing and teetering movement to Wandering but is often found on mudflats as well as rocky shores. **P&R** 40,000. Breeds in northern Asia east to Kamchatka. **T&M** Loss of habitat on migration routes. **BV** Widespread around coast, but very few in numbers; may overwinter occasionally.

Oriental Pratincole *Glareola maldivarum* **LC NBM**

FAMILY Glareolidae | L 23–24cm WS 54–57cm Bill 1.1–1.7cm Tarsus 3.0–3.5cm Wt 75g

Distinctive, *short-legged, short-billed, fork-tailed wader*. Non-breeding (photo) head, neck and upperparts dull brown, *throat buff enclosed in dark ring*. Upper breast greyish fading into white belly and undertail. *Bill dark, short and slightly hooked, legs dark*. In flight, shows *white rump and black forked tail*, underwing coverts chestnut. Flight very distinctive, buoyant and tern-like. Breeding similar but *black line around throat patch more distinct and bordered white, breast cinnamon*. **VOICE/CALL** Sharp *kyik, chik-chik* or *chet*. **FEEDING** Insects caught mainly while on the wing. Appears like a large swallow with more tern-like flight. **P&R** *c.*3 million. Breeds in southern Asia, partial migrants, rare vagrant to NZ, 10 records to date. **T&M** No known threats. **BV** Coastal areas most likely, but often seen over grasslands.

Red-necked Phalarope *Phalaropus lobatus* **LC V**

FAMILY Scolopacidae

L 18–19cm WS 31–34cm Bill 1.9–2.3cm Tarsus 1.9–2.2cm Wt (M) 30g (F) 35g

Very small, graceful swimming wader. Non-breeding (A) *dark crown extending down nape* and blending into pale grey back, *black eye-stripe,* head, neck and underparts white. *Bill black, short and fine*, legs blue-grey, with *lobed toes*. Flight fast and erratic, shows *white wing bar and white on either side of rump*. Breeding female (B – upper bird) grey upperparts *with bright rufous patch* running from behind eye to throat and upper breast, *chin white*, back flecked with *pale chestnut*. Male (B – lower bird) similar but paler and rufous does not extend to breast. Immature like non-breeding but rather pinkish cinnamon with dark crown and eye-patch, darker on back. **VOICE/CALL** Short *clip* or *tchwik*. **FEEDING** Zooplankton and other marine invertebrates; feeds by swimming jerkily and in circles. **P&R** 3.6–4.5 million. Breeds in northern Europe, Asia and North America; migrates south during winter. **T&M** Loss of habitat on migration routes. **BV** Coastal saltwater lagoons and harbours, and offshore. Rare vagrant to NZ.

Wilson's Phalarope *Phalaropus tricolor* **LC V**

FAMILY Scolopacidae

L 22–24cm WS 35–38cm Bill 2.7–3.6cm Tarsus 2.9–3.6cm Wt (M) 50g (F) 68g

Very small, delicate swimming wader, largest of the phalaropes. Non-breeding (photo) very similar to Red and Red-necked phalaropes, but has *grey rather than black crown and eye-stripe*. *Bill much longer and finely pointed and legs dull yellow*. In flight, shows *broad white rump and feet protrude beyond tail*. Breeding female very varied plumage, forehead and cheek dark, *crown and nape pearl grey, rich buff or chestnut on ear coverts and side of neck down to upper breas*t, back grey with buff markings, undersides white. Bill is fine and pointed, and legs are dark. Male similar but less dramatic and lacks pearl grey on head. Immature similar to non-breeding but much browner on back. **VOICE/CALL** Not very vocal but may give a soft *aangh* in flight. **FEEDING** Small crustaceans and invertebrates. Feeds while swimming, but also wading in shallow water, or on edges of lagoons and on land. **P&R** 1.5 million. Breeds on prairie marshes of northern North America; migrates south in winter. **T&M** Loss of breeding habitat. **BV** Coastal wetlands, harbours and estuaries. A very rare visitor to NZ.

Red Phalarope *Phalaropus fulicaria* **LC V**

ALTERNATIVE NAME Grey Phalarope | FAMILY Scolopacidae

L 20–22cm WS 37–40cm Bill 2.0–2.5cm Tarsus 2.0–2.3cm Wt (M) 42g (F) 57g

Very small, delicate pelagic wader. Non-breeding (A) virtually identical to Red-necked Phalarope, but *lacks white on sides of rump* and bill is slightly longer and heavier, legs greyish or brownish. Breeding female (B) has *rich rust-red underparts and neck, cheeks and ear coverts white, black on forehead and crown extends down nape to back, which is mixed buff and black*. Bill all orange-yellow apart from dark tip. Male similar but much paler, back greyer. Immature similar to non-breeding but with buff wash on sides of neck, breast and on back. **VOICE/CALL** Short, shrill *wit wit*. **FEEDING** Zooplankton and other marine invertebrates. **P&R** 1–2 million. Breeds in Arctic Asia and North America; migrates south in winter. **T&M** No known threats. **BV** Coastal harbours, estuaries and lakes, but more likely offshore.

Grebes – Podicipedidae

Australasian Crested Grebe *Podiceps cristatus* **LC** (local NT) **N**

ALTERNATIVE NAME Puteketeke | L 48–61cm Bill 4.2–5.4cm Wt 1.1kg

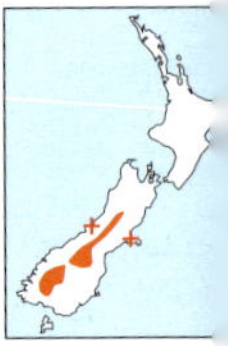

Medium-sized, *long-necked, diving* waterbird with *long dagger-shaped bill*. Adult (A) male upperparts dark brown, *crown black with elongated crest, face white with black lores, back of head chestnut merging to black and forming a distinctive ruff, front of neck, breast and undersides white*. In flight, prominent white patches on leading edge and secondaries, *legs and feet extend well beyond very short tail*. Bill pinkish brown, legs dark olive green, toes broadly lobed. *When swimming, appears to float very low in water*. Female similar but smaller, especially crest and ruff. Immature (B) lacks crest and ruff and has brown and white vertically striped neck. **VOICE/CALL** Vocal only during display, a guttural bark *rah-rah-rah*, a loud drawn-out *ghaaar* or during courtship a soft crooning. **BREEDING** Varied and often dramatic water-courtship display, often with ruff extended and crest erect. Builds large floating nest of twigs and vegetation, mainly in high country lakes, lays up to 7 eggs September–February, hatching after 3.5–4.5 weeks. Chicks travel on adult's back when young. **FEEDING** Mainly fish with some aquatic invertebrates caught by diving. Dives usually last 25–35 seconds, but have lasted up to 85 seconds. **P&R** Worldwide species. NZ population (subspecies *P. c. australis*) numbers about 350 individuals, found SI only, in high country lakes and Banks Peninsula. Vagrant to NI. **T&M** Nationally threatened due to small population, modification of lakes for hydropower, recreational use and competition from introduced fish species. Also mammalian predators and use of monofilament gill nets. Susceptible to avian influenza. **BV** SI only, high country lakes, and Lake Forsyth, near Christchurch.

New Zealand Dabchick *Poliocephalus rufopectus* **VU E**

ALTERNATIVE NAME Weweia | L 30cm Bill 1.9–2.8cm Wt 170–295g

Small, dark, dumpy waterbird with *long, upright neck*. Breeding adult (A) upperparts dark black-brown apart from *chestnut-brown neck*, often held very upright. Underparts pale brownish grey, tail very short, *tufted and white*. Head black with silver-grey streaking. Bill short and dark brown, *eye bright yellow*, legs and lobed feet dark grey. In flight, *wings short and rounded*, underwing shows white and *feet and legs extend well beyond tail*. Non-breeding and immature much lighter with pale chin and throat, eye less yellow. Younger immatures and chicks (B) show *striking black and white head pattern*. **VOICE/CALL** Not very vocal, a shrill *wee-eee ee*, the source of the Maori name, also a low *tuk tuk tuk* or *kra kra kra*. **BREEDING** Elaborate water-courtship with a variety of movements, including diving. Builds floating nest in reeds or similar. 2 or 3 eggs laid June–March but especially September–December. Hatching after 3+ weeks, fledging after 10 weeks. Small young may ride on parent's back. **FEEDING** Aquatic invertebrates, but also small fish and crustaceans, by diving and some surface feeding. **P&R** 1,700–1,800 decreasing, NI only. Widespread in coastal and inland lakes, especially Rotoiti and Taupo. An occasional visitor to SI, mainly outside of breeding season. In autumn and winter, birds gather on a few lakes and sewage oxidation ponds, among others Masterton, Waikanae and Marton. **T&M** Human interference and activity on breeding lakes, introduced mammalian predators. **BV** Lakes Rotoiti, Taupo, Okareka, Hatuma, Horowhenua, and in Hawke's Bay and Masterton.

Australasian Little Grebe

Tachybaptus novaehollandiae novaehollandiae **LC N**

L 23–25cm WS 39cm Wt 100–235g

Very small, *dumpy, furtive, diving* waterbird. Breeding bird (photo) upperparts largely dark brown, fading gradually to pale fawn underparts, tail very short, white and tufted. *Head and throat black with distinct rufous patch on sides of neck. Well-defined patch of yellow skin from base of lower mandible to below eye*. Bill *black with cream tip*, legs and lobed feet olive green. In flight, *white underwing* visible and feet and legs extend well beyond very short tail. Non-breeding generally paler and lacks rufous neck patches, neck and throat pale buff. Immature body similar to non-breeding but has striking *black and white head and neck pattern*. Very wary and dives frequently, especially when disturbed; the smallest waterbird in NZ. **VOICE/CALL** Not very vocal except during courtship and breeding. Clear metallic trill *tititititititi* or *zizizizizizi* or more aggressive *diyg-diyg-diyg* or, when alarmed, a sharp *pit*. **BREEDING** Elaborate water-courtship with a variety of postures and calls. Builds floating nest in reed beds or similar. Lays up to 5 eggs, hatching after 3–4 weeks and fledging after about 8 weeks. **FEEDING** Fish, snails and aquatic invertebrates, mainly by diving but also surface feeding. **P&R** Up to 1 million throughout Australasia. Recent arrival, 1968, in NZ, population 100–150, found mainly NI, especially dune lakes in Northland, but also Rotorua area and in Canterbury. **T&M** No specific threats, but alien predators and shortage of habitat likely to restrict numbers. **BV** Northland dune lakes, Kaipara Harbour, Lake Rotoiti.

Hoary-headed Grebe *Poliocephalus poliocephalus* **LC V**

A
B

L 29–30cm WS 46cm Wt (F) 220g (M) 260g

Small, rather drab and dumpy diving waterbird. Similar to New Zealand Dabchick but much paler. Breeding bird (A) has dark head streaked silver-grey, neck long and buff, upperparts dark grey-brown, underparts much paler. Bill dark brown with pale tip (breeding) or pinkish (non-breeding), eye yellow (but not contrasting), legs and lobed feet greyish yellow. Non-breeding similar but has dark cap with no streaking, bill yellowish or greenish, chin, throat, sides of face and neck pale buff. Immature (B) similar but may have black and white head pattern of chicks. **VOICE/CALL** Not at all vocal; range of low guttural calls, including *hrow* or *eeow*. **BREEDING** Has been recorded breeding in NZ (1970s), but in very small numbers and not recently. **FEEDING** Chiefly aquatic arthropods, mainly by deep diving. **P&R** Up to 1 million. Found throughout Australia but a vagrant to NZ. **T&M** No known threats. **BV** Lakes from Northland to Southland, but most likely on SI.

Herons, Egrets and Bitterns – Ardeidae

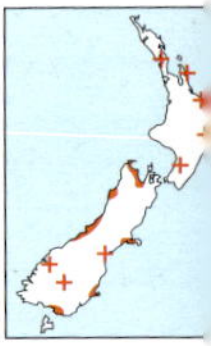

White Heron *Ardea modesta* LC N

ALTERNATIVE NAME Kotuku | PREVIOUSLY *Casmerodius albus, Egretta alba, Ardea alba*
L 83–103cm WS 150cm Tarsus 13–16.8cm Wt 700g–1.2kg

Very large, all-white bird with very long neck and very long legs. Plumage all white in all stages. Breeding adult (A) develops long filoplumes or aigrettes on back, which extend beyond tail and folded wings. *Neck has a distinctive kink c.*$1/3$ way down. Breeding adult has *long (96–116mm), dagger-like, black bill,* lores pale olive green to blue-green, iris red, legs black with reddish or yellowish above knee. Non-breeding (B) lacks filoplumes, *bill yellow,* lores yellow, iris yellow, *legs and feet slate grey.* In flight, long *neck held back in 'S' and legs and feet extend well beyond tail.* Immature same as non-breeding. **VOICE/CALL** Not very vocal; a range of harsh and guttural croaks. **BREEDING** Builds large platform of branches and twigs in upper branches of trees, in or on the edge of a lagoon or lake. 3–5 eggs laid September–October, hatching after 3–4 weeks, chicks fledge 6 weeks later. Single breeding colony in NZ at Okarito Lagoon in Westland. **FEEDING** Mainly fish, eels, shrimp and aquatic invertebrates, but known to eat mice, lizards and small birds. Hunts by walking stealthily or by standing motionless and waiting. **P&R** Worldwide up to 2 million. NZ population *c.*200 with occasional additions from Australia. Out of breeding season found throughout the country in shallow lagoons, estuaries, lakes, harbours and waterside pastures. **T&M** No specific threats. **BV** Okarito Lagoon in Westland during breeding season, widespread at other times.

Little Egret *Egretta garzetta* LC NBM

L 55–65cm WS 90cm Tarsus 9.5–11.2cm Wt 300g

Small, sleek, all-white heron with very long legs and long, dagger-shaped bill. Non-breeding (A) all white, bill black, lores yellow with buff patch at base of lower mandible. Legs and feet dark slate grey with yellow soles. Breeding (B) similar but with two long, 15–16cm, white plumes on crown and long filoplumes on neck, breast and back; lores pinkish, sometimes red. Immature as non-breeding but bill has more yellow on it and legs and feet dark olive green. **VOICE/CALL** Low-pitched gargling *wulla-wulla-wulla,* also harsh squawks. **FEEDING** Fish and also frogs and insects; may hunt standing motionless like other herons, but often chases after prey with high-stepping gait and wings open. **P&R** Up to 3 million. Widespread in Africa, Eurasia and Australasia; very small numbers visit NZ each year. **T&M** No specific threats in NZ, but loss of habitat through wetland drainage elsewhere is a threat. **BV** Harbours and estuaries, prefers saltwater areas.

Plumed Egret *Ardea intermedia* LC V

PREVIOUSLY *Egretta intermedia* | L 56–70cm Bill 5.4–8.3cm Tarsus 8.7–11.4cm Wt 400g

Medium-sized, all-white heron with heavy, pointed bill. Non-breeding (photo): *all white, bill and lores orange or yellow, legs black, pale grey above 'knees'.* Breeding similar but with distinct *bib formed by long filoplumes on upper breast and very long ones on back,* extending well beyond folded wings. *Bill red or magenta with yellowish tip, lores green or greenish yellow, iris red. Upper leg red, lower leg blackish.* Immature similar to non-breeding but legs all dark. **VOICE/CALL** Not very vocal; a variety of soft rasping, croaking or buzzing calls. **FEEDING** Mainly fish, grasshoppers and lizards. **P&R** To 1.3 million worldwide in Africa and Asia. **T&M** No known threats. **BV** Occasional visitor, prefers freshwater wetlands.

Cattle Egret *Ardea ibis* **LC NBM**

PREVIOUSLY *Bubulcus ibis*

L 70cm WS 88–91cm Bill 5–5.9cm Tarsus 8–9cm Wt 340–390g

Small, all-white, rather stocky heron. Non-breeding (photos) *all white with short, powerful orange-yellow bill and yellow lores and iris. Legs and feet green-grey to black*. Breeding similar but develops *buff, sometimes orangey, feathers on head and neck* and similarly coloured filoplumes on upper breast and back, *legs dull grey, yellowing towards top*. During courtship bill and lores turn magenta and iris red, legs somewhat pinkish. Immature as non-breeding but with black bill. **VOICE/CALL** Not very vocal, but has a range of croaking calls. **FEEDING** Wide variety of food, including lizards, grasshoppers, earthworms and mice; often seen with cattle. **P&R** 3–7 million worldwide. Range has increased in past 50 years; first recorded NZ 1963, now a regular winter visitor in significant numbers, with some remaining year-round but no records of breeding. **T&M** No known threats. **BV** Widespread, mainly coastal, but some inland lowland regions, often on farms, but also close to lakes, lagoons and estuaries.

White-necked Heron *Ardea pacifica* **LC V**

L 80–106cm WS 150–160cm Bill 7.5–9.0cm Tarsus 12.0–14.5cm Wt 860g

Large, distinctive, black and white heron. Non-breeding (photo) *upperparts dark slate grey with greenish sheen and reddish plumes. Head and neck white with dark irregular line down front of neck and upper breast*. Underparts white, becoming brownish grey under tail. Breeding has all-white neck and more prominent maroon plumes on back. In flight, *white patch on wing joint. Bill black*, bare skin at base of bill extends back behind eye, dark grey to light blue. *Legs and feet dark grey*. Immature similar to non-breeding but neck more spotted and barred, bill yellowish. **VOICE/CALL** Not very vocal; harsh, guttural alarm call, also a loud *oomph* during display. **FEEDING** Fish, crustaceans and other invertebrates. **P&R** To 100,000. Breeds in Australia, a vagrant to NZ. **T&M** No known threats. **BV** Freshwater swamps, farm ponds, generally inland.

White-faced Heron *Egretta novaehollandiae* **LC N**

L 66–68cm WS 106cm Bill 6.7–8.7cm Tarsus 8.0–10.1cm Wt 550g

Slim, rather elegant heron with long legs and *long, fine, dagger-like bill* (A). Upperparts generally blue-grey, *forehead, face and throat white*, neck and *upper breast pinkish brown*, becoming grey on belly and undertail. Long lanceolate plumes on back and breast, especially during breeding season. *In flight shows dark primaries and secondaries. Bill black, legs and feet yellow*. Immature (B) as adult but paler and duller, and lacks white on head, legs dull yellow. **VOICE/CALL** Not very vocal; variety of loud, rather guttural calls, may shriek when alarmed or at nest and with other herons. **BREEDING** Builds loose platform of sticks high up in tree, often close to water, solitary or in small, loose colonies. 3–5 pale blue-green eggs laid June–February, hatching after 3–4 weeks, fledging after 6–7 weeks. **FEEDING** Very wide range, mainly fish, crustaceans and insects, but will take mice, lizards and earthworms. Hunts either stationary or by deliberate stalking, occasionally pursues prey. **P&R** Up to 1 million. Found throughout Australia and NZ; a relatively recent arrival, first recorded breeding in NZ in 1941, now throughout country. **T&M** No known threats. **BV** Widespread, especially near estuaries and harbours, but also in open country by ponds, streams and in wet pastures.

Reef Heron *Egretta sacra* **LC N**

ALTERNATIVE NAME Matuku Moana

L 60–65cm WS 90–100cm Bill 8–9cm Tarsus 65–90cm Wt 330–450g

Medium-sized, all-dark heron with a characteristic *hunched appearance*. Plumage *uniformly slate grey but with distinct reddish-brown tinge*. Bill darkly yellow, *long and heavy*, legs and feet yellow. Develops long filoplumes on neck and back during breeding season. Immature similar but browner and may have a 'dark-capped' appearance. White morph, as above but all-white plumage, is found in the islands of the southwest Pacific but is rarely recorded in NZ. **VOICE/CALL** Not very vocal. Range of guttural croaks and caws. **BREEDING** Solitary nester in caves and crevices or in vegetation on cliffs. 2–4 pale blue-green eggs laid September–December, hatching after 3–4 weeks and fledging after 5–6 weeks. **FEEDING** Fish and eels, but also crabs, molluscs and marine invertebrates. **P&R** To 1 million. Southeast Asia and Australasia. In NZ entirely coastal, mainly NI, especially Bay of Plenty northwards, but also in Marlborough Sounds and Fiordland. **T&M** Loss of habitat and increased disturbance by human interference. **BV** Coastal harbours and estuaries.

Adult

Nankeen Night Heron *Nycticorax caledonicus* **LC N**

L 55–65cm WS 95–110cm Wt 550–900g

Medium-sized, stocky, brown heron. Upperparts *rich cinnamon brown*, underparts pale fawn. *Neck and face pale cinnamon, crown and nape black* with 2 long white plumes during breeding season (photo). *Bill stoutly pointed and black, facial skin and lores pale green*, becoming blue during courtship, iris yellow or orange, legs and feet dull yellow. In flight, wings very rounded and tail short. Immature mid-brown, spotted and streaked pale fawn all over apart from black cap and nape, bill horn coloured with dark tip, legs and feet pale yellow. **VOICE/CALL** Not very vocal, hoarse croaking call *quaark* or *quaak*, especially when disturbed. **BREEDING** Nests colonially in dense cover of trees, especially mangroves, in wetlands or by water. 2–5 pale green-blue eggs laid spring and summer, hatching after 3 weeks, fledging after 6–7 weeks; however, little information available. **FEEDING** Fish, frogs, crustaceans and insects, often at night, but more diurnal during breeding season. **P&R** To 1.1 million, mainly Micronesia, Indonesia, New Guinea and Australia. Birds breeding at Wellington Zoo were released in 1982, plus vagrants occasionally arrive from Australia. Some 50–100 birds present. **T&M** No known threats. **BV** Whanganui River, NI.

Australasian Bittern *Botaurus poiciloptilus* **EN N**

ALTERNATIVE NAME Matuku | L 66–76cm WS 105–118cm Wt (M) 1.4kg (F) 1.0kg

Medium-sized, stocky, short-necked, skulking, secretive heron. Adult plumage (photos) all *brown and heavily flecked, darker on back, neck and head, chin off-white, with pale streaking on throat, breast and belly*. Ear coverts buff, eye golden, *bill dull yellow, short and dagger-like*, facial skin grey or blue-grey, legs and feet yellowish or olive green. In flight, has broad, rounded wings. Immature paler and more subdued. Males significantly larger than females. **VOICE/CALL** *Loud foghorn-like booming* by males to advertise territory, otherwise a rather typical heron-like guttural croak. **BREEDING** Builds nest in dense stand of Raupo (*Typha alba*) or similar reed bed, by lake or in swamp. 3–5 olive-brown eggs laid September–November, hatching after 3.5 weeks, with chicks fledging after 7 weeks. **FEEDING** Mainly fish and eels, but also frogs, crustaceans and aquatic invertebrates, feeding mainly at night. **P&R** To 2,500, also in Australia and New Guinea. Australian population in serious decline, New Guinea almost extinct while NZ *c.*750 individuals, but difficult to survey due to secretive habits. **T&M** Loss of habitat especially due to wetland drainage for agriculture and grazing of wetlands. Some conservation measures being taken. **BV** Widespread in wetlands, but hard to observe; commoner in NI, especially Volcanic Plateau northwards.

Little Bittern *Ixobrychus minutus* **LC V**

L 25–36cm WS 41–49cm Wt 85g

B A

Very small, secretive, brown and black, freshwater heron. Male (A) upperparts, *back and tail black with buff upperwing coverts, neck rich chestnut, chin white*, breast and belly pale buff with *broad central dark brown stripe*. *Bill yellowish green with dark culmen, lores and base of bill yellow*, iris yellow, legs and feet greenish. In flight, buff wing coverts contrast strongly with black flight feathers. Female (B) lacks black back, which is brown, streaked pale, while cap and nape are dark brown. Immature as female but more striated. **VOICE/CALL** Not very vocal; if flushed, a sharp, repeated *cuck-cuck-cuck*. **FEEDING** Small aquatic invertebrates including crustaceans, and some fish. **P&R** 100,000–610,000, mainly in Europe and Africa, Australian subspecies. One NZ record, 1987 Westport. **T&M** No known threats. **BV** Chance sighting, freshwater wetlands.

Spoonbills, Ibis and Cranes

SPOONBILLS AND IBIS – THRESKIORNITHIDAE

Royal Spoonbill *Platalea regia* **LC N**

L 74–81cm WS 120cm Bill 16–22cm Tarsus 10–13cm Wt 1.5–1.8kg

Very large, upright, long-legged, all-white waterbird with an *immensely long, laterally flattened bill*. Plumage *all white* but male in breeding season develops a cream crescent on upper breast and striking crest with long, to 20cm, plumes. Facial skin, which extends past eye, black, with yellow eye-patch. *Bill black, very wide, ribbed, broadens at tip to 50–55mm*, iris red, legs and feet black. In flight, pink along leading edge of underwing visible. Immatures have black tips to primaries and lack yellow eye-patch. **VOICE/CALL** Not very vocal, variety of soft grunts and groans. Greeting call a soft honking *huh-huh-huh-huh*. **BREEDING** Colonial nester in variety of locations from tall trees to shrubby bushes or on the ground. Eggs white with brown blotches, 2–4 laid September–December, hatching after 3–3.5 weeks. **FEEDING** Mainly small invertebrates with some small fish and frogs; often feeds at night, in shallows in coastal lagoons, sweeping bill from side to side. **P&R** Up to 100,000, mainly Australia, a recent arrival to NZ, first breeding record 1949 in Okarito. Now widespread but with a total population of around 1,000 birds. Breeds mainly SI, Okarito on west coast, Marlborough and along southeast coast, also in NI at Kapiti I. and in Parengarenga Harbour in Northland. **T&M** No known threats. **BV** At breeding areas, but widespread in winter in coastal lagoons and harbours, Nelson and Welcome bays and around Christchurch in SI, and in many coastal harbours and estuaries in NI.

Yellow-billed Spoonbill *Platalea flavipes* **LC V**

L 76–92cm Bill 18.6–23.8cm Wt 1.9kg

Very large, all-white, long-legged, wading bird with very long, laterally flattened bill. Non-breeding plumage entirely white or pale creamy white, facial skin white with faint dark edge, iris pale yellow, bill pale yellow, lacks ribbing of *P. regia*. Legs and feet pale greyish yellow. Breeding has cluster of yellow plumes on upper breast and wispy greyish plumes on back, red patch at base of bill and the black around facial skin more prominent. Immatures lack black on facial skin. Males significantly larger than females. **VOICE/CALL** Not very vocal; variety of soft coughing hisses and low *woofing*. **FEEDING** Very similar to Royal Spoonbill. **P&R** 25,000–100,000. Found only in Australia. **T&M** No known threats. **BV** A vagrant, most likely in coastal harbours and estuaries.

Glossy Ibis *Plegadis falcinellus* **LC V**

L 55–65cm WS 80–95cm Bill 9.8–14.0cm Wt 500g

Large, *long-legged, long-necked, dark-plumaged bird with very long, slender, down-curved bill*. Non-breeding largely dark brown with *strong purple iridescence on upperparts. Head and neck heavily streaked with white*, especially below eye, faint white line bordering facial skin. Bill pinkish to greenish brown, legs and feet yellow-green to brown or grey. Breeding *head and body rich chestnut brown*, with strong green and purple iridescence, white line on facial skin more distinct. Immature as non-breeding but has variable white mottling on head and neck. **VOICE/CALL** Not very vocal; occasional grunts or a soft chattering call. **FEEDING** Mainly aquatic invertebrates and pasture insects, taken by probing into mud and soft sediments. **P&R** 1.2–3.2 million, worldwide distribution. Vagrant to NZ from Australia. **T&M** Loss of habitat through wetland drainage, susceptible to avian influenza, hunted in some areas. **BV** Chance sighting in coastal harbours and estuaries.

Australian White Ibis *Threskiornis molucca* LC V

L 65–75cm WS 110–125cm Wt (M) 1.7–2.5kg (F) 1.4–1.9kg

Large, black and white, *long-legged, long-necked bird with long, down-curved bill.* Plumage *mainly white, often looking stained and dirty. Head and upper neck black and unfeathered.* Long dark frilly tertials hang down over tail when on ground. *Bill black, legs dark, sometimes with reddish tinge.* In flight, tips of primaries black. Immature similar but head grey and legs grey. **VOICE/CALL** Not very vocal; most likely a harsh guttural honk, when alarmed a shorter, shriller honk. **FEEDING** Variety of small aquatic animals including fish, crustaceans, insects, also earthworms. **P&R** Up to 1 million. Breeds in Australia, a vagrant to NZ but fairly regular in small numbers. **T&M** No known threats. **BV** Coastal wetlands, harbours and estuaries.

CRANES – GRUIDAE

Brolga *Grus rubicundus* LC V

L (M) 105–134cm (F) 77–113cm WS 170–240cm Bill 15–18cm Wt (M) 4.7–8.7kg (F) 3.7–7.3kg

Very large, extremely long-legged, long-necked bird. *Plumage all grey, head lacks feathers; grey crown and forehead, red band around back of head to base of bill with contrasting blue-grey, feathered ear coverts.* Bill olive-grey, very long and dagger-like, iris yellow to reddish orange, small but distinct dewlap on throat. Legs and feet dark grey. In flight, shows black primaries and secondaries. Immature head feathered with pink cap but lacks red wrap-around and dewlap, legs paler. **VOICE/CALL** Loud trumpeting, aided by dewlap, and a variety of croaks, and grating, guttural sounds. **FEEDING** Omnivorous, including grain crops, invertebrates, frogs, crustaceans, molluscs, lizards and small mammals. **P&R** 26,000–100,000. Breeds in Australia and New Guinea. **T&M** No known threats. **BV** Wetlands, or pasture close by; a rare vagrant to NZ.

Pelicans – Pelecanidae

Australian Pelican *Pelecanus conspicillatus* LC V

L 160–180cm WS 230–250cm Bill 35–49cm Wt 4.0–6.8kg

Very large, *heavy-bodied*, broad-winged bird with a *huge pouched bill.* Non-breeding *largely white but with grey on nape and back of neck, and black wings* with large white patch on coverts. Bill pinkish, very large with capacious pink gular pouch, iris yellow. In flight, shows dramatic black and white wing pattern on both surfaces. Legs and webbed feet slate grey. Breeding develops cream patch on breast and gular pouch becomes red-orange. Immature as non-breeding but wings browner. **VOICE/CALL** Not very vocal; hoarse grunts and whispers. **FEEDING** Mainly fish, but also invertebrates, crustaceans; surface feeding but also by rather ungainly but effective plunge-diving. **P&R** To 1 million. Widespread in Australia. **T&M** No known threats. **BV** Coastal lakes and harbours, mangrove lagoons; a vagrant to NZ.

Rails and Swamp Hens – Rallidae

Western Weka *Gallirallus australis australis* **VU E**

L (M) 50–60cm (F) 45–50cm Bill 4.5–5.4cm Wt (M) 1kg (F) 700g

Large, brown, feisty, *flightless* bird with *long dagger-shaped bill* and an *enquiring nature*. Upperparts mid to dark *rufous brown with black streaking and flecking on neck and back, barring on primaries and tail*, underparts lighter, chin and throat greyish, pale eyebrow, eye red-brown. Bill powerful, pointed, reddish brown; legs sturdy, orange-brown. Female has generally lighter bill, legs and feet than male, immature generally darker all over. **VOICE/CALL** Shrill *coo-eet*, also a booming *doon-doon-doon*, both calls carry a long way. **BREEDING** Territorial, can breed at any time depending on weather, food supply and population pressure; up to 4 broods a year. Nest on ground, in base of tree, hollow log, short burrow or under thick vegetation. Up to 6 cream eggs laid 2–3 days apart, incubation lasts 4 weeks; young leave nest when 2–3 days old, are fully grown after 6–10 weeks and may breed as young as 5 months. **FEEDING** Omnivorous, mainly invertebrates and fruit, also seeds, lizards, young birds and eggs. **P&R** Low thousands, widespread but localised in northern and western SI and in Fiordland. **T&M** Loss of habitat, alien predators; previously viewed as pest by farmers and gardeners, now protected; difficult to relocate to sanctuaries due to predatory feeding habits. **BV** Northwest Nelson, northern Westland, Marlborough Sounds, Fiordland.

Western Weka is the most widespread and numerous of the 4 subspecies of weka, the others are: **North Island Weka** (A) *G. a. greyi*, greyer below and with brown legs. Previously found throughout NI; now restricted to the East Cape, inland from Opotiki and Gisborne. Introduced to island sanctuaries, Kapiti, Mokoia (Lake Rotorua), Pakatoa and Kawau islands (Hauraki Gulf). **Buff Weka** (B) *G. a. hectori*, much lighter coloured than the other wekas and found only in the Chatham Is, where it was introduced. Now extinct in its natural range of eastern SI. Recently reintroduced to two SI sanctuaries. **Stewart Island Weka** (C) *G. a. scotti*, slightly smaller that the others and darker than all but the Western Weka; found only on Stewart I. and surrounding islands.

Auckland Island Rail *Lewinia muelleri* **VU E**

L 21cm WS *c.*20cm Bill 2.5cm Wt 90g

Tiny, secretive, near-flightless bird. *Head, neck and upperparts chestnut with dark streaking on back*. Throat, foreneck and undersides grey with black and white barring on flanks and undertail. Bill long, reddish and sharply pointed, legs pinkish grey. **VOICE/CALL** A sharp *crek crek*, ascending and then descending; up to 20 in series. Loud repeated whistle. **BREEDING** Ground nester in dense vegetation, 2 or more eggs, cream coloured with blotches, laid in October–November. No information on incubation or fledging. **FEEDING** Unknown, but likely to be mainly invertebrates such as worms, insects, snails. **P&R** *c.*2,000, stable. Once thought extinct but rediscovered and found only on Adams (1966) and Disappointment (1993) in the Auckland Is. Inhabits dense vegetation. **T&M** Adams and Disappointment are predator-free, but Auckland I., only a few hundred metres away, has cats, mice and pigs, any of which would be a serious threat. **BV** Adams and Disappointment islands.

Banded Rail *Gallirallus philippensis assimilis* **LC N**

ALTERNATIVE NAME Mohu-pereru | L 30–33cm WS 40–52cm Wt 130–230g

Medium-sized, secretive, strikingly plumaged rail. Head clearly patterned, with *forehead, crown and nape dull chestnut, broad white eye-stripe above eye, broad chestnut stripe from bill, through eye and round neck*. Back and upperparts olive-brown flecked with black and white. *Chin, throat and upper breast grey, lower breast and belly barred black and white with variable buff band across breast*. Bill pinkish with darker culmen and tip, iris red, legs and feet greyish pink. **VOICE/CALL** Mainly silent, an occasional harsh squeaky *preeep* repeated up to 5 times. **BREEDING** Territorial year-round, ground nester, up to 6 pale buff-pink, spotted eggs laid September–March, hatching after 3–3.5 weeks; young leave nest almost immediately and fledge some 8–9 weeks later. **FEEDING** Mainly molluscs, crustaceans, spiders, beetles and worms, but also seeds, fruit and succulent vegetation. **P&R** To 200,000. Found throughout southwest Pacific; 15 subspecies. NZ subspecies found mainly in northern NI from Bay of Plenty and Raglan northwards. Also northwest of SI and Stewart I. **T&M** In NZ the continued loss of wetland habitat poses a serious threat, along with introduced mammalian predators, such as Stoats, cats and rats. **BV** Swamps and wetlands around estuaries and harbours, also Great Barrier I.

Spotless Crake *Porzana tabuensis tabuensis* **LC N**

ALTERNATIVE NAMES Puweto, Putoto | L 17–20cm WS 26–29cm Wt 400–500g

Very small, secretive, *all-dark bird with bright red eye*. Head, neck and underparts glossy lead grey, *upperparts dark reddish brown*. Tail near black, *undertail barred black and white*. Bill black, quite stout and pointed, *iris and orbital ring red, legs pink*. Immature paler and browner with white on chin and throat. **BREEDING** Territorial year-round, ground nester, lays up to 5 creamy-brown eggs, hatching after 3 weeks; young leave nest soon after hatching and are looked after by both parents for 4–5 months. **FEEDING** Wide range of invertebrates as well as fruit and seeds. **P&R** Widespread in southwest Pacific. In NZ, subspecies found mainly on NI, especially north of Palmerston North–Dannevirke. Rarely observed due to secretive nature. **T&M** Loss of habitat combined with introduced mammalian pest species. **BV** More frequently heard than seen. Wetlands, coastal and inland, especially on some island sanctuaries such as Tiritiri Matangi.

Marsh Crake *Porzana pusilla affinis* **LC N**

ALTERNATIVE NAME Koitareke | L 15–18cm WS 23–25cm Wt 30–40g

Tiny, miniature, secretive version of Banded Rail. Male *forehead, crown, neck and upperparts rich cinnamon, crown streaked black, back and wings streaked black and white*. *Faint white eyebrow*, face, chin, throat, foreneck and belly mid-grey, becoming near white on belly and *heavily barred black and white on flanks and undertail*. *Bill green* with dark culmen and tip, short and pointed, *legs and feet olive-yellow*. Female similar but rather duller olive-brown on back. Immature upperparts similar but grey of underparts is replaced by light brown and chin and throat whitish, breast somewhat barred. **VOICE/CALL** Rough, ratchet-like *krekkkkkkk*. **BREEDING** Ground nester in dense vegetation near water, up to 7 olive-brown eggs laid October–December, incubation takes up to 3 weeks. **FEEDING** Variety of invertebrates and seeds of aquatic or water-loving plants. **P&R** 13,000–37,000. Widespread in Europe, Africa, Asia and Australia. NZ subspecies is found in scattered localities in NI and SI; may be more widespread, but habits make observation and recording difficult. **T&M** Loss of wetland habitat and introduced alien pests. **BV** Raupo swamps and saltmarshes, but most records are vocal rather than visual.

South Island Takahe *Porphyrio hochstetteri* **EN N**

L 63cm Wt (M) 2.7kg (F) 2.3kg

Very large, unmistakable, *flightless* rail with massive, vertically flattened, *red bill. Head, neck, breast and belly rich purplish blue*. Back and flanks olive-green with a variety of hues and sheens, *undertail white. Bill and frontal shield red, legs, which are impressively stout, and feet red*. Looks rather like a large blue and green football. **VOICE/CALL** Most commonly a loud monosyllabic *klowp*; also a low resonating *oomp*. **BREEDING** Very territorial, ground nester, lays up to 3 large, 74mm long, pale buff eggs in a deep bowl, October–December, hatching after 4–4.5 weeks. Young may stay with parents for up to 2 years and may help rear next brood. **FEEDING** In native habitat feeds on snow tussock and in winter fern rhizomes. In protected sanctuaries, mainly introduced grasses. A surprisingly modest diet for such a massive bill. **P&R** 230. Thought extinct until rediscovered in 1948 in Murchison Mountains in Fiordland. A third of the population is found on island sanctuaries mainly around NI and they will be gradually reintroduced to safe mainland sanctuaries; they are already at Maungatautari in the Waikato. The North Island Takahe *P. mantelli* is extinct. **T&M** Very vulnerable to alien mammalian predators, particularly Stoats and rats, but also deer, which compete for food. They are subject to an intensive recovery programme, including pest eradication in their natural home in Fiordland as well as captive breeding and the use of predator-free sanctuaries. **BV** Tiritiri Matangi, Mana and Kapiti islands, Maungatautari.

Pukeko *Porphyrio melanotus melanotus* **LC N**

L 45–51cm WS 70–88cm Tarsus 8.8–10.6cm Wt (M) 1.05kg (F) 850g

Large, dark, *long-legged, upright bird with prominent red bill and faceplate. Crown, nape and face black, back and tail black, neck, breast and belly deep royal blue, undertail white*, underwing black. Bill large, 4–4.5cm, vertically flattened, and frontal shield bright red, iris red, legs and feet, which have exceptionally long, 10–11cm, delicate toes, pink or dull pink. In flight, legs often hang down. Immature generally dark black-brown, bill and frontal plate dull red. **VOICE/CALL** Wide variety of calls, including a soft *n'yip*, a harsh low-pitched *hic-cup*, a loud harsh squawk, and a loud yell and a crow. **BREEDING** Ground nester, often nesting communally, nest built in or beside clump of sedge or similar tussocky grass. Up to 13 olive-brown, somewhat blotched eggs laid August–February, hatching after 3.5–4 weeks. **FEEDING** Omnivorous; wetland and farmland vegetation but also insects, spiders, frogs and even small birds and bird eggs. **P&R** Up to 3 million worldwide, mainly South and Southeast Asia, Africa and Australia. Subspecies found in NZ is widespread and found throughout the country, especially wetlands and NI, but not alpine areas or native forest. A species that has adapted well to the agricultural environment. **T&M** Partially protected, but significant numbers shot legally each year during hunting season and a common roadkill. **BV** Widespread in wetlands and in lowland agricultural areas.

Half-grown chick

3/7/12 - Rotorua, Sulphur Bay

Australian Coot *Fulica atra australis* **LC N**

L 35–39cm WS 56–64cm Wt (M) 570g (F) 520g

Medium-sized, *all-black waterbird with white bill and frontal shield* (A). Head and neck deep black, rest of body deep charcoal grey. *Bill and frontal shield white, iris red or red-brown*, legs and lobed feet dark grey. Immatures (B) a little paler and may have some white on chin and throat. **VOICE/CALL** Typically a loud harsh *crark*; also a chopping sound *kratack krat krat*. **BREEDING** Builds floating nest anchored to vegetation at edge of freshwater lake. Up to 8 cream eggs laid August–February, hatching after 3–4 weeks; young become independent at *c*.5 weeks but may stay with parents until following spring. **FEEDING** Largely aquatic weeds but some invertebrates, largely by diving, which is initiated with an upwards jump, entering the water head first. **P&R** Up to 3 million worldwide. A relatively recent arrival from Australia, first recorded breeding in 1958. Now widespread at scattered locations on larger lakes but largely absent from Northland, the West Coast and Southland. **T&M** No known threats. **BV** Larger lakes in NI and SI, especially around Rotorua and Taupo (NI), St Anne's Lagoon and Ashburton Lakes (SI).

Dusky Moorhen *Gallinula tenebrosa* **LC V**

L 35–40cm WS 55–65cm Wt (M) 570g (F) 495g

Medium-sized, all-dark, coot-like waterbird. Breeding has *head, neck and body slate black, upperwing olive-brown, and a broken line of white along flank, extending to outertail feathers. Bill and frontal shield red with yellow tip*, iris red-brown, legs red, toes olive-yellow. Non-breeding *bill and shield olive-green*, legs and feet olive-green. Immature as non-breeding but browner and more white on flanks and belly. **VOICE/CALL** Raucous crowing *kurk* and a short soft *kook*. **FEEDING** Mainly vegetable matter, seeds, fruits, but also molluscs, invertebrates; feeds in water, dabbling but not diving, and on land. **P&R** Breeds in Australia, a vagrant to NZ. **T&M** No known threats. **BV** Marshy areas and water edges, freshwater wetlands; chance sighting.

Black-tailed Native-hen *Gallinula ventralis* **LC V**

L 30–38cm WS 55–66cm Wt (M) 410g (F) 370g

Medium-sized, all-dark, upright rail with *tail often held cocked*. Male *head, nape and upperparts dark olive-brown, tail black*. Face, throat and undersides charcoal with *white flashes on flanks*. Underwing dark grey with white edges to coverts. *Bill and frontal shield greenish yellow with base of lower mandible orange-red, iris bright yellow, legs and feet coral pink*. Female similar but paler and duller with less white on flank. Immature as female but paler on throat and neck and lacks red on lower mandible. **VOICE/CALL** Not well known, but a sharp *kak* and a rapid harsh metallic *yapyapyapyap*. **FEEDING** Mainly plant and plant material with some insects; often immerses head and neck when feeding in water. **P&R** Up to 1 million. Breeds in Australia, vagrant to NZ. **T&M** No known threats. **BV** Chance observation, coastal or inland wetlands.

Swans, Ducks and Geese – Anatidae

B | A

Mute Swan *Cygnus olor* **LC I** (Eur)

L 130–160cm WS 240cm Wt (M) 11.8kg (F) 9.7kg

Very large, all-white waterbird with a very long neck. Adult plumage (A) all white though head and neck may have creamy appearance. Head white with *black facial skin around bill and back to eye, iris brown, bill orange with prominent black knob* at base of upper mandible; female bill and iris are paler than male. Legs and webbed feet black. Immature (B) generally somewhat smaller and all greyish brown, bill brown and lacks knob. **VOICE/CALL** A variety of soft honks, snorts and hisses. **BREEDING** Generally solitary. Builds large floating nest of Raupo, flax and reeds. Up to 11 large white eggs laid September–December. Hatch after *c.*5 weeks, young leave nest within 24 hours and stay with parents until fledging after 17–21 weeks. **FEEDING** Mainly aquatic plants, but also some invertebrates, and occasionally frogs and fish. **P&R** 600,000, mainly northern Europe and Asia, introduced to NZ in 1866. NZ population probably a few hundred individuals, especially in urban parks. **T&M** No specific threats in NZ, not a known pest. **BV** Lake Ellesmere near Christchurch, also Napier and Hastings.

Adult pair and cygnets

✓

A | A
A | B

Black Swan *Cygnus atratus* **LC N/I** (Aus)

L 110–140cm WS 160–200cm Wt (M) 6kg (F) 5kg

Very large, *mainly black waterbird with very long neck.* Adult (A) plumage all black apart from *primaries and outermost secondaries which are white,* but visible only in flight. *Facial skin, lores and bill red with white bar across it close to tip,* iris red, legs and webbed feet black. Immature (B) dark ashy brown with dull orange bill. **VOICE/CALL** Loud hisses and occasionally a whistle, also trumpeting while in flight and to protect territory near nest. **BREEDING** Large nest made of Raupo and other vegetation, on land within 100m of water. Nesting time varies, with individual pairs mainly July–October while colonies tend to nest later depending on water level of lake or wetland. Up to 14 pale green eggs laid, hatching after 5–6 weeks, cygnets take to water within a day of them all hatching, fledging after 13–20 weeks. **FEEDING** Aquatic vegetation by dabbling and up-ending, also waterside pasture. **P&R** Up to 1 million, mainly in Australia. Introduced to NZ in 1860s but also arrived naturally. Now well established and found throughout the country, sometimes in large numbers. **T&M** Can be an agricultural pest, consuming large amounts of grass and fouling pastures. Some hunting and culling takes place each year. **BV** Widespread on lakes, harbours and estuaries throughout the country.

3/5/12 - Lake Rotorua

Canada Goose *Branta canadensis* **LC IP** (N. Am)

L 55–100cm WS 122–183cm Wt 3–6kg

Large, *long-necked, brown, black and white waterbird*. Upperparts mid-brown. *Neck black, head black apart from broad white chin-strap running from behind the eye*. Upper breast buff, underparts buff barred brown, undertail white. Bill black, legs and webbed feet dark grey. *In flight, tail dark with white 'V' on rump*, primaries and secondaries show dark. Immature very similar but greyer and chin-strap brownish. **VOICE/CALL** Loud, rather guttural honk, male's louder and longer than female's. Also in flight, short, nasal *kum kum kum* and a commoner double *ah honk ah honk*. **BREEDING** Builds nest on ground from available vegetation, up to 10 white eggs laid mid-September to late October, hatching after 4 weeks, goslings leave nest within 24 hours and fledge after 11–12 weeks. Known to hybridise elsewhere with domestic geese. **FEEDING** A largely terrestrial grazer of grasses, clover, Lucerne, brassicas and other crops. Some aquatic plants. **P&R** *c*.5 million, mainly North America but introduced in Europe. First introduced to NZ in 1876, more successfully in 1920. NZ population likely 50,000+. Partially migratory within NZ, moving north in winter, forms large flocks in autumn and winter. **T&M** A pest species that is hunted and sometimes culled due to damage caused to crops and pasture from foraging and droppings. **BV** Widespread near lakes and rivers, especially SI.

Cape Barren Goose *Cereopsis novaehollandiae* **LC I** (N. Am)

L 75–91cm WS 137–162cm Wt 4–6kg

Large, all-grey, rather bulky, short-necked goose. Plumage all mid-grey with large, oval, darker grey spots on wings. Bill quite short, black but with a greenish-yellow cere or covering. Legs pinkish, feet partially webbed and black. **VOICE/CALL** A low-pitched grunt, also a hissing sound and a soft honk; male also makes a disyllabic trumpeting honk. **BREEDING** A winter breeder in its native Australia, there are few details of its breeding in NZ. **FEEDING** A terrestrial feeder, pasture grasses, herbs and legumes. **P&R** 16,000–18,000. Native of Australia, introduced in small numbers to NZ, may also appear as a vagrant. **T&M** No known threats. **BV** Scattered locations on NI and SI, especially around Kaipara Harbour in NI and Lake Ellesmere in SI.

✓

Feral Goose *Anser anser* **LC I** (Eur)

L 80cm WS 150–165cm Wt 3kg

Large, bulky, white or brown and white bird. Male normally *all white* but may have *some barring on neck. Bill, legs and webbed feet orange*. Female similar but with *brown on upperwing and thighs*. Immature generally all brown, with duller bill, legs and feet. A domesticated variety of the European Greylag goose. **VOICE/CALL** Loud honking, especially in flight and in groups. **BREEDING** Ground nester, often colonial; no information from NZ, but elsewhere lays 4-6 creamy-white eggs. **FEEDING** Grass, clover, weeds and other vegetation in pastures, often away from water. **P&R** *c*.1 million in Europe. Brought to NZ in 19th century as farm animals, now established throughout the country, especially in rural farming areas. **T&M** Not a known pest species in NZ. **BV** Widespread, mainly in rural agricultural and semi-urban areas, also Auckland Domain, Auckland.

3/7/12 - Lake Rotorua

Paradise Shelduck *Tadorna variegata* **LC E**

ALTERNATIVE NAMES Putangitangi, Pari

L 65cm WS 90–120cm Wt (M) 1.7kg (F) 1.4kg

Large, heavy-bodied, goose-like duck with striking plumage. Male (A) *head and neck black, back and flanks dark grey with vermiculations*, some green and chestnut gloss/iridescence, which feathers show at rest, chestnut undertail. In flight, *upperwing shows black primaries, green secondaries, chestnut tertiaries with white secondary and tertiary coverts*. Bill black, legs and webbed feet dark grey. Female breeding (B) largely *rich chestnut with white head and neck*, somewhat darker outside breeding season; in flight, wing pattern similar to male. Immature similar to male, but duller and female shows white on head (photo C shows a chick). **VOICE/CALL** Very vocal, especially during courtship; male has a loud trumpeting *zonk zonk* while the female has a shorter disyllabic honk, more of a *zeek zeek*. **BREEDING** Solitary nester, on ground or sometimes high up in hollow tree, normally close to water, often a farm pond. Up to 10 white eggs laid August–mid-November, hatching after some 5 weeks, young leave nest within 24 hours and head for nearest water, fledging some 8 weeks later. **FEEDING** Feed on grass, clover, weeds and other vegetation, including arable crops, can cause some damage. **P&R** 150,000–180,000. Found throughout the country apart from alpine and heavily forested areas. The species has benefited from the development of western agriculture but is still only partially protected and sadly hunted legally in season. **T&M** Not fully protected, restricted hunting is allowed; may cause some crop damage but little reliable information. **BV** Widespread in open country, especially near water.

Chestnut-breasted Shelduck *Tadorna tadornoides* **LC V**

L (M) 59–72cm (F) 56–58cm WS (M) 96–132cm (F) 94–116cm Wt 1.3–1.6kg

Large, distinctly coloured shelduck. Male (A) *head and neck black with narrow white ring separating it from chestnut lower neck and breast*. Back, mantle and tail black-brown with vermiculations, shows some white, green and chestnut wing feathers when on ground. In flight, very similar to Paradise Shelduck with *black-brown primaries, green secondaries and green tertiaries with white coverts on secondaries and tertiaries*. Bill, legs and webbed feet are black. Female (B) very similar but has *broad white eye-ring and white mask around bill*. Immature rather browner and lacks white neck-ring and white on head of female. **VOICE/CALL** Honk, rather similar to Paradise Shelduck. **BREEDING** Nests in hole in tree, or under log or similar, lays up to 10 white eggs, which hatch after *c*.4.5 weeks; young leave nest immediately and fledge after 10 weeks. Only 1 NZ breeding record. **FEEDING** Grazes on grass, clover, weeds and other vegetation, sometimes on edge of lagoons. **P&R** 340,000–1.2 million, almost entirely in southern Australia. Vagrant to NZ in small numbers and has bred, but population very small and very scattered. **T&M** No known threats, fully protected but probably mistaken for Paradise Shelduck during the shooting season. **BV** Wetlands, or pastures close by; chance sighting.

Blue Duck *Hymenolaimus malacorhynchos* **EN EG**

ALTERNATIVE NAME Whio | L 53cm Wt (M) 900g (F) 750g

Large, rather heavy-looking duck with *grey plumage and an unusual bill*. Adult blue-grey overall with greenish tinge on crown, mantle and upper back and *reddish spots on breast*. *Bill pale pink with dark lip and soft lobe on both sides*. Iris yellow, legs and webbed feet pinkish grey. Immature similar but paler, lacks greenish tinge and less spotted on breast. **VOICE/CALL** Male has a high-pitched, whistling *whio whio (fee-o fee-o)*, female a rather rattling or guttural growl. **BREEDING** Ground nester, builds simple nest in hollow log or cavity or thick vegetation near fast-flowing stream. Up to 9 creamy-white eggs are laid from late July–December, incubation takes 4.5–5 weeks; on hatching, young immediately take to the water and fledge after 10 weeks. **FEEDING** Aquatic invertebrates, caddisfly, mayfly and stonefly larvae, caught by dabbling and up-ending in fast-flowing streams and rivers. **P&R** 1,200. Originally found throughout NZ, now restricted to mainly fast-flowing streams and rivers in native bush areas in central and eastern NI and western and northern SI. **T&M** Loss of habitat and introduced mammalian predators have resulted in a serious decline in population, particularly serious is loss of females as they do all the incubation and are thus more vulnerable to Stoats and ferrets. Fully protected and subject to captive breeding and recovery programmes, particularly pest control. **BV** Central and eastern NI, Te Urewera NP; northern and western SI, Kahurangi NP, Nelson, Mt Arthur, Fiordland.

Maned Duck *Chenonetta jubata* **LC V**

B A L 48cm WS 80cm Wt 800g

Medium-sized, predominantly grey duck with *rather small bill*. Male breeding (A) body generally *grey with dark spotting and flecking on lower neck and breast*, rump, tail and undertail black. *Head and upper neck rich brown with short black mane on nape*. Bill grey-black, legs and feet brownish grey. In flight, *primaries show dark and secondaries white with black bar*. Non-breeding male head less brown, lacks black mane and has pale lines above and below eye. Female (B) similar to non-breeding male but has whitish lines above and below eye, and brown vermiculations along flanks. **VOICE/CALL** Male makes soft, wheezy *wee-ow*, female has long, drawn-out *neeoow* or *naaa-wh*. **FEEDING** Grazes grass, clover and other herbs, also grain and insects; feeds mainly on land but may catch insects from surface of water. **P&R** Up to 2 million. Widespread in Australia, a vagrant to NZ. **T&M** No known threats. **BV** Grasslands and agricultural areas, near water, chance sightings.

Plumed Whistling-duck *Dendrocygna eytoni* **LC V**

L 40–60cm WS 75–90cm Wt 600g–1.4kg

Medium-sized brown duck with *long neck and upright goose-like posture*. Overall brown apart from white belly and undertail. *Crown and hindneck cinnamon, throat and foreneck pale buff, breast cinnamon, barred brown especially towards flanks, which have long cream-coloured plumes curving upwards towards back*. In flight, tail dark brown and *feet and legs extend well beyond*. *Bill pink with black mottling on upper mandible, legs and feet pink*. Immature similar but plumes and barring less distinct and bill and legs duller. **VOICE/CALL** Loud, distinctive high-pitched whistle. **FEEDING** Mainly terrestrial feeder, grass, clover and other herbs, but also dabbles. **P&R** Up to 1 million. Widespread in eastern and northern Australia, a vagrant to NZ. **T&M** No known threats. **BV** Chance sighting near lagoons or wetlands.

Grey Duck *Anas superciliosa* **LC N**

ALTERNATIVE NAME Parera | L 47–60cm WS 80–100cm Wt 1.0–1.1kg

Large, all-brown duck with striking head pattern. Adult *all brown and buff with pale throat and foreneck, green or purple (changes with light) speculum* often visible when on land, visible as green/purple secondaries in flight. *Head conspicuously striped brown-black and pale brown. Bill grey with black 'nail' at tip*, feet and legs grey-green to dull orange. Plumage of breeding female highlighted by buff edges to feathers. Immature similar but less marked and with uniformly streaked underparts. Very similar to female Mallard but generally darker and with striking head pattern and green/purple speculum; however, due to interbreeding, there are large numbers of variously plumaged hybrids. **VOICE/CALL** Similar to Mallard, male a fairly high-pitched *queck*, female a more raucous *quack quack*. **BREEDING** Ground nester, or in hollow or fork in tree near water. Up to 13 pale green eggs laid late August–December, hatching after 4 weeks; young leave nest immediately and head for the water, fledging after 8–9 weeks. **FEEDING** Seeds and aquatic vegetation by dabbling, also grazes on grass, clover and other herbs; may also take small aquatic invertebrates and molluscs. **P&R** Up to 1.2 million. Australia and islands to the north. NZ population thought by some to be a subspecies *A. s. superciliosa*. Population less than 500,000, in decline, found throughout country but cannot compete with Mallard and so mainly in more remote areas. **T&M** Loss of habitat and competition with introduced Mallard, with which it hybridises readily (see below). Also introduced alien mammals impact heavily on females and young. Still legally hunted in season. **BV** Widespread on all 3 islands, but especially Northland, Gisborne area in NI and Fiordland in SI. Prefers small lakes, slow flowing rivers and tidal areas rather than farming and urban areas.

Mallard *Anas platyrhynchos* **LC I** (Eur)

B A
C

L 50–70cm WS 75–100cm Wt (M) 1.3kg (F) 1.1kg

Large, archetypal duck. Male breeding (A) has *glossy green head and neck separated from rich chestnut breast by narrow white ring; body grey with vermiculations*, back and wings brownish grey with *blue speculum* formed by green secondaries, which are visible in flight. Bill yellow, legs and webbed feet orange. Female generally streaky mid-brown with faint darker eye-stripe, bill brown. Male non-breeding similar to female (B) but grey head and pale yellow bill; males start moulting in November. Immature similar to female. Readily hybridises widely with native Grey Duck, resulting in many plumage variations (C). **VOICE/CALL** Male has a rather soft, high-pitched *quek*, while female has a more raucous *quaack*, often repeated frequently. **BREEDING** Generally on ground or hollow tree or log; up to 16 pale greenish eggs laid late July–December, hatching after 4 weeks; young leave nest almost immediately and fledge after 8–9 weeks. **FEEDING** Mainly aquatic vegetation by dabbling, but also grazes on grass, clover and other herbs; ducklings and pre-laying females take aquatic invertebrates; also grain from standing and stubble crops. **P&R** Native of northern hemisphere, introduced to NZ from UK and North America, widespread throughout the country in all areas apart from alpine regions and native forest. **T&M** No known threats, partially protected, shot in considerable numbers during hunting season and under licence as a gamebird and agricultural pest. **BV** Widespread and abundant.

Australasian Shoveler *Anas rhynchotis* **LC N**

ALTERNATIVE NAME Kuruwhengi | L 45–55cm WS 70–80cm Wt 600–650g

Medium-sized, vari-coloured duck with very large, *55–65mm, spathulate bill*. Breeding male (A) has *dark grey head and neck with white crescent at base of bill. Breast pale with dark brown spotting and mottling, flanks chestnut and scalloped with clear white patch at base of tail*. Back black-brown with buff edges to feathers. Bill slate grey, *legs and feet orange*. Male non-breeding largely all brown with grey head. Female (B) similar but with pale brown head and paler cheeks. In flight, male shows pale *blue secondary coverts separated from green secondaries by white band, female similar but secondary coverts pale brown*. Immature similar to female but paler. **VOICE/CALL** Not very vocal; a distinctive soft *cuck cuck cuck*. **BREEDING** Ground nesters in rough pasture, sedge or reeds, away from water. Up to 13 very ice-blue eggs laid October–January, hatching some 3.5 weeks later; female leads young to water almost immediately, young fledge after 7–9 weeks. **FEEDING** Largely aquatic plants, seeds and zooplankton sieved from water by dabbling; larger invertebrates are also taken. **P&R** Up to 150,000. Found in western and eastern Australia and in NZ. Widespread in NZ, breeding mainly northern and southeastern NI and eastern SI, but widely distributed at other times. Prefers wetlands and shallow reed-fringed lakes. **T&M** Loss of habitat; introduced alien mammals impact heavily on eggs and young; legally hunted in season. **BV** Shallow and secluded lakes in Northland, Lower Waikato, Rotorua, Hawke's Bay in NI, and in Canterbury and Otago in SI.

Northern Shoveler *Anas clypeata* **LC V**

L 45–55cm WS 70–85cm Wt 650g

Medium-sized duck with *very large spathulate bill*. Breeding male (A) has *rich green head and neck and white breast, flanks chestnut and undertail black. Bill dark grey, legs and feet orange*. Non-breeding male generally brown but with face greyish, barred and mottled. Upper breast and flanks reddish brown with dark crescent-shaped markings. *In flight, wing pattern similar to Australasian Shoveler*. Female (B) difficult to distinguish from Australasian Shoveler, generally pale brown with mottling and scalloping, and white outer tail feathers. Bill olive grey with orange sides. **FEEDING** Very similar to Australasian Shoveler. **P&R** 5–6 million. Breeds across northern hemisphere, migrates south in winter; occasional vagrant to NZ. **T&M** No known threats. **BV** Chance sighting, freshwater lakes and ponds, possibly harbours and estuaries.

Northern Pintail *Anas acuta* **LC V**

L 50–65cm (excl. tail streamers) WS 80–95cm Wt 800g–1.2kg

Large, slim, dabbling duck with very long central tail streamers to 100mm. Male breeding (photo): *head and neck rich chocolate brown, lower foreneck, breast and underparts off-white, flanks and upperparts pale greyish brown, finely vermiculated with dark, scapulars dark, edged buff. Tail feathers long, fine and black*. Bill blue-grey with black markings around tip and on culmen. Legs and feet pale grey with black webs. Male non-breeding: pale brown flecked and mottled mid-brown but pale on head and neck. Female similar to non-breeding male, noticeably smaller and with rather more cinnamon on head. Immature as female but darker with less clear markings. **VOICE/CALL** Variable, rather wheezy *geee geee* and a disyllabic *twer-dip*. **FEEDING** Aquatic invertebrates, algae and water weeds. Feeds mainly by dabbling but also by diving. **P&R** *c*.5 million. Breeds north northern hemisphere, migrates south for winter; a vagrant to NZ. **T&M** No known threats. **BV** Chance sighting, quiet lakes, estuaries or other wetlands.

Grey Teal *Anas gracilis* **LC N**

ALTERNATIVE NAME Tete | L 42–44cm WS 60–67cm Wt (M) 525g (F) 420g

Small, slender, upright, grey-brown dabbling duck. Overall greyish brown with buff tips to darker feathers, *head darker and faintly streaked, throat and foreneck off-white, breast blotchy,* green speculum sometimes visible. *Bill bluish grey with short nail, eye red.* Legs and feet dull grey. In flight, white wing bar and trailing edge, white patch under wing. Immature as adult but breast uniformly streaked. **VOICE/CALL** Male makes a loud whistling *gedee-oo* and during courtship *cuc-cuc-cuc-cuc-ooo* or *thew-thew-thew-theeeoo* whistle. Female a soft *cug-cug-cug* or an alarmed *wreee-ak.* **BREEDING** Nests on ground in dense vegetation or in tree hole, close to water. Up to 9 cream eggs laid June–January, hatching after 4–4.5 weeks, fledging after 8 weeks. **FEEDING** Largely aquatic vegetation, seeds, flowers, but also invertebrates, mainly by dabbling or dredging in shallow water. **P&R** 1 million; 50,000+ in NZ. NI apart from west. SI, mainly east coast and lakes in Otago and Canterbury. **T&M** Protected but some shot 'accidentally' during hunting season. **BV** Widespread in lakes and ponds, also estuaries and coastal wetlands.

Chestnut Teal *Anas castanea* **LC V** (Aus)

B A

L (M) 40–50cm (F) 35–45cm Wt (M) 700g (F) 600g

Small, compact, large-headed dabbling duck. Male breeding (A) *head and neck rich glossy green, breast and underparts rich chestnut* with dark centres to feathers, *large white patch either side of tail.* Back dark brown, rump, tail and undertail black. In flight, shows *green secondaries with white triangle in front* and fine white trailing edge, underwing has *large white armpit* and dark leading edge. *Bill blue-grey, iris red,* legs and feet greenish grey. Male non-breeding brown all over, *head darker and streaked, breast cinnamon, flanks paler,* with feather centres *darker.* Female (B) as male non-breeding but more uniformly brown all over, with light margins to feathers. Immatures similar to female. **VOICE/CALL** Very similar to Grey Teal. **FEEDING** Mainly seeds and insects, but some molluscs and crustaceans in estuarine habitats. **P&R** 110,000. Breeds Australia. **T&M** No known threats. **BV** Chance sighting, estuaries, wetlands or inland lakes.

Brown Teal *Anas chlorotis* **EN E**

ALTERNATIVE NAME Pateke | L 48cm Wt 600–700g

D A
C B

Medium-sized, brown dabbling duck. Male breeding (A), *head and neck dark green with glossy sheen, narrow white neckband;* back dark brown with pale brown scalloping, *breast and flanks rich brown* with dark spotting, becoming vermiculations, *white patch either side of tail.* Rump, tail and undertail dark black-brown. In flight, shows *dark green speculum, narrow light bar in front* and white trailing edge; *underwing shows large white armpit. Bill blue-black, white eye-ring, iris black,* legs and feet slate grey. Non-breeding male (B) all brown, dark brown on head and back, lighter on breast and undersides, eye-ring less obvious. Female (C) similar to non-breeding male but with white eye-ring and slightly paler plumage overall. Immature (D) similar to female but darker with heavy blotching on breast. **VOICE/CALL** Male a wheezy trisyllabic *mmm-yea;* also high-pitched whistle after copulation. Female series of rapid 'quacks' or a high-pitched chirping when young threatened. **BREEDING** Year-round ground nester in dense vegetation close to water. Up to 8 creamy eggs laid mainly June–October. Hatching after 4–5 weeks, and young fledge after 7–8 weeks. **FEEDING** Mainly freshwater or marine invertebrates by dabbling in shallow water and mud. **P&R** Under 1,000. Restricted to Great Barrier I., Fiordland and Northland. Reintroduced to a number of island and mainland sanctuaries. **T&M** Loss of habitat and introduced mammalian predators; subject to an intensive captive breeding and reintroduction programme. **BV** Great Barrier, Tiritiri Matangi and Kapiti islands, Tawharanui, Karori Sanctuary.

Auckland Island Teal *Anas aucklandica* **VU E**

L 43cm Wt (M) 425–620g (F) 375–435g

Small, dark brown, flightless duck, very similar to Brown Teal but significantly smaller, and flightless. Plumage similar to Brown Teal but *lacks white neck-ring*, and white flank mark on breeding male much less obvious. **VOICE/CALL** Series of whistles, similar to Brown Teal. **BREEDING** Very little information, but similar to Brown Teal, with 3–4 eggs laid December–January and similar hatching and fledging periods. **FEEDING** Largely marine crustaceans with some freshwater insect larvae and algae; forages along shore, in seaweed; also known to dive to *c*.1.5m. Largely crepuscular and nocturnal. **P&R** 1,000–2,000, found only in the Auckland Is, on Ewing, Enderby, Rose, Ocean, Adams, Disappointment and Dundas islands. **T&M** Extinct on Auckland I. itself due to feral pigs and cats; population currently stable on offshore islands but, being flightless, the species is very vulnerable to introduction of mammalian predators. It is intended to reintroduce them to the main island once cats and pigs have been eradicated. **BV** Auckland Is.

Campbell Island Teal *Anas nesiotis* **CE E**

L 40cm WS 12.8-13.3cm Wt 315–500g

Small, dark brown, flightless dabbling duck. Plumage very similar to Auckland Island Teal. **VOICE/CALL** Little information but similar to Auckland Island and Brown teals. **BREEDING** Similar to Auckland Island Teal; in captivity, females may lay 2 clutches of up to 4 eggs. **FEEDING** Very little information; similar to Auckland Island Teal, not restricted to coast but forages in tussock grass all over the islands. **P&R** *c*.200, found only on Dent and Campbell islands in the Campbell I. Group and on Codfish I., where they have been moved for protection and captive breeding. In 2004 and 2005, 105 individuals were returned to Campbell, where they appear to be establishing a viable population. Found all over the island, not restricted to coast. **T&M** Driven to extinction on Campbell I. by rats, rediscovered 1975 on nearby Dent I. Subject to captive breeding programme, and reintroduced to Campbell I. in 2004 and 2005 after rats were eradicated. **BV** Campbell I.

New Zealand Scaup *Aythya novaeseelandiae* **LC E**

ALTERNATIVE NAME Papango | L 40cm WS 60cm Wt (M) 700g (F) 600g

Small, all-dark diving duck with a 'toy-like' jizz. Male (A) all dark, *head, breast, neck and upperparts near black with rich purplish, sometimes green, sheen*, underparts dark to mid-brown, near white on belly. In flight, *broad white wing bar covering primaries and secondaries*. Bill blue-grey with black nail, *iris golden yellow*, legs and feet black. Female (B) *all mid- to dark brown apart from white around base of bill*, on belly and wing bar. Immature (C) similar to female but lacks white around bill and with dark mottling on underparts. **BREEDING** Nests on ground, in dense vegetation close to water, up to 12 pale cream eggs laid late October–early February, hatching after 4–4.5 weeks; young leave nest for water soon after hatching and can dive immediately and fledge after some 10–11 weeks. **FEEDING** Aquatic plants and invertebrates by diving to at least 3m, probably more, and can last up to 1 minute. Also dabbles and surface feeds. **P&R** 5,000–10,000. Widespread but patchy distribution, dictated by location of suitable large, deep lakes, though increasingly they are also found in harbours, sewage ponds, some rivers and estuaries. **T&M** Loss of habitat and disturbance by human activities, water sports, etc., and predation by introduced mammalian predators. **BV** Kaipara Harbour, Rotorua lakes, Lakes Taupo and Waikaremoana, Farewell Spit, around Christchurch including Avon River, and high country lakes in Southern Alps.

3/7/12 Rotorua

Australian White-eyed Duck *Aythya australis* **LC V**

L 45–60cm WS 65–70cm Wt 800–900g

Medium-sized, *all-dark, chocolate-brown diving duck*. Male has crown, neck and upper back dark brown, chestnut on sides of head and neck and black-brown on lower back and rump; *lower breast, belly and undertail white*. In flight, *broad white wing bar covering primaries and secondaries. Bill dark at base, blue-grey at tip, iris white*, legs and feet dark grey. Female as male but paler on head and neck, bill similar but blue-grey band narrower. Immature as female but paler, especially chin and throat and some mottling on upperparts. **VOICE/CALL** A wheezy whistling *whirrrr*, female a loud, harsh rattling noise. **FEEDING** Aquatic vegetation, invertebrates, especially crustaceans and molluscs, mostly by diving. **P&R** Up to 1 million; breeds in Australia, a vagrant to NZ. Some suggestion, due to Maori name, that it may have previously bred in NZ. **T&M** No known threats. **BV** Chance sighting, deeper lakes, similar habitat to New Zealand Scaup.

Pink-eared Duck *Malacorhynchus membranaceus* **LC V**

L 36–45cm WS 57–71cm Bill 8cm Wt 300–480g

Small, *rather hunched* dabbling duck with large square-ended bill. Adult forehead, crown and nape grey-brown, *face white with fine barring and large chocolate-brown eye-patch* with small patch of pink feathers just behind it. Lores, chin and throat white. *Neck, breast, flanks and mantle white with dark variegated barring*, upperwing brown with *white trailing edge visible in flight. Rump white*, tail brown with fine white terminal band. *Bill long, dull grey, spathulate, with soft flaps that hang down from upper mandible*. Legs and feet dark grey. Immature similar but paler and less barred, lacks pink ear patch. **FEEDING** Largely invertebrates and seeds, but also aquatic vegetation, especially pondweeds; uses broad bill to strip seeds and flowers from plants and then uses flaps to guide invertebrates into bill. **P&R** 1 million. Found only in northeast Queensland, a vagrant to NZ. **T&M** No known threats. **BV** Freshwater wetlands, sewage ponds, chance sightings.

Muscovy Duck *Cairina moschata* **N/A I** (Mex)

L (M) 86cm (F) 64cm Wt (M) 4.6–6.8kg (F) 2.7–3.6kg

Very large, rather ungainly duck with distinctive red caruncles around base of bill and eye. Male is largely black with dark blackish green on back and with large white wing-patches, head and neck black with low erectile crest, much of face bright red and unfeathered, and red caruncle at base of bill. Bill pink, legs and heavily clawed feet grey-pink. Female significantly smaller with similar plumage and lacks caruncle and crest. Immature duller, with much less red facial skin. Being escaped domestic birds, plumage varies considerably and some domestic varieties are almost all white, so jizz and red facial skin probably the best identifiers. **BREEDING** No information on wild breeding in NZ. **FEEDING** Grazer of grasses, clover and other herbs, generally fairly close to water. **P&R** Up to 500,000. Native of Mexico, domesticated worldwide. Found in scattered locations around NZ, in NI and eastern SI. **T&M** Not known to be a pest species. **BV** Most likely in open rural and semi-urban areas, near water.

Landbirds

Kiwi – Apterygidae

There are five species of kiwi: three brown kiwi – Tokoeka, Rowi and North Island Brown; and two spotted – Great Spotted and Little Spotted. Tokoeka is further split into two, or possibly four, races or subspecies. All are very similar physiologically and differ mainly in size, coloration and location.

Kiwi are large, flightless, nocturnal birds that have hair-like feathers and very long down-curved bills with nostrils close to the tip. Brown kiwi are just that, but near-black feather shafts often give them a much darker appearance and they may have white patches and be slightly grey around the head and neck. Spotted kiwi are grey with bands of brown, grey and off-white feathers, giving a mottled or spotted appearance. Kiwis' legs are short, very stout and muscular with large, heavily toed feet. Long, sensitive rictal hairs at the base of the bill probably act as sensors for night feeding. The bill may take up to five years to be fully grown. The sexes are indistinguishable.

BREEDING The nest is in a burrow, hollow log or in dense vegetation. Females lay one or occasionally two extremely large white eggs weighing 300–530g, which is up to 25% of their body weight. The eggs are laid up to four weeks apart. Brown kiwi lay June–December, Great Spotted Kiwi July–December and Little Spotted September–January. Incubation takes 2–3 months, and the young leave the nest after a few days, becoming independent after 2–5 weeks and fully grown after 2–5 years. They start breeding after anything up to eight years. **VOICE** They can be quite vocal, with the male making a variable but often repeated and ascending *kee wee*, the origin of its name; there is considerable variation in tone and note length between different species and populations. The female has a hoarse cry. **FEEDING** Kiwi feed mainly on soil invertebrates, which they hunt using their long probing bill, the nostrils at the tip probably helping to locate prey. They may also feed on fallen fruit. **HABITAT** Native bush from sea-level to the subalpine zone (1,000–1,500m), but generally lower down in winter. Sometimes swamplands, pine forests and farmlands. **T&M** Loss of habitat and introduced mammalian predators, particularly dog, cat, pig, possum, Stoat and ferret.

Great Spotted Kiwi *Apteryx haastii* VU EF

L 45–55cm Bill (M) 8.3–10.4cm (F) 10.3–13.5cm Wt (M) 2.4kg (F) 3.3kg

Largest kiwi, with distinctive grey-mottled appearance. **P&R** Up to 20,000 individuals. Found only in northwest of SI, in higher altitude forest and tussock grasslands. **BV** Nelson Lakes and Kahaurangi national parks; Buller and Hurunui rivers, Arthur's Pass and Lewis Pass.

Little Spotted Kiwi *Apteryx owenii* CE EF

L 35–45cm Bill (M) 6.2–7.3cm (F) 7.5–9.4cm Wt (M) 880g–1.45kg (F) 1.01–1.92kg

The smallest kiwi, the female's egg/body ratio is the largest of any bird species. **P&R** Seriously affected by introduced predators and now extinct in its native SI. Breeding populations have been established on a number of NI offshore islands. Total population of around 1,600 birds. **BV** Karori Sanctuary and island reserves such as Kapiti, Tiritiri Matangi and Long islands.

Tokoeka *Apteryx australis* **VU EF**
L 40–50cm Bill (M) 8.1–12.0cm (F) 11.1–15.7cm Wt (M) 2.2kg (F) 2.8kg

Tokoeka translates as 'weka with a walking stick'. Most numerous kiwi, with 4 geographically distinct races: **Stewart Island Brown Kiwi** (A) *A. a. lawryi*, Stewart I., a population of around 20,000 individuals, mainly on southern and western part of the island. **South Island Brown Kiwi** *A. a. australis*, with three distinct populations, considered by some to be races or subspecies:

Southern Fiordland Population of around 5,000 individuals, from coast to above snowline.

Northern Fiordland Very similar to Southern, population of around 10,000 individuals.

Haast Prefers higher ground to above snow line. Plumage more rufous.

P&R Up to 35,000 individuals. Largest population is on Stewart I., remoteness of habitat making it difficult to estimate accurately. Very restricted geographically from coast to subalpine zone, or lower down in winter. **BV** Haast in Westland, Fiordland, Mason Bay and The Neck on Stewart I.

Rowi *Apteryx rowi* **CE EF**
L 40–50cm Bill (M) 8.1–12.0cm (F) 11.1–15.7cm Wt (M) 2.2kg (F) 2.8kg

Previously considered a race of the Tokoeka. Greyer plumage with some white on face. **P&R** Around 250 individuals, with very restricted range near Okarito on the west coast of SI. **BV** Okarito in Westland.

✓ **North Island Brown Kiwi** *Apteryx mantelli* **VU EF**
L 45–55cm Bill (M) 8.1–12.0cm (F) 11.1–15.7cm Wt (M) 2.2kg (F) 2.8kg

The only kiwi found on mainland NI. **P&R** Localised remnant populations in native bush and occasionally in pine plantations and farmland. Subject to intensive pest control operations wherever there are significant numbers. **BV** Tongariro, Taranaki, Te Urewera and Whanganui national parks; localised populations in Northland, Coromandel, Bay of Plenty.

Trounson Kauri Park Reserve

Raptors – Birds of Prey

OWLS (STRIGIDAE) AND BARN OWLS (TYTONIDAE) There were originally two native owls in New Zealand; only one survives, the other, the Laughing Owl *Sceloglaux albifacies* became extinct in 1914. Two other species are found, an introduced European species and an Australian species that may be becoming resident.

Little Owl *Athene noctua* **LC I** (Eur)

L 21–23cm WS 54–58cm Wt 175–180g

Small, *rather rotund* owl, often seen perched on post or shed ridge during the day. Plumage *mid-greyish brown, heavily streaked off-white, especially on belly*. Facial mask paler with *distinct white eyebrows*. Bill short, horn coloured and hooked, *iris bright yellow with large black pupils*. Legs feathered white. *Flight undulating, wings very rounded*. **VOICE/CALL** Clear, high-pitched *kieww*. **BREEDING** Nests in hole in tree, old building, bank or quarry; up to 5 white eggs laid October–November, hatching after 4 weeks and young fledge after 4–5 weeks. **FEEDING** Mainly insects and other invertebrates, some small birds, lizards or mice. Mainly nocturnal but also feeds during day. **P&R** 5–15 million. Europe, Africa and Asia; probably German subspecies *vidalii* introduced to SI 1906. **T&M** No known threats; no information on its impact on native species. **BV** SI only, widespread in lowland areas of eastern SI, and scarce in Westland and Fiordland. Prefers open country to bush.

Morepork *Ninox novaeseelandiae* **LC N**

ALTERNATIVE NAME Ruru | L 29–35cm WS 56–82cm Wt (M) 250g (F) 315g

Small, dark brown, nocturnal owl with *characteristic call*. Overall mid- to dark brown, *back dark brown with some buff flecking, breast mid-brown, heavily flecked with light brown and off-white, especially on belly*; tail long, with barring on feathers. *Facial disc dark brown with pale eyebrows*, bill heavily hooked and horn coloured, *iris golden yellow*, pupils black. Legs feathered, feet yellowish. **VOICE/CALL** Haunting 2-note *More-pork*, less frequently a repeated *more-more-more*, or when hunting a penetrating *cree*. **BREEDING** Hole in tree or in epiphytes in tree, or tree fork. Up to 3 white eggs laid, hatching after 3–4 weeks, young fledging after 5 weeks. **FEEDING** Mainly large insects, but also mice, young rats and small birds. **P&R** Widespread throughout country but mainly in forested areas. **T&M** Loss of habitat is chief restricting factor. **BV** Areas of native bush throughout country; nocturnal, but often viewed in daytime on branch or tree fern.

Barn Owl *Tyto alba delicatula* **LC N**

L 29–38cm WS 70–100cm Wt (M) 350g (F) 360g

Medium-sized, very pale owl. *Upperparts and head pale yellowy brown with darker flecking, underparts white*. *Facial disc white*, bill horn coloured and sharply hooked, iris dark brown, legs white-feathered, feet yellowish. Largely nocturnal, *appears all white* in car headlights. **VOICE/CALL** A rasping, screeching *skirrr*. **BREEDING** First recorded breeding in Northland in 2009–10. Elsewhere breeds in hollow trees, old buildings, caves, etc. Opportunistic breeders laying 3–6 white eggs, hatching after 4–5 weeks and fledging 7–8 weeks later. **FEEDING** Mice, small rats, small birds, reptiles and insects, though no information available on NZ birds. **P&R** 5 million. Worldwide; Australian subspecies. Occasional records from places other than Northland; open country and forest margins. **T&M** No known threats and its impact on native wildlife is unknown. **BV** Chance sighting, open country and farmland.

HARRIERS, FALCONS AND KITES There are only two surviving native species of diurnal raptors, one of which is endemic. The two extinct species are the giant Haast's Eagle *Aquila moorei*, which became extinct some 600 years ago, and Eyles' Harrier *Circus teauteensis* (previously *C. eylesi*), which was probably extinct before Cook arrived. The other three species recorded are Australian vagrants. Females are generally larger than males.

Swamp Harrier *Circus approximans* **LC N**

FAMILY Accipitridae | ALTERNATIVE NAMES Kahu, Australasian Harrier
L 50–60cm WS 120–145cm Wt (M) 630g (F) 850g

Large, long-winged, long-tailed bird of prey. Adult male (A) is all mid-brown apart from *white rump*, female darker and with *barring on tail*. Head brown with some white flecking, bill sharply hooked, *yellow at base, black at tip, legs long and yellow, feet yellow*. Males become paler with age. In flight, *wings held upwards in shallow 'V'* (B), tips fingered and tail square. Immature (C) darker than female with whitish patch on nape. **VOICE/CALL** Chattering *chit-chit-chit* or *kit-kit-kit*, also *kee-uu, kee-uk* and *kee-oh* in courtship. **BREEDING** Ground nester in wetlands, and in rank grass of young pine plantations or roadsides, rarely in tree, after prolonged aerial courtship. Up to 7 off-white eggs laid September–December, hatching after 4–5 weeks; young fledge after 6–7 weeks. **FEEDING** Carrion and live prey, former mainly sheep, possum and other road kill; live prey mainly small mammals, small introduced bird species also frogs, fish, lizards and large insects. **P&R** *c*.100,000. Widespread in Australasia and South Pacific. **T&M** No known threats, this species has benefited from the destruction of native bush and its conversion to farmland, the introduction of small mammals and birds, and the frequent availability of road kill. **BV** Widespread throughout the country, especially wetlands, agricultural pasture and forest margins. Frequently seen soaring with wings in shallow 'V' or feeding on road kill.

Black Kite *Milvus migrans* **LC V**

FAMILY Accipitridae | L 45–55cm WS 120–140cm Wt (M) 570g (F) 600g

Large, dark brown raptor with *long, slightly forked tail*. Adult all dark brown, but *paler and greyer on face, forehead, chin and throat, pale shoulder patches* visible at rest. *Bill black, cere yellow*, iris dark brown, legs and feet yellow. In flight, *fingered wing-tips and forked tail distinctive*. Immature generally paler than adult. **VOICE/CALL** Hoarse, rather querulous whistle, *seee-ee-ee* or *see-i-i-i*. **FEEDING** Scavenger, but will also take small birds, reptiles, fish and insects. **P&R** Up to 6 million. Worldwide apart from Americas, NZ and Pacific islands. **T&M** No known threats. **BV** Chance sighting, open country, wetlands.

New Zealand Falcon *Falco novaeseelandiae* **NT E**

FAMILY Falconidae | ALTERNATIVE NAME Karearea
L 40–50cm WS (M) 60cm (F) 80cm Wt (M) 350g (F) 550g

Medium-sized, slender, *fast-flying, long-tailed raptor with pointed wings*. Adult (A) dark brown on head, nape and back with pale feather edges on back. *Throat and breast white heavily streaked dark brown, belly and undertail dark cinnamon. Distinct dark drooping moustache either side of throat*. Slim rufous eyebrow, iris dark, *bill dark but white around base. Legs and feet yellow*. Flight direct and fast, with wings flat or swept back. Immature (B) is darker all over, with pale throat and eyebrow. **VOICE/CALL** Distinctive *kek kek kek*. **BREEDING** Very territorial year-round, nesting on cliff ledge, under overhang or in 'nest epiphytes' in large tree. Up to 4 buff to reddish-brown eggs laid September–December, hatching after 4 weeks; young fledge after 4–5 weeks. **FEEDING** Small birds, small mammals and large insects. **P&R** *c*.5,000 pairs. Three forms: Bush Falcon (650 pairs) found in forest in NI and northwest SI; Eastern Falcon (3,150 pairs) found in open country on eastern SI; Southern Falcon (200 pairs)in Fiordland, Stewart I. and Auckland Is. These have not been taxonomically described and are not considered races or subspecies. **T&M** Loss of habitat, predation of eggs and chicks by introduced pest mammals and, more seriously, shooting by ignorant and uninformed humans. **BV** Eastern SI and central NI.

Black Falcon *Falco subniger* **LC V**

FAMILY Falconidae | L 45–55cm
WS 95–115cm Wt (M) 630g (F) 900g

Medium-sized *very dark* falcon. Plumage quite *uniform brownish black apart from pale chin and throat and streaking on upper breast*, the latter more evident in adult female. Bill dark brown with paler base, iris dark brown, legs and feet grey. **VOICE/CALL** Repeated *gak gak gak*. **FEEDING** Small birds, mammals, reptiles and insects. **P&R** *c*.10,000. Endemic to Australia, a vagrant to NZ. **T&M** No known threats. **BV** Chance sighting, open country, wetlands, forest margins.

Nankeen Kestrel *Falco cenchroides* **LC V** (Aus)

FAMILY Falconidae | L 30–35cm WS 60–80cm Wt (M) 165g (F) 185g

Small raptor with *long narrow wings, long tail and pale underparts*. Male head and neck grey, *back rich chestnut with black primaries*, tail grey with *black bar and white tip. Undersides white* apart from pale buff with dark streaking on upper breast. Forehead white, *dark tear mark below eye*, bill blue-grey with dark tip, *orbital ring yellow*, iris brown, legs and feet yellow. *Hovers in flight*, from below all white apart from black band on tail. Female (photo) similar but head and neck brown, and tail rufous. Immature similar to female but more streaking on breast. **VOICE/CALL** A variety of chatters, twitters, screams and trills, *Kee kee kee, ki ki ki*, etc. **FEEDING** Small rodents and lizards by hovering and diving, also small birds and insects in flight. **P&R** 1 million. Endemic to Australia, vagrant to NZ. **T&M** No known threats. **BV** Chance sighting, open country.

Pigeons and Doves – Columbidae

There are two species of native pigeon in the New Zealand region, the Kereru of the mainland and adjacent islands, and the Parea found only in the Chatham Islands. There are three other introduced species but only one, the Rock Pigeon, is at all widespread.

Kereru *Hemiphaga novaeseelandiae* **NT EG**

ALTERNATIVE NAMES Wood Pigeon, New Zealand Pigeon, Parea (Chatham Is)

L 51cm WS 750cm Wt 600–700g

Large, *heavy-bodied, colourful, long-tailed* forest bird. *Head, neck, upperparts and upper breast varied mix of rich iridescent green with purple and bronze patches*. Lower *breast and underparts white*. Bill quite fine and red, iris and orbital ring red, legs feathered, feet red. Immature similar but rather duller. In flight, broad wings with fingered tips, makes distinctive swishing sound. **VOICE/CALL** Not very vocal, occasional soft but penetrating *coo*. **BREEDING** Forest breeders, in rough platform in fork of tree or similar. May breed at any time, depending on availability of food, but mainly September–February. Single white egg hatches after 4 weeks, young fledge after 5–6 weeks. May lay 2 or 3 clutches in season and start second clutch while still feeding earlier chick. **FEEDING** Entirely herbivorous, mainly flowers, foliage and fruit of a variety of forest trees, especially Miro, Tawa, Taraire, Puriri, Karaka and Pigeonwood. They are an important distributor of seeds for many trees. **P&R** Endemic to NZ, widespread, mainly in native bush, on all 3 islands. Not found in alpine or grassland areas. **T&M** Loss of habitat, but particularly predation of eggs and nestlings by alien mammals, especially possum, Stoat, Black Rat and feral cats. Some competition for food with possum, and hunting by humans. Fully protected and gradually recovering in numbers thanks to habitat restoration schemes and pest control. **BV** Native forest, but also parks and gardens, especially in non-breeding season, when fruits of native and some non-native trees are available. **Chatham Island Pigeon** *Hemiphaga chathamensis*, or Parea, is similar but about 25% larger (680–965g) and less colourful. It is found only in the Chatham Is. Once reduced to around 40 individuals, it is now recovering, but is still an endangered species.

Rock Pigeon *Columba livia* **LC I** (Eur, Afr)

L 31–34cm WS 63–70cm Wt 295–400g

Medium-sized, heavy bodied pigeon with *very variable plumage*. Wild or ancestral form plumage is largely *dark bluish grey with a green or purplish sheen on neck and upper breast*, and pale grey upperwing with 2 black bars. Bill short, grey-black, cere off-white, *iris orange-yellow to red, legs and feet pink or red*. Wide variation in plumage due to domestication. Immature similar but duller. **VOICE/CALL** Long, vibrant, moaning *oorh* or *oh-oo-oor*, display call *oo-ru-cu-t'coo*. **BREEDING** In wild on cliffs and in caves, but in urban areas on ledges on buildings. Can breed at any time, and may do so up to 5 times a year. Usually 1 or 2 white eggs laid, but occasionally 3 or 4 eggs, which hatch after 2.5 weeks; young fledge after 4 weeks. **FEEDING** Mainly seeds, but some invertebrates; also scavenges human food, bread, etc. **P&R** 260 million. Originally Europe, Asia, Africa, but now worldwide. Introduced to NZ in 19th century. **T&M** Can be a serious pest species, damaging crops. **BV** Widespread, including urban areas, inland cliffs; not found in native bush or alpine areas, and rare along western half of SI.

Spotted Dove *Stigmatopelia chinensis* **LC I** (Asia)

L 30–33cm WS 40–46cm Wt 160g

Medium-sized pigeon with distinctive black and white 'shawl'. *Head and nape grey, tinged pink*. Distinctive *broad, white-spotted, black partial collar*, back and tail mid-grey-brown, flecked paler on wings, undersides and *breast pinkish brown*. Bill short and black, *iris orange-yellow with dark outer ring, legs and feet pink-red*. Immature similar but lacks collar and generally duller. **VOICE/CALL** A variety of cooing calls: *croo-croo, cuck-croo-cuck, cu-cu-croo-cruk* etc. **BREEDING** Food-dependent year-round breeder, nest a flimsy platform of twigs in small tree or shrub. 2 white eggs laid, hatching after 2.5 weeks, young fledging after 2–3 weeks. **FEEDING** Largely grass and weed seeds, but also grain and occasional invertebrates. **P&R** Native of Asia, introduced to NZ as cage birds; small number of escapees and deliberately released birds found in Auckland area. **T&M** No known threats. Not known to have impact on native species or on agricultural or horticultural crops. **BV** Urban areas, specifically Whangarei, Auckland and Bay of Plenty, locally common in parks and gardens.

Barbary Dove *Streptopelia roseogrisearisoria* **LC I** (Eur, Afr)

ALTERNATIVE NAME African Collared Dove

L 28–30cm WS 45–50cm Wt 140–150g

Smallest pigeon in NZ. Largely *pale sandy buff*, paler on head and neck with noticeable *narrow black partial collar*. Bill short, purplish black, iris dark red, orbital ring light grey, *legs and feet deep red*. Immature similar but duller and lacks partial collar. Domesticated version of African Collared Dove. **VOICE/CALL** Mellow *ku-krroo* or *ku-kurroo*. **BREEDING** Opportunistic year-round breeder, nest a flimsy platform of twigs in shrub or small tree. 2 white eggs laid, hatching after 2.5 weeks, young fledging after 2–3 weeks. **FEEDING** Seeds and fruit, also scavenges human food such as bread. **P&R** Native of Africa, introduced to NZ as cage birds, now escapees or released. **T&M** No known threats. Not known to have impact on native species or on agricultural or horticultural crops. **BV** Close to urban areas, especially Whangarei, Auckland, Hamilton, Tauranga, Hastings, Napier.

Parrots

New Zealand boasts nine species and four subspecies of native parrot. There are a further four species introduced from Australia.

STRIGOPIDAE (PREVIOUSLY PSITTACIDAE)

Kakapo *Strigops habroptilus* **CE EG**

L 58–64cm WS *c.*90cm Wt (F) 1.2–2.0kg (M) 1.6–3.5kg

Large, unmistakable, flightless, nocturnal parrot. Plumage: *moss green upperparts, yellowish-green underparts, vermiculated on head, nape and back with dark brown*. Owl-like, *light brown facial discs*, iris dark brown, bill pale grey and surrounded by soft hairs or 'vibrissae', legs feathered, feet dark grey. Immature similar, olive-green and plumage more finely barred. **VOICE/CALL** Male makes a loud, repetitive booming call and a high-pitched *chinging* as part of its nocturnal mating display, as well as a range of harsh *skrarking* calls throughout the year. **BREEDING** Irregular, breeding in synchrony with periodic abundant supply of fruit or seed every 3–5 years. Lek or arena mating system: males display communally, making loud booming calls to attract females to their track and bowl systems; mates and leaves female to lay and incubate eggs and feed chicks alone. Ground nester, in natural cavity or under tussock; female lays 2–4 white eggs that hatch after 4 weeks, young fledge after 10–12 weeks but may stay with female for a further 4–6 months. **FEEDING** Entirely herbivorous, eats fruit, seed, nectar, leaves stems, sap, roots and leaves. Preferred foods are tussock grass blades and seeds, beech, Rimu and Pink Pine fruit. **P&R** *c.*122, increasing slowly. Previously widespread on all 3 islands, now confined to offshore island sanctuaries. **T&M** Extinct throughout natural range due to predation by Stoats and other alien predators, and habitat loss. Subject of an intense recovery programme involving relocation of all individuals to predator-free islands for close-order management, including manipulation of breeding, artificial insemination, captive rearing when natural food supply fails and supplemental feeding. **BV** Codfish and Anchor islands, off Stewart I.; individuals occasionally available for public viewing on Ulva I. and at Auckland Zoo.

Kea *Nestor notabilis* **VU EG**

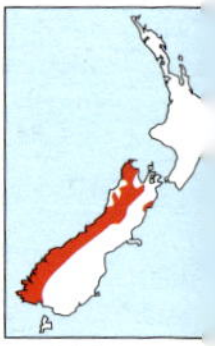

L 46–50cm Wt (M) 1,000g (F) 800g

Large, gregarious, inquisitive parrot with very *long down-curved upper mandible*. Adult plumage (A) *olive-green with dark edges to feathers giving scalloped appearance. Upperwing feathers brighter olive-green, underwing coverts scarlet*. Bill black, very long, 5.5cm, upper mandible significantly longer than lower, especially in males. Iris dark, *orbital ring yellow*, legs and feet grey-brown. Immature (B) similar but has yellow cere and at base of lower mandible. Adept at using long upper mandible to remove windscreen seals, open tramping packs, etc.; often acrobatic in flight. **VOICE/CALL** Loud, echoing onomatopoeic *keee-aah*. **BREEDING** Solitary ground nester in holes, under logs, rocks, etc. Up to 4 white eggs laid July–January, female incubates for 3–4 weeks while male feeds her. Young fledge after 12–14 weeks. **FEEDING** Mainly herbivorous, berries, shoots, etc., but also scavenges and will eat carrion – known to dig into sick or snow-bound sheep above kidneys to get at subcutaneous fat, and to prey upon nestling Hutton's Shearwaters. **P&R** *c.*5,000, SI only. Montane and alpine areas. **T&M** Fully protected but suffers from some loss of habitat, and predation by Stoats and other alien mammalian predators of eggs and nestlings. Subject to lead poisoning from proclivity for eating lead off roofs and nail-heads. Still subject to human predation due to its occasional habit of killing sheep. **BV** Alpine areas on SI, Arthur's Pass, Nelson Lakes.

3/12/17 Fox Glacier Carpark

Kaka *Nestor meridionalis* **EN EG**

L 38–45cm WS 72–86cm Wt (M) 475g (F) 425g

Medium-sized, rather *noisy* forest parrot (A). Plumage *olive-brown above with lighter crown and gold coloration on face and red on neck, undertail and belly*. Dark feather edges give scalloped look all over. In flight, *crimson underwing* visible (B). *Bill large, sharply hooked*, dark grey, longer in male, iris dark brown, legs and feet dark grey. Immature less colourful and has yellow cere and at base of lower mandible. Two distinct subspecies exist. **South Island Kaka** *N. m. meridionalis*, which is found on SI and Stewart I., is brighter with a near-white crown compared to the **North Island Kaka** *N. m. septentrionalis*, which is found only on NI. **VOICE/CALL** Loud and varied series of whistles and harsh screams. **BREEDING** Nests in hollow tree or tree bowl; up to 8 white eggs laid September–March, eggs incubated by female while male feeds her, hatching after 3–4 weeks, young fledge at 9–10 weeks. **FEEDING** Wide range: fruit, nectar, invertebrates; uses powerful beak to break up rotting logs. **P&R** Up to 10,000, probably decreasing. Found on all 3 islands in native bush; visits urban areas in winter and early spring, when exotic trees are fruiting. **T&M** Loss of habitat is a major problem, along with introduced mammalian pest species, especially Stoats and possums. Introduced wasps compete for food, especially honeydew. **BV** Native bush areas in all 3 islands, especially Great Barrier, Mayor and Kapiti islands, Coromandel, Whirinaki and Pureora forest parks, in northwest and southwest of SI and on Stewart I.

PSITTACIDAE

Yellow-crowned Parakeet *Cyanoramphus auriceps* **NT E**

ALTERNATIVE NAME Kakariki

L (M) 23–27cm (F) 20–24cm WS (M) 32–36cm (F) 31cm Wt (M) 50g (F) 40g

Small, *long-tailed*, green forest parrot. *Bright yellow-green all over, somewhat paler on breast, crown golden yellow, red band from eye to eye across base of bill, crimson patch on underside of rump*, bright blue outer wing feathers. Bill grey with dark tip, iris red, legs and feet dark grey. Flight fast and direct. **VOICE/CALL** High-pitched chatter *ki-ki-ki-ki*. **BREEDING** Nests in holes in trees; opportunistic breeder but up to 9 white eggs are laid mainly October–December, female incubates while male feeds her. Hatch after 2–3 weeks, young fledge after 5–6 weeks. **FEEDING** Mainly insects but also flower and leaf buds, flowers and seeds. **P&R** 10,000–20,000, widespread but scarce throughout 3 main islands and on Auckland Is. **T&M** Loss of habitat and the usual invasive alien mammalian predators, especially Stoats, rats and possums. No specific programmes in force but benefits from ongoing pest-control programmes. **BV** Native forest on all 3 islands; not normally found in logged or regenerating areas, appears to need mature trees.

Orange-fronted Parakeet *Cyanoramphus malherbi* **CE E**

L 23–25cm WS 31–36cm Wt (M) 50g (F) 40g

Small, *long-tailed*, green forest parrot. Virtually identical to Yellow-crowned Parakeet, but has *paler yellow crown and an orange band across base of bill and orange patch on side of rump*. Previously considered a phase of *C. auriceps*. **VOICE/CALL** High-pitched chatter. **BREEDING** No specific information but likely to be similar to *C. auriceps*. **FEEDING** As for *C. auriceps*. **P&R** Up to 250, probably decreasing; found only in inland North Canterbury and the Nelson region. **T&M** Loss of habitat and alien predators are the main threats; specific pest-control programme in place in Hurunui River catchment and a population established on Chalky I., Fiordland. **BV** Native bush in Canterbury.

Forbes' Parakeet *Cyanoramphus forbesi* **EN E**

L 23–25cm WS 31–36cm Wt (M) 50g (F) 40g

Larger than, but virtually identical to, Yellow-crowned Parakeet and found only on Mangere and Little Mangere islands in the Chatham Is. **P&R** Less than 250 individuals, but population stable. Restricted to Mangere and Little Mangere islands in Chatham Is. **T&M** No direct threats as habitat recovering and islands are pest-free; however, very susceptible to changes due to very small population. Some hybridisation with *C. novaezelandiae chathamensis*. **BV** Mangere and Little Mangere islands.

Red-crowned Parakeet *Cyanoramphus novaezelandiae* **VU E**

ALTERNATIVE NAME Kakariki

L (M) 25–27cm (F) 21–26cm WS 32–38cm Wt (M) 80g (F) 70g

Small, *long-tailed, bright green parrot*, very similar to Yellow-crowned Parakeet but with *bright red forehead and crown, and red stripe from bill through eye to ear coverts*. **VOICE/CALL** Similar to *C. auriceps* but lower-pitched. **BREEDING** Nests in holes in trees, or in cliffs or among rocks, also in burrows in ground or dense vegetation. Up to 9 white eggs laid October–December, sometimes March, hatching after 3–3.5 weeks; female incubates and male feeds her. Young fledge after 6–7 weeks. **FEEDING** Mainly herbivorous, especially seeds and flowers of NZ flax, beech and grasses, fruit, invertebrates and occasionally carrion. **P&R** 20,000–25,000, probably decreasing. Previously widespread on all main islands, now found almost entirely on predator-free offshore islands. **T&M** Loss of habitat, but mainly alien mammalian predators. Subject to recovery programme and reintroduced to several islands sanctuaries, including Matiu/Somes and Tiritiri Matangi. **BV** Tiritiri Matangi and Kapiti islands. Subspecies **Kermadec Parakeet** *C. n. cyanurus* is found in the Kermadec Is while the **Chatham Island Red-crowned Parakeet** *C. n. chathamensis* is found in the Chatham Is; they are virtually indistinguishable from the mainland race.

Reischek's Parakeet *C. hochstetteri* is found on Antipodes and Bollons islands and all adjacent islets. It is virtually indistinguishable from the mainland species, though it has a rather more orange-red crown and eye-stripe.

Antipodes Island Parakeet *Cyanoramphus unicolor* **VU E**

L (M) 32cm (F) 29cm WS 38–43cm Wt (M) 170g (F) 130g

Small, *all-yellow-green, long-tailed* parrot, head rather brighter green and outer primaries blue, though less noticeable than *C. auriceps* and *C. novaezelandiae*. Immature has shorter tail than adults. **VOICE/CALL** Similar to *C. novaezelandiae*. **BREEDING** Ground nester in burrows in base of tussock grasses; up to 6 white eggs laid October–January, female incubates for 4 weeks while male feeds her. Little information available on breeding in wild where clutch size may be smaller. **FEEDING** Leaves of tussock, sedge and other grasses, also seeds, berries, flowers and sometimes carrion in penguin colonies. **P&R** 2,000–3,000, stable. Found only on Antipodes and Bollons islands in the Antipodes Is. **T&M** No specific threats though small population and limited habitat make the species very vulnerable. **BV** Antipodes Is.

CACATUIDAE (PREVIOUSLY PSITTACIDAE)

Sulphur-crested Cockatoo *Cacatua galerita* **LC I** (Aus)

L 48–55cm WS 103cm Wt 815–975g

Large, noisy, *white parrot with bright yellow forward-curved crest.* Underwing and undertail have slight yellow tinge. Bill black and strongly down-curved, eye dark brown. Strong flier with fingered wing-tips. **VOICE/CALL** Raucous screech, especially when in flight. **BREEDING** High up in hole in tall tree. Up to 3 white eggs laid August–November, hatching after 4 weeks with young fledging after a further 6 weeks. **FEEDING** Wide variety, from grass seeds and cereals to fruit, nuts and invertebrates. **P&R** Native to Australia. Introduced in NZ in early 1900s. **T&M** No known threats, not a serious pest species due to small numbers. **BV** Scattered populations, mainly NI, Auckland, Waitakere Ranges, Raglan, Bay of Plenty, Whanganui and in SI on Banks Peninsula.

Galah *Eolophus roseicapillus* **LC I** (Aus)

L 35–36cm WS 75cm Wt 330g

Medium-sized parrot. Adult largely *rosy pink with pale pink head and blue-grey flight feathers*. Bill horn coloured, eye dark brown, orbital ring white, legs and feet grey. Immature similar but duller with grey face. **VOICE/CALL** Very varied, including a short *chet*, a high-pitched *chill-chill* and a pigeon-like *choot-choot, choot-choot*. **BREEDING** No NZ information but in Australia nest is in tree, up to 8 white eggs laid late July–November, hatching after 3–4 weeks, young fledge after 7 weeks. **FEEDING** Mainly ground feeders; grass seeds, cereals, fruit and some insects. **P&R** Native of Australia, introduced to NZ as cage birds and escaped. **T&M** Agricultural pest in Australia, but numbers too small in NZ to be of concern. **BV** Auckland and northern Waikato.

PSITTACIDAE

Eastern Rosella *Platycercus eximius* **LC I** (Aus)

L 28–33cm WS 38–47cm Wt 100–110g

Medium-sized, very brightly coloured parrot. Male *head, neck, breast and undertail bright red, chin and throat white, belly yellow, back yellow, scalloped with black, outer upperwing blue, tail green with blue outer feathers*. Bill off-white, iris dark brown, legs and feet dark grey. Female and immature darker on back and red duller. Flight fast and direct, often noisy. **VOICE/CALL** Loud chattering *kwink kwink* and strident screeching, especially in groups and in flight. **BREEDING** Nests in holes in trees; female incubates up to 9 white eggs for 3–3.5 weeks. Young fledge after 4 weeks. **FEEDING** Wide range of seeds, fruit, flowers and occasionally insects. **P&R** Native of Australia, introduced to NZ as cage birds, but escaped. **T&M** Not known to be a serious pest. **BV** Northern NI and Wellington region, also Dunedin.

Crimson Rosella *Platycercus elegans* **LC I** (Aus)

L 35–38cm WS 44–53cm Wt 120–150g

Medium-sized, very colourful, long-tailed parrot. Adult very largely *crimson apart from blue chin and throat, blue flight feathers and black scalloping on back*, tail green with blue outer feathers. Bill pearl grey, iris dark brown, legs and feet grey. Immature largely green with red crown, breast and undertail and blue chin. **VOICE/CALL** Low-pitched *kweek-kweek-kweek*. **BREEDING** Nest in hollow in tree, up to 8 white eggs laid and incubated by female for 3 weeks, young fledge after 5 weeks but remain with parents for several months. **FEEDING** Wide range of seeds, fruit and some insects. **P&R** Native of Australia, introduced to NZ as cage birds. **T&M** Not a known pest species. **BV** Urban areas. Wellington, Dunedin, few sightings.

Ring-necked Parakeet *Psittacula krameri* **LC I** (Asia)

L 38–42 cm WS42–48cm

Gregarious, noisy, medium-sized, all-green parrot with distinctive *neck ring and very long (19–28cm) tail*. Male (A) plumage all green, lime green about face and on wings, paler on upper breast and back. Black neck band turns red on nape, which is bluish green. *Black bib from neck band to bill, bill bright red with dark tip*, red eye ring, iris yellow, feet and legs grey. In flight, long tail and *yellowish-green underwing coverts* obvious. Female (B) smaller, more uniform green and lacks dark neck band or has a very pale one, and bib. **VOICE/CALL** Very noisy; wide variety of shrieks and whistles. **BREEDING** Nests in hole in tree, 2–6 white eggs, hatching after 3–4 weeks, fledging after 6–7 weeks. **FEEDING** Variety of flower buds, fruits, vegetables, nuts, berries and seeds. **P&R** Native of Africa and Asia, 4 subspecies. Small population in NI. **T&M** No known threats, a potential horticultural pest. **BV** Rotorua, Tauranga, Bay of Plenty.

Cuckoos – Cuculidae

There are two native cuckoos; both are parasitic breeders and migratory, coming to New Zealand to breed. The other five species are vagrants, mainly Australian.

Shining Cuckoo *Chrysococcyx lucidus* **LC BM**

ALTERNATIVE NAME Pipiwharauroa | L 13–18cm WS 25–32cm Wt 250g

Small, *short-tailed* cuckoo. Adult (A) head, nape and mantle purplish burnished brown, *rest of upperparts bright iridescent green*. Underparts *white, narrowly barred brown, undertail broadly barred*. Face white with fine brown spotting. Bill black, iris brown, sometimes reddish, legs and feet dark grey. Immature (B) much duller and barring less distinct. **VOICE/CALL** High-pitched increasing whistles, *coo-ee coo-ee*, and a decreasing *tsee-ew*; normally stop calling in December. **BREEDING** Parasitic breeder; single olive-green egg in nest of a Grey Warbler (Chatham Island Warbler in Chatham Is), removing one warbler egg. Hatching after 2 weeks, 4 days before host's eggs, chick then evicting host eggs or chicks, fledging after 3 weeks. **FEEDING** Invertebrates, especially caterpillars. **P&R** Breeds NZ, but in March migrates to western Indonesia, New Guinea and the Bismarck Archipelago, returning in September–October. A few individuals overwinter in Northland. **T&M** Cats and other alien predators, also loss of habitat in wintering grounds. **BV** Widespread especially in native bush and on NI.

Long-tailed Cuckoo *Eudynamys taitensis* **LC BM - E**

ALTERNATIVE NAME Koekoea | L 40–42cm WS 47–52cm Wt 120–125g

Large, brown, *long-tailed*, skulking cuckoo. Adult (A) *head and upperparts rich brown, barred black. Underparts off-white with bold brown and black striations. Undertail barred*. Bill dark cream with dark brown ridge. Iris yellow to red-brown, orbital ring olive-green, legs and feet olive greenish grey. Juvenile (B) similar but dark grey rather than brown. **VOICE/CALL** A loud, penetrating whistling, sometimes harsh *whiz-z-z-zt* or *zzwheesht*. **BREEDING** Parasitic breeder; single creamy-white egg in November–December, in the nest of Whitehead (NI), Yellowhead (SI) and Brown Creeper (SI, Codfish and Stewart islands). Hatches after 2.5 weeks, before host's eggs, and ejects other eggs or chicks; fledges 3 weeks. **FEEDING** Mainly large invertebrates (weta, stick insects), also lizards, small birds, eggs and fruit. **P&R** Endemic to NZ, found throughout, mainly in native bush. Migrates in winter to southwest Pacific islands. **T&M** Alien mammalian predators and loss of habitat, especially in its wintering grounds. **BV** Native bush, especially central NI and western SI, also offshore islands, Kapiti, Little Barrier and Mayor.

B A **Oriental Cuckoo** *Cuculus optatus* **LC OV**

L 30–32cm WS 53–55cm Wt 90–115g

Medium-sized, long-tailed, grey cuckoo. Adult male (A) *head, upper breast and upperparts grey, lower breast, belly and undertail white barred grey-black*. Bill black with orange at base of lower mandible, iris and orbital ring yellow, legs and feet yellow or orange-yellow. Female has 2 morphs: grey is similar to male with *rufous on upper breast*; rufous morph (B) *upperparts largely brown with black barring*. Immature heavily barred, brown or grey depending on morph. **FEEDING** Invertebrates, especially caterpillars. **P&R** Native of central, eastern and southeastern Asia, partially migratory, vagrant to NZ. **T&M** No known threats. **BV** Chance sighting during October–April, most likely in open woodlands or forest margins.

Pallid Cuckoo *Cuculus pallidus* **LC V**

L 30–31cm WS 52cm Wt 80–85g

Medium-sized, *all-grey, long-winged* cuckoo. Adult male all mid-grey with *barring on undertail. White spot on nape and dark eye-stripe and pale eyebrow*. Bill grey-black, paler at base, gape orange, iris brown, orbital ring yellow, legs and feet pale yellow. Dark grey morph is darker with touch of rufous on nape and upperparts. Female *browner than male*, has pale and dark rufous morphs. Immature strikingly black, brown and white barring, especially on back. **VOICE/CALL** Loud, clear series of rising, whistled notes: *too..too..too..too*. **FEEDING** Mainly insects, especially caterpillars, also beetles, grasshoppers and sometimes plant matter. **P&R** Native of Australia, vagrant to NZ. **T&M** No known threats. **BV** Chance sighting.

Fan-tailed Cuckoo *Cacomantis flabelliformis* **LC V**

L 24–28cm WS 34–42cm Wt 50g

Small grey and brown cuckoo with *long, rounded tail, which is often fanned on landing*. Adult male *head, neck and upperparts uniform blue-grey*, paler on chin and upper throat. *Underparts rufous brown, darker on upper breast, paler on belly, underside of tail distinctly barred grey and white*. Bill black, gape orange, iris dark brown, orbital ring yellow, legs and feet yellow. Female similar but less rufous on breast and paler on belly. **VOICE/CALL** A sad, slow, downward trill *peeeeer*; also a repeated whistle *pwhoo* or *pwheee*. **FEEDING** Mainly insects, especially caterpillars; frequently swoops on prey from perch. **P&R** Native of Australia and New Guinea, vagrant to NZ. **T&M** No known threats. **BV** Chance sighting.

Channel-billed Cuckoo *Scythrops novaehollandiae* **LC V**

L 56–71cm WS 88–107cm Wt 560–935g

Very large cuckoo with *very long tail* and a *huge bill. Head, neck and upper breast light bluish grey*, back and tail mid-grey with dark scalloping, *tail end has broad black band with white tip*. Lower breast and belly light grey, undertail silver-grey with black barring. Bill grey with cream tip, iris red, orbital ring and lores red, legs and feet grey. Female similar but with smaller bill. Immature has buff-coloured head and much browner body and wings. **VOICE/CALL** Loud rasping scream *cree-cree-cree*, also raucous *ee-awk ee-awk* or *crerk-crerk-crerk*. **FEEDING** Not well known, mainly fruit but also insects and occasionally eggs and nestlings. **P&R** Native of Australia, vagrant to NZ. **T&M** No known threats. **BV** Chance sighting.

Kingfishers – Halcyonidae (previously Alcendinidae)

Only two kingfishers are found here; one is a widespread native, the other is introduced and very restricted in range.

New Zealand Kingfisher *Todiramphus sanctus vagans* **LC N**

ALTERNATIVE NAME Kotare | L 24cm WS 37cm Wt 55–65g

Distinctive, small, colourful bird with *very large bill*, frequently seen sitting on wires or posts. *Head blue-green with broad dark band running through eyes around back of head, white neck collar*. Back and tail blue and blue-green, *undersides white with buff flanks*. Bill very large, up to 4.8cm long and 1.1cm deep, dark and with *boat-shaped lower mandible*, iris dark brown, legs and feet grey or slightly pinkish. Immature duller with mottling on breast. **VOICE/CALL** Loud, penetrating *kek-kek-kek-kek*. **BREEDING** Nests in holes in trees or riverbanks and coastal cliffs. Up to 7 white eggs laid October–January, hatching after 3 weeks, young fledge after 3.5–4 weeks. **FEEDING** Wide variety of terrestrial and marine vertebrates and invertebrates, including lizards, mice, small birds, small crabs, large insects. Perches on wire, post or tree whilst watching out for prey. **P&R** 60 million. Widespread in Australasia. NZ subspecies is found throughout the country, especially NI; not common in central Otago, Southland or in alpine areas. **T&M** No known threats, one of the few species that has adapted quite well to human intervention in the ecosystem. **BV** Widespread, but especially near water.

Laughing Kookaburra *Dacelo novaeguineae* **LC I/V**

L 40–48cm WS 66–80cm Wt 310–380g

Large, unmistakable kingfisher with *long tail and massive bill*. Head off-white with some brown flecking, *a brown cap and brown eye-stripe back to ear coverts*. Upperparts brown with light edges to feathers giving scalloped appearance. *Tail long with dark and light brown barring*. Underparts off-white with some light barring on flanks. *Bill huge, up to 6.9cm long and 2.3cm deep*, dark upper mandible, pale lower one strongly upturned near tip. Immature generally browner with more barring. **VOICE/CALL** Loud, raucous laughing *kooaa-cackle-kooaa-haha-kooaa* and variations, often in a noisy family chorus. **BREEDING** In hole in tree; up to 4 white eggs laid November–February, hatching after 3 weeks, young fledge after 4.5–5.5 weeks. **FEEDING** Invertebrates and vertebrates, snails, insects, crayfish, frogs, lizards, mice and small birds. **P&R** 65 million. Native of Australia. Small population in Auckland area, mainly to north. Occurs elsewhere as a vagrant. **T&M** No known threats and not a known pest species. **BV** North Auckland.

Dollarbirds – Coraciidae

Dollarbird *Eurystomus orientalis* **LC OV**

L 26–29cm WS 55–65cm Wt 125–143g

Medium-sized, rather stocky bird with large, rounded head. Head and neck dark olive-brown, *upperparts bluish green*, underparts dull greenish blue with *large purplish-blue throat patch*. In flight, shows *large white patches on primaries, tail square with dark tip*. Bill red-orange with small black tip, iris dark brown, legs and feet orange-brown to red-brown. Immature much browner all over and lacks red bill, legs and feet. **VOICE/CALL** Strident *kek-kek-kek*; also *yap-yapapapap*. **FEEDING** Mainly flying insects, taken on the wing. **P&R** Migratory native of Australia, small numbers reach NZ most years, especially immature birds in autumn and adults in spring, as they migrate respectively north and south. **T&M** No known threats. **BV** Chance sightings, especially NI, most likely in open woodlands or shrublands.

Gamebirds – Phasianidae

The term 'gamebird' refers to species that are hunted for food; most of these, and all that are included in this section, are members of the order Galliformes, which includes the Domestic Chicken. There are no extant native gamebirds in New Zealand; some 18 species have been introduced since 1840, either for domestic, ornamental or sporting purposes. Acclimatisation societies still existed into the 1980s, attempting to establish new species in a land that needed none. Of the 18 species, the ten included here are the survivors, and while some, such as the California Quail and Ring-necked Pheasant, are common and widespread, many are quite rare and very localised. It is good to know that not all introduced aliens thrive.

Ring-necked Pheasant *Phasianus colchicus* **LC I** (Eur, Asia)

L 55–100cm WS 70–90cm Wt (M) 1.4kg (F) 1.2kg

Large, distinctive, ground-loving gamebird with *very long tail*. Male (A) very colourful; *body, wings and tail chestnut brown with black flecking on breast and brown and white flecking on wings. Tail very long, 25–60cm, brown with black barring. White neck band* separates body plumage from *head and neck, which are dark glossy green,* crown often olive-green. *Large, bright red facial wattles,* bill pale horn, iris yellowish, legs and feet dark grey. Female (B) smaller and light to mid-brown with darker flecking. Immature as female but duller and less flecking and barring. Flies abruptly and noisily, glides after short flight on short, rounded wings. Owing to the interbreeding of up to 40 subspecies, male plumage can be quite variable and at times the white collar is absent, or nearly so. **VOICE/CALL** Male makes a loud crowing sound *ko-or-ok korrk-ok* or *kok-ok-ok* and a harsh squawking noise when disturbed. **BREEDING** Ground nester with long breeding season. Up to 15 olive-brown eggs laid August through March, hatching after 3.5 weeks; young leave nest soon after hatching, and can make short flights after only 12–14 days. Males polygamous. **FEEDING** Mixture of vegetation, seeds and berries, with some insects. **P&R** Up to 300 million worldwide; originally from Asia, it has been introduced widely in Europe and North America. NZ population about 250,000, mainly NI, where it is widespread; SI mainly Kaikoura south to Waitaki River and around Nelson. First introduced to NZ in 1842. Some captive breeding to release for sport. **T&M** Not a significant pest species. Large numbers are killed each year during hunting season. **BV** Open country, scrublands; NI, especially north of Volcanic Plateau.

Indian Peafowl *Pavo cristatus* **LC I** (Eur, Asia)

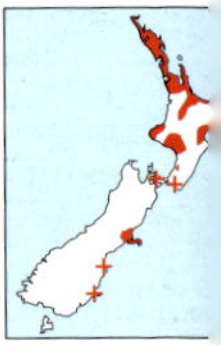

(Peacock [M], Peahen [F]) | L (M) 200–225cm (F) 90cm WS (M) 130–160cm (F) 80–130cm Wt (M) 4.0–6.0kg (F) 2.8–4.0kg

Very large, unmistakable, ground-loving gamebird with fan-shaped crest on head. Male *head, neck and breast glossy metallic blue and green with white face and blue lores*. Body and wings colourful mix of brown, chestnut and green with a *huge green train or tail, which is spectacular when displayed* (photo). Bill greyish, iris brown, legs and feet grey. Female smaller and generally grey-brown and white with short tail. Immature duller with very short crown. **VOICE/CALL** Male has loud screaming, trumpeting *pe-hawn pe-hawn* or *ki hai ki hai*, also an explosive *kok kok kok*. **BREEDING** Ground nester, up to 6 cream or pale buff eggs laid spring and incubated for 4 weeks; little information on NZ breeders. **FEEDING** Omnivorous: seeds, fruit, shoots, flower buds, invertebrates and small vertebrates. **P&R** Native of Indian subcontinent, first introduced to NZ in 1840s as ornamental, now feral and found mainly north of a line from Whanganui to Gisborne in NI. **T&M** Not a known pest, though may be a nuisance locally. **BV** Firth of Thames north to Aupouri Peninsula, Whanganui, Hawke's Bay, Napier.

Wild Turkey *Meleagris gallopavo* **LC I** (N Am)

L (M) 120cm (F) 90cm Wt (M) 5.0–11.0kg (F) 3.0–5.0kg

Very large, black, upright, long-legged, ground-loving gamebird with bare head. Male (A) *largely black with white on primaries and white tip to tail. Head bare, loose red and grey skin,* colour varies significantly during the year. Primaries show barring when displaying. Bill grey to blue-grey, covered at times by drooping bare skin, iris red, brown legs and feet pinkish grey. Female (B) smaller and browner, head only has bare skin. Immature as female but more vermiculated and barred. Rarely flies except to roost. **VOICE/CALL** A loud *gobble* when displaying, clucking and trilling when alarmed. **BREEDING** Ground nester, little information available in NZ. **FEEDING** Mainly vegetation, seeds, fruit, berries, some insects and other invertebrates. **P&R** Native of North America, introduced to NZ 1890s, now widespread especially in NI open country, farmland; in SI, mainly inland Otago and Marlborough. **T&M** Not known to be a pest, some shot during hunting season. **BV** NI, open country, especially Northland.

Helmeted Guineafowl *Numida meleagris* **LC I** (Afr)

L 60cm Wt 1.5kg

Large, *distinctly rounded, short-legged* gamebird. Body *dark slate grey with white spotting and spangling.* Head unfeathered with *flattened horn-coloured crest, pinkish cap, red around base of bill and red wattles, face bluish or pale bluish grey.* Amount of red on head varies. **VOICE/CALL** Short, harsh cry. **BREEDING** Ground nester but no information available on breeding in NZ. **FEEDING** Vegetation, seeds, fruit and insects; in native range noted for eating ticks. **P&R** Worldwide up to 2.5 million. Introduced to NZ from 1864. Small population found mainly northern NI. **T&M** Not a known pest species. **BV** Northland, Auckland, Hunua Ranges.

Grey Partridge *Perdix perdix* **LC I** (UK)

L 30cm Wt 500g

Medium-sized, rather *rotund* gamebird. Male generally brown on back and grey underneath, near white on belly, with *dark chestnut-coloured horseshoe-shaped patch on breast.* Face and throat dull orange, bill horn, iris brown, *legs and feet grey.* Female paler with less distinct, or no, patch on breast. Immature as female. Flight *low, fast and with short, rapid wing-beats,* interspersed with glides. **VOICE/CALL** Loud, high-pitched, grating *keev* or *keev-it,* and a rapid *it-it-it* when flushed. **BREEDING** Ground nester in short cover; up to 20 eggs laid, hatching after 3.5 weeks, the young leaving the nest soon after hatching. **FEEDING** Mainly grains and other seeds, though young eat only insects at first. **P&R** Up to 10 million. Native of Europe. Introduced to NZ on several occasions, most recently 1970, but continued presence uncertain; last confirmed sighting 1975. **T&M** Not a known pest species. **BV** Small numbers may still exist in Canterbury, Otago or Southland.

Male

Red-legged Partridge *Alectoris rufa* **LC I** (Eur)

L 34–38cm WS 47–50cm Wt (M) 480–547g (F) 391–514g

Medium-sized, *rotund*, short-legged gamebird. Adult upperparts largely soft brown. *Head has white eye-stripe, chin and throat, with black border and black streaking down the breast.* Rufous band around neck below the streaking, lower breast and belly grey with heavy black, brown and white barring on flanks. Bill short and red, iris red, *feet and legs red.* Immature much duller. **VOICE/CALL** Loud, challenging *chukka chukka*. **BREEDING** Ground nester, very similar to Grey Partridge. **FEEDING** Mainly seeds, some insects, especially just after hatching. **P&R** Up to 14 million worldwide. A native of Europe. Introduced to NZ on a number of occasions, most recently 1991, mainly to northern NI, especially Hawke's Bay, Bay of Plenty, Kaipara Harbour, also Nelson, Marlborough and Canterbury; small isolated populations remain. **T&M** Not known to cause any problems. **BV** Small isolated populations, recent sightings in Pirongia, Taupo and Kerikeri.

Chukar *Alectoris chukar* **LC I** (India)

L 33cm WS 50cm Wt (M) 650g (F) 550g

Medium-sized, *rotund*, short-legged gamebird. Adult largely grey with a *rufous tinge on neck, mantle and wings. Black eye-band, which curves down to form a necklace below and encircling the white throat, chin and face.* Flanks grey with broad black and buff barring, belly cinnamon. *Bill short and red,* iris red, legs dull red. Immature like adult but duller and with all markings less distinct and lacks black eye-band. **VOICE/CALL** Series of repeated *chuk chuk* and variations. **BREEDING** Ground nester, grassland, in rocks or scrub. Up to 18 cream eggs with reddish flecking, laid September–January, hatching after 3.5 weeks. Young leave nest almost immediately and may remain in family group over winter. **FEEDING** Seeds, leaves and occasional insects. Young initially eat insects only. **P&R** Up to 10 million in native Eurasia. Introduced to NZ at various times, most recently 1987, but with very limited success. Well established in rocky country of eastern SI from Marlborough to Central Otago. Small numbers possibly in Bay of Plenty and Hawke's Bay on NI. **T&M** Not known to cause any problems. **BV** Central Canterbury, Twizel, Tekapo.

Bobwhite Quail *Colinus virginianus* **NT I** (N Am)

L 23cm Wt 180g

Small, rounded gamebird. Male (A) largely brown with distinctive *black and white head markings and slight crest; white chin, black throat and strongly striated breast with strong lateral markings along flanks.* Female (B) head markings brown and buff and lacks crest, body rather duller brown with less distinctive striations on flank. Immature as female, only duller. **VOICE/CALL** Male, a clear, rising whistle *bob-white* or *bob-bob-white* and a range of rather squeaky whistles. **BREEDING** Ground nester, in grassland or scrubland, may lay more than 20 white eggs, hatching after 3.5 weeks. Young leave nest soon after hatching. **FEEDING** Mainly seeds and vegetation, some insects. **P&R** Up to 9 million, decreasing in its native North America. Introduced to NZ on a number of occasion, but no recent records. **T&M** Not known to be a problem species. **BV** Probably no longer survives in the wild in NZ.

California Quail *Callipepla californica* **LC I** (N Am)

L 25cm WS 32–35cm Wt 150–200g

Small, active gamebird with *forward-curved plume*. Male (A) has very varied plumage, *crown chestnut with black club-shaped plume* curving forward from it, *white band above eye and round forehead, black chin and throat encircled by white band running from eye to eye*. Nape dark grey, speckled white, back largely greyish brown. *Breast grey, belly buff and white with black scalloping*, flank brown with heavy white streaking. Bill short and black, legs and feet greyish brown. Female (B) much plainer; all brown with *heavy buff barring on breast and flanks, crest smaller*, brown, and less obvious. Immature as female but paler and with very short plume. **VOICE/CALL** Loud, rather melodious crowing *cu-ca-cow*, or a metallic *pit* as an alarm call. **BREEDING** Ground nester, in thick vegetation; up to 20 cream-coloured eggs laid September–February, hatching after 3.5 weeks; young leave nest almost immediately, able to fly short distances at 3–4 weeks, adult size by 4 months. **FEEDING** Mainly seeds and some leaves, also insects; young entirely insectivorous when first hatched. **P&R** Up to 1 million. Native of North America, introduced to NZ from 1860s onwards. Most successful of smaller gamebirds, now widespread, especially northern and central NI, and northern and eastern SI. **T&M** Not known to be a pest species. **BV** Grasslands and scrublands, not common in lowland pastures or native bush.

Brown Quail *Coturnix ypsilophora* **LC I** (Aus)

L 17–22cm WS 26–36cm Wt 90–120g

Very small all-brown gamebird. Male *crown and nape reddish brown*, rest of body uniformly mid-brown with *fine black and fawn barring*. *Bill blue-grey with black tip*, iris bright red-brown, legs and feet dull orange-yellow. Female similar but with *bolder black markings on back*. Immature as female but spotted rather than striated underneath. **VOICE/CALL** A 2-note whistle *f-weep*, *tu-eee*, or *bee-quick*. **BREEDING** Ground nester, in thick vegetation, tussock grass and shrublands. Up to 14 bluish-white eggs laid September–January, hatching after 3 weeks, only female incubates; young leave nest almost immediately and able to fly short distances after 10 days, attain adult size at 6 weeks and adult plumage at 3 months. **FEEDING** Seeds and foliage, some insects and occasionally small reptiles. Young feed on only insects initially. **P&R** Population unknown; widespread in its native Australia, introduced to NZ from 1860s onwards. Found NI only, especially Northland with some populations around Auckland and in Coromandel, Bay of Plenty and East Cape. **T&M** Not a known pest species. **BV** Small, localised populations exist, particularly in Northland, also Tiritiri Matangi I.

Feral Chicken

Gallus gallus gallus

Small populations of feral chickens exist throughout the country, often associated with human activity, car parks, campsites, etc. Plumage varies considerably but they are hard to mistake for anything else.

Passerines

Of the 49 species in this section only 22 are native. However, 20 of the 22 native species are endemic, so emphasising the unusual nature of the New Zealand avifauna, which evolved in geographic isolation over a very long period. Of the remaining species, 16 have been deliberately introduced and 11 are vagrants.

SWALLOWS, MARTINS, WOODSWALLOWS AND SWIFTS There is just one native swallow; all other swifts, swallows, woodswallows and martins seen here are vagrants. Some taxonomists have proposed nomenclature changes for some species, but these are not yet generally accepted. Swifts are not actually passerines, but are included here for convenience.

Hirundinidae

Welcome Swallow *Hirundo neoxena* **LC N**

L 14–16cm WS 26–31cm Wt 9–20g

Very small, *graceful, fast-flying* bird (A). *Head, nape and upperparts metallic blue-black*, underparts dull white, *forehead, throat and upper breast rufous. Tail long and deeply forked.* Immature (B) duller upperparts and less rufous on throat, tail shorter and only slightly forked. **VOICE/CALL** High-pitched chittering or tweeting. **BREEDING** Nest is a cup of mud and dried grass attached to vertical surface, often under a bridge or in a building, on roof beams or wall. Up to 7 pale speckled eggs laid August–February, hatching after 2.5 weeks; young fledge after a further 3 weeks. **FEEDING** Almost exclusively insects, taken on the wing, often very low down and over water. **P&R** Found throughout the country apart from the far southwest, also in Australia and Pacific islands. A relatively recent arrival, first recorded breeding in 1958, now everywhere including occasionally over native bush. Partially migratory within NZ with some individuals moving northwards in winter. **T&M** No known threats, protected native. **BV** Widespread, especially in wetlands, open country and suburban areas.

Previously considered a subspecies of the Pacific Swallow *H. tahitica*, but now accepted as a separate species.

Australian Tree Martin *Petrochelidon nigricans* **LC V**

L 10–13cm WS 28cm Wt 15g

Very small, rather dull-coloured swallow. Head and back dull blue-black, wings and tail murky brown, *rump large and dirty white, forehead rufous*. Underparts off-white with some fawn on flanks, chin grey-brown, *tail short with a very shallow 'V'*. Bill short, black, iris dark, legs and feet pinkish grey. Immature much duller and forehead more yellow. **VOICE/CALL** Rather pleasant chittering and twittering. **FEEDING** Almost entirely insects, caught on the wing. **P&R** Native of Australia, a vagrant to NZ. **T&M** No known threats. **BV** Chance sighting, most likely open country or suburban area.

Fairy Martin *Petrochelidon ariel* **LC V**

L 12cm WS 22cm Wt 11g

Minute bird, smallest martin recorded in NZ. *Head and nape dark cinnamon, back metallic blue-black*, wings dark brown, *small off-white rump*. Undersides off-white with some colouring on flanks. Bill dark, iris dark, legs and feet pinkish (left photo shows adult left and juvenile right). **VOICE/CALL** High-pitched twittering. **FEEDING** Insects taken on the wing. **P&R** Native of Australia, a vagrant to NZ. **T&M** No known threats. **BV** Chance sighting, most likely open country, wetlands or suburban parks.

Artamidae

White-browed Woodswallow *Artamus superciliosus* **LC V**

L 19cm WS 31–34cm Wt 35g

Small, starling-like bird with *graceful swallow-like flight*. Adult male head, nape, throat, upper breast and upperparts, including wings and tail, mid- to pale grey, *face somewhat darker* with distinctive *white eyebrow, undersides rufous, underwing and tail pale grey*. Bill pale grey with *black tip*, iris dark, legs and feet dark. Female similar but both grey and rufous are paler. **VOICE/CALL** Quite varied, high-pitched whistle or twitter. **FEEDING** Mainly insects taken on the wing and on the ground, but also nectar and fruit. **P&R** Native of Australia, vagrant to NZ. **T&M** No known threats. **BV** Chance sighting, possibly in exotic forestry.

Masked Woodswallow *Artamus personatus* **LC V**

L 18–20cm WS 32–34cm Wt 37g

Small, grey, starling-like bird with *graceful, swallow-like flight*. Adult male *head, nape, back and tail dark blue-grey, forehead, face, chin and throat black with white edge from behind eye to throat*. Underparts pale grey. Bill pale grey with *black tip*, iris dark with pale orbital ring, legs and feet mid-grey. Female similar but more uniform *grey*, face mask and white border less prominent. **VOICE/CALL** High, descending *chirrup* and loud, penetrating *chyet*. **FEEDING** Mainly insects taken both on the wing and on the ground, but also nectar and occasionally fruit. **P&R** Native of Australia, vagrant to NZ, though a pair may have bred near Naseby, Central Otago, in 1972–73. **T&M** No known threats. **BV** Chance sighting, most likely in open country near woods, but not in dense native bush.

Apodidae

Spine-tailed Swift *Hirundapus caudacutus* **LC V**

L 20cm WS 49cm Wt 115–120g

Large, *fast-flying* swift with *long, swept-back wings and cigar-shaped body*. Adult mostly dark olive-brown with greenish-blue sheen on head and upperwings. *Chin, throat and undertail white. Tail short, dark and square-ended*. Bill black and very short. Short, fine spines project beyond tail, not easily seen except in the hand. **VOICE/CALL** High-pitched chittering *chee-chee-chee*. **FEEDING** Insects taken on the wing. **P&R** Native of Asia, migrating to Australasia for northern winter, occasional vagrant to NZ. **T&M** No known threats. **BV** Chance sighting, most likely NI in open country.

Fork-tailed Swift *Apus pacificus* **LC V**

L 18–21cm WS 40–42cm Wt 30–40g

Small, fast-flying dark swift. Adult all dark blackish brown apart from *triangular off-white patch on chin and throat and white rump, tail deeply forked*. Bill black, iris dark, legs and feet black but not normally visible. **VOICE/CALL** High-pitched screaming *skreee-ee*. **FEEDING** Insects caught on the wing. **P&R** Native of Asia, migrates south to Australasia and Pacific islands in winter, vagrant to NZ. **T&M** No known threats. **BV** Chance sightings, most likely on NI.

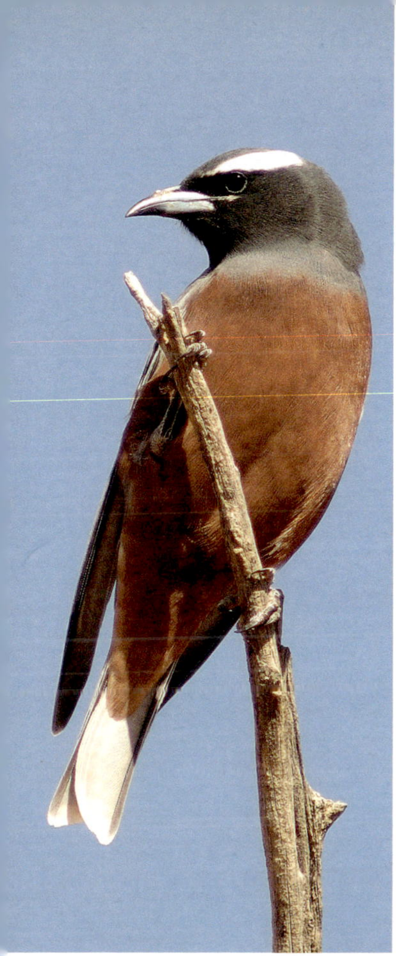

Monarchidae

Black-faced Monarch

Monarcha melanopsis

LC V

L 16–19.5cm WS 25–29cm
Wt 23–25g

Small, slim, colourful, *long-tailed flycatcher*. Adult head, upper breast and back soft lead grey with *black forehead, chin and throat. Lower breast and underparts rufous*. Bill pale grey, iris and orbital ring black, legs and feet grey. **VOICE/CALL** Loud, clear *why-you* or *wichye-oo* and a mellow descending *why-you*. **FEEDING** Invertebrates, taken in the air or from foliage and branches. **P&R** Native of Australia, a vagrant to NZ. **T&M** No known threats. **BV** Chance sighting.

Satin Flycatcher *Myiagra cyanoleuca* LC V

L 16.5–18cm WS 20–25cm Wt 17g

Small, slim flycatcher with a *small head crest*. Male all *dark glossy blue-black apart from white lower breast and belly*. Bill and iris black, legs and feet grey. Female head and upperparts bluish grey, chin, throat and breast rufous, merging into white belly. Very mobile, often swaying while perched on a branch. **FEEDING** Insects, caught in flight, darting out from perch. **P&R** Native of Australia, vagrant to NZ. **T&M** No known threats. **BV** Chance sighting.

Campephagidae

Black-faced Cuckoo Shrike *Coracina novaehollandiae* LC V

L 33cm WS 54cm Wt 115g

Large, grey, *long-tailed* woodland bird. Adult head, nape and upperparts soft blue-grey, *forehead, face and throat black. Underparts grey-white. Bill black*, iris black, legs and feet dark grey. Flight strong and undulating, tends to fold and refold wings on alighting. Immature similar but black facial mask reduced to broad black eye-stripe, also faint barring on throat and upper breast. **VOICE/CALL** A soft, rather croaky *purr*. **FEEDING** Mainly insects, taken on the wing from a perched position. **P&R** Native of Australia, a vagrant to NZ. **T&M** No known threats. **BV** Chance sighting, edge of bush, most likely spring or autumn.

White-winged Triller *Lalage tricolor* LC V

L 18cm WS 30cm Wt 26g

Small, *slim flycatcher* with variable plumage. Breeding male, *crown, back and tail black, upperwing black with white shoulder, rump grey, underparts white*. Bill dark, iris dark with orbital ring, legs and feet dark grey. Female mainly brown with white belly and undertail, non-breeding male similar but with black and white wings. **VOICE/CALL** Very vocal, male sings on perch or in flight, rather like a high-pitched pneumatic drill. **FEEDING** Insects, caught either on the wing, or on the ground. **P&R** Native of Australia, vagrant to NZ. **T&M** No known threats. **BV** Chance sighting.

NATIVE PASSERINES There are relatively few native passerines in New Zealand, possibly due to the long isolation of the archipelago. Many passerines are small and so not well equipped for crossing large expanses of water. A significant proportion of them are now extinct thanks to the impact of humans through forest clearance and introduced mammalian predators.

New Zealand Wrens – Acanthisittidae Of the original seven species of wren, only two survive. The extinct species included the Stephens Island Wren *Traversia lyalli*, which was flightless and never observed in the wild, all known specimens having been caught by the lighthouse keeper's cat, and the Bush Wren *Xenicus longipes*, which was nearly flightless, the last race of which, Stead's Bush Wren *X. l. variabilis*, became extinct in or soon after 1972 (*see* page 7).

Rifleman *Acanthisitta chloris* LC EG

ALTERNATIVE NAME Titipounamu | L 7–9cm WS 13.5–14.5cm Wt (M) 6g (F) 7g

Minute, *almost tailless* bird with short, rounded wings and *up-turned bill*. Male (A) *head and back bright olive-green with distinct white eyebrow*. Underparts off-white with some flecking on breast. Bill black, very fine and slightly upturned, iris dark brown, legs and feet dark but sometimes orange-yellow. Female (B) similar but *head and upperparts brown*. Immature (C) as female but more flecked and spotted especially on breast and underparts. **VOICE/CALL** Very high-pitched *zip zip zip*, beyond the hearing range of many people. **BREEDING** Nests in hole in tree; male may start building several nests before female assists with building. Some pairs have 1 or more helpers when nesting. Up to 5 white eggs laid September–December, hatching after 2.5–3 weeks; young fledge after 3.5 weeks and continue to be fed by parents for a further 4–5 weeks. **FEEDING** Invertebrates, largely moths, beetles, spiders, flies and caterpillars. **P&R** 2 subspecies: **North Island Rifleman** *A. c. granti* is found on NI only, in areas of native bush especially in central and eastern areas and offshore islands, Mayor and Little Barrier; **South Island Rifleman** *A. c. chloris* is found on SI, in native bush mainly in north and west, and on Stewart I. **T&M** Major threats are loss of habitat and predation by introduced pests, especially Stoats and rats. **BV** Native bush on NI in Whirinaki FP, Tiritiri Matangi I. and Mayor I., SI and Stewart, native bush in most national parks.

Rock Wren *Xenicus gilviventris* VU EG

ALTERNATIVE NAME Matuhi | L 9–10cm WS 14–16cm Wt (M) 15.5g (F) 19g

Very small, *tailless, long-legged*, ground-loving bird with short, rounded wings. Adult male (A) *head olive-brown, becoming greener on back and upperparts*, tail virtually non-existent, underparts off-white or fawn, paler on throat, *yellowish on flanks, distinctive off-white eyebrow*. Bill black and finely pointed, iris dark brown, legs, which are long, and feet pinkish brown. Female (B) similar but generally browner. Immature similar to female but duller, also little known. Some colour variation between different populations. Prefers to hop and run, but does fly short distances. **VOICE/CALL** 3-part call – very high-pitched *tzee-tzit-tzit*. **BREEDING** Builds an enclosed nest in hollow in rock bank, crevice or ledge; up to 5 cream-coloured eggs, hatching after 3 weeks; young fledge after 3–4 weeks but continue to be fed by parents for a further 2–4 weeks. **FEEDING** Mainly invertebrates, especially beetles, spiders, centipedes and caterpillars, but some fruits including those of coprosmas and *Gaultheria*. **P&R** 5,000–10,000, probably declining. Previously widespread, now found on only SI, in alpine and subalpine areas. **T&M** Greatest threat is alien mammalian pests, especially Stoats and rats; being very terrestrial they are particularly at risk. Fully protected and helped by trapping of alien pest species. **BV** Alpine and subalpine areas on SI.

Zosteropidae

B A Silvereye *Zosterops lateralis lateralis* LC N

ALTERNATIVE NAMES Tauhou, White-eye | L 12cm WS 17cm Wt 11–13g

Very small, warbler-like bird with *conspicuous white eye-ring*. Adult (A) head, neck, upperwings and rump light olive-green, *nape mantle and breast bluish grey*, belly pale, flanks pale cinnamon, undertail white. Bill fine, tapering and grey-brown, *orbital ring white*, legs and feet grey. Immature (B) similar but lacks white eye-ring. Out of breeding season travels in small flocks. **VOICE/CALL** High-pitched, rather excited *clee-clee-clee* or a plaintive *cree*; also has a varied warbler-like song. **BREEDING** Builds a suspended cup nest in tree or shrub; up to 5 pale blue eggs laid, hatching after 1.5–2 weeks, young fledge after 1.5 weeks but are fed by parents for a further 2–3 weeks. **FEEDING** Varies seasonally, largely invertebrates, especially insects, but also fruit and nectar. Will willingly feed from a bird-table. **P&R** Found throughout Australasia and the Pacific islands. First recorded in NZ in 1832, but not in numbers until 1856. Now widespread and found in all areas apart from highest alpine areas and inland Otago. **T&M** No specific threats, but alien mammalian predators have an impact on the population. **BV** Widespread throughout the country, especially urban areas.

Acanthizidae

Grey Warbler *Gerygone igata* LC E

ALTERNATIVE NAME Riroriro | L 10cm WS 12–14cm Wt 6.5g

Very small, rather drab warbler. Upperparts all brownish grey, *with whitish-grey eyebrow, tail darker near end with white tip*, underparts off-white. *Bill black, short and sharply pointed*, iris red-brown, legs and feet black. Immature similar but duller. **VOICE/CALL** Song a soft, sweet, trilling warble. Call varies regionally, but *chee-ree* and variations appear to be the basic. **BREEDING** Builds hanging, enclosed nest in dense vegetation, laying up to 5 white to pink, reddish-brown-speckled eggs August–January, hatching after 2.5 weeks; young fledge after a further 2.5 weeks and parents may continue to feed young for a further 35 days. Occasionally hosts chick of Shining Cuckoo. **FEEDING** Largely invertebrates, especially insects, and some fruit. **P&R** Endemic to NZ and found throughout the country apart from high alpine areas and tussock lands of Otago. **T&M** No specific threats, but alien mammalian predators have an impact on the population. **BV** Widespread on the 3 main islands, including bush and urban areas.

Chatham Island Warbler *Gerygone albofrontata* LC E

L 12cm WS 18cm Wt (M) 11g (F) 9.5g

Small, drab warbler, *similar to mainland Grey Warbler* but larger, with larger bill and more *prominent white eyebrow, forehead and underparts*, and found only in Chatham Is. **VOICE/CALL** Repeated 4-note phrase. **BREEDING** Nest is enclosed and hanging, up to 4 red-speckled white eggs laid September–December, hatching within 3 weeks, young fledge after 3 weeks and are fed by parents for a further 3–4 weeks. **FEEDING** Invertebrates, mainly insects and spiders. **P&R** Small numbers. Found only in the Chatham Is, especially South East and Mangere islands. Less widespread than previously. **T&M** No immediate threats, but with a small population and the existence of alien predators the population will always be vulnerable. **BV** Chatham Is.

Motacillidae

New Zealand Pipit *Anthus novaeseelandiae* **LC N**

ALTERNATIVE NAME Pihoihoi | L 13–18cm WS 22–29cm Wt 28–39g

Small, brown, *long-tailed, upright,* ground bird (A). Adult head and upperparts brown, *heavily streaked darker and paler, prominent white eyebrow, breast white, heavily striated brown,* belly and undertail white. In flight, *white outer tail feathers visible.* Bill short, dark, paler at base, and fine, iris dark, legs pinkish brown. Runs and then flies a short distance. Immature very similar but darker upperparts. **VOICE/CALL** Pleasant, soft, high-pitched trilling warble, also shrill *screee* and longer *zweee,* and sometimes *tzree-tzit-it-it.* **BREEDING** Nests on ground near tussock or in Bracken or under shrub; up to 5 brown-blotched, cream-coloured eggs laid August–February, hatching after 2 weeks, young fledge after 2–2.5 weeks. Generally 2 or 3 clutches per season. **FEEDING** Mainly invertebrates, but some seeds. **P&R** Found in Australia and throughout NZ and the sub-Antarctic islands. Four subspecies in NZ: *A. a. novaeseelandiae* is found on the 3 main islands; **Chatham Island Pipit** (B) *A. n. chathamensis* is found in the Chatham Is; **Auckland Island Pipit** *A. n. aucklandicus* on the Auckland Is; and **Antipodes Island Pipit** (C) *A. n. steindachneri* in the Antipodes Is. All are very similar to the mainland variety. **T&M** No known threats. **BV** Widespread but patchy, preferring open natural areas, such as beaches, riverbeds, and alpine and subalpine tussock lands. Not found in industrialised agricultural areas.

Auckland Island Pipit

Megaluridae (was Sylviidae)

Fernbird *Bowdleria punctata* **LC BE**

ALTERNATIVE NAME Matata | L 18cm Wt 35g

Small, heavy-bodied, *long-tailed,* skulking bird. *Adult has reddish-brown upperparts heavily streaked dark black-brown, thin white eyebrow,* underparts white, *heavily streaked brown,* especially on breast. *Tail very long, up to 10cm, and rather ragged-looking.* Bill dark with paler base to lower mandible and slightly down-curved, iris dark reddish brown, legs and feet greyish brown. A reluctant flyer, preferring to skulk in reed beds. **VOICE/CALL** Sharp metallic *uu-tick,* also *tchip, tcheong* and *zrup.* **BREEDING** Nests in tussock of rush or sedge; up to 4 brown-flecked, pale pink eggs laid August–January, hatching after 2 weeks, young fledge after 2.5 weeks. Further south, breeding starts later and takes longer. **FEEDING** Mainly invertebrates. **P&R** Widespread but localised due to preferred wetland habitat. **North Island Fernbird** *B. p. vealeae* is found chiefly in northern and central NI, while **South Island Fernbird** (A) *B. p. punctata* is found mainly along the West Coast and in Southland. **Stewart Island Fernbird** (B) *B. p. stewartiana* is found on Stewart I., **Codfish Island Fernbird** (C) *B. p. wilsoni* is found on Codfish I. and **Snares Island Fernbird** (D) *B. p. caudata* on the Snares Is. All are very similar and distinguished mainly by their location. **T&M** Loss of habitat is a major concern, as is predation by alien mammalian predators. **BV** Wetlands and shrublands, occasionally young forestry plantations.

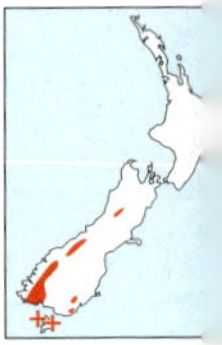

Brown Creeper *Mohoua novaeseelandiae* **LC EG**

ALTERNATIVE NAME Pipipi | L 13cm WS 14–15cm Wt (M) 13g (F) 11g

Small, rather nondescript, brown bird. Adult *head and upperparts reddish brown apart from nape and face which are grey, fine white stripe behind eye*. Undersides pale pinkish brown apart from much *paler chin and throat*, slightly darker on flanks, *dark bar near end of tail.* Bill short, pinkish grey, darker on top, iris dark, legs and feet pinkish or grey-brown. Immature head greyer and eye-stripe minimal. Often in small, noisy flocks in canopy. **VOICE/CALL** Short, attractive warble, *chee-roh-ree-roh-ree-ree*. **BREEDING** In dense shrub or in canopy; up to 4 white or pinkish eggs, speckled reddish brown, laid late September–January, hatching after 2.5–3 weeks; young fledge after 3 weeks. Young often form autumn and winter flocks. Main host of Long-tailed Cuckoo in SI and Stewart I. **FEEDING** Mainly invertebrates, but some fruit. **P&R** Only lowland and montane native forest, exotic plantations and scrublands. Previously widespread in NI. **T&M** Population apparently stable, but only anecdotal evidence available. **BV** Native bush, scrublands and forestry, SI and Stewart I.

Whitehead *Mohoua albicilla* **LC EG**

ALTERNATIVE NAME Popokatea | L 15cm WS 18cm Wt (M) 18.5g (F) 14.5g

Small, distinctive, brown and white bird. Adult male (A) *white head, neck and underparts*, though fawn on flanks. *Upperparts light brown*. Female (B) similar but *crown and nape brownish*. Bill short and black, iris, legs and feet black. Immature similar to female but crown and nape browner. Often in small family groups, or larger, noisier, feeding flocks high in canopy. **VOICE/CALL** Series of harsh, chattering calls, also a clear Canary-like *peek-o peek-o peek-o*. **BREEDING** Nests in shrub, or more often the canopy; up to 4 speckled white eggs laid late September–December, hatching after 2.5 weeks. Occasionally host or foster parents to Long-tailed Cuckoo. **FEEDING** Mainly invertebrates, but includes some fruit. **P&R** NI only. Now restricted to central areas, the eastern ranges and offshore island sanctuaries. **T&M** Loss of habitat and predation by introduced alien pest species. **BV** Native bush in central NI, Taranaki, Whirinaki, Kapiti, Tiritiri Matangi, Little Barrier and Kawau islands.

Yellowhead *Mohoua ochrocephala* **EN EG**

ALTERNATIVE NAME Mohua | L 15cm Wt (M) 30g (F) 26g

Small, unmistakable, yellow bird. Adult male (A) *all bright yellow apart from dark yellow-brown on wing feathers. Tail often worn, giving spiky appearance*. Bill short and black, iris, legs and feet black with grey soles to feet. Female (B) similar but *mottled brownish on crown and nape*. Immature as female but browner and also on flanks. Often in small, noisy flocks in canopy. Lacks head markings of Yellowhammer. **VOICE/CALL** Attractive Canary-like trill, sometimes sounds like a pneumatic drill, or coin spinning on hard surface. **BREEDING** Nests in holes high up in trunks and branches. Usually breeds as pairs but sometimes with 1 or more 'helpers'. Up to 5 pink eggs, freckled reddish brown, laid October–January, hatching after 3 weeks, young fledge after a further 3 weeks. Pairs will often produce 2 clutches in a season. Occasionally host to Long-tailed Cuckoo. **FEEDING** Mainly invertebrates, but also some fruit. **P&R** Remoter areas of Fiordland and West Coast beech forests plus a few isolated populations. **T&M** Loss of habitat, especially from selective logging, and predation by Stoats and rats. Currently part of conservation programme involving predator control and transfer to offshore island sanctuaries. **BV** Fiordland and selected isolated areas of mature beech forest in SI.

New Zealand Grey Fantail *Rhipidura fuliginosa* LC E

ALTERNATIVE NAME Piwakawaka | L 16cm WS 21cm Wt 8g

Very small, brownish bird with *very long (8cm), frequently fanned, tail.* 2 distinct morphs. Pied morph (A), head dark grey with *white eyebrow*, and white and black bands across throat or upper breast, fawn to yellow-brown underparts, darker on flanks, paler undertail. Upperparts mid- to dark brown, *tail very long with 2 central feathers blackish, and outer feathers (4 each side) white with grey outer edge. Beak black and very short*, iris black, legs and feet grey-black. Immature (B) generally duller with more rufous breast and indistinct black and white bands; wing coverts have brown tinge. Dark morph (C) *all black-brown, slightly lighter undersides, often with white spot behind eye*. Found mainly in SI with a few around Wellington. Erratic bouncing flight with frequent tail fanning characteristic; may follow trampers in bush. **VOICE/CALL** Penetrating *cheet cheet*, and a saw-like *tweet-a-tweet-a-tweet*. **BREEDING** Nests in shrub or tree fern; up to 5 speckled white eggs laid late August–February on main islands but later on offshore islands. Eggs hatch after 2 weeks and young fledge after 2–2.5 weeks. Pairs may raise up to 5 broods in a season. **FEEDING** Almost entirely insectivorous, insects caught on the wing or by foraging in foliage and on the forest floor. Some fruit also. **P&R** Throughout the country; 3 subspecies: **North Island Fantail** (A) *R. f. placabilis*, **South Island Fantail** (B and C) *R. f. fuliginosa* and **Chatham Island Fantail** (D) *R. f. penitus*. Previously considered conspecific with the Australian Grey Fantail *R. albicilla*. **T&M** Well adapted to human activity and has prospered in spite of loss of habitat and predation by introduced mammalian predators. **BV** Almost anywhere, but especially native bush; not found in alpine areas or tussock grasslands. It has adapted well to suburban areas.

Pied morph, South Island Fantail, showing fanned tail

Willie Wagtail *Rhipidura leucophrys* LC V

L 20cm WS 29cm Wt 18g

Distinctive and very active, black and white, *long-tailed flycatcher*. Adult *head, neck, upper breast and upperparts black, bold white eyebrow* and some fine, but variable, white flecking on chin and throat. Dark brown flight feathers on wing, *tail long, black and frequently fanned and flicked. Lower breast and underparts white*. Bill black, iris dark brown, legs and feet black. Immature head and upperparts browner, eyebrow cream-coloured, chin and throat pale brown. Rather like a large New Zealand Grey Fantail. **VOICE/CALL** A scolding *chick-a chick-a chick* and a short musical song similar to the New Zealand Grey Fantail. **FEEDING** Almost entirely invertebrates, caught on the wing and while foraging on ground. **P&R** Native of Australia, vagrant to NZ. **T&M** No known threats. **BV** Chance sighting.

Petroicidae

B A / D E / G C / F

South Island Tomtit *Petroica macrocephala macrocephala* LC E

ALTERNATIVE NAMES Miromiro (NI), Ngiru-ngiru | L 13cm Wt 11g

Very small, *dumpy*, black and white, *short-tailed* forest bird. Adult male (A) *all-black head, neck, upper breast and upperparts, small white dot at base of upper mandible.* White flashes on wings and outer tail feathers visible in flight. *Lower breast bright lemon yellow, often almost orange where it meets black upper breast, and fading to pale yellow on belly.* Bill fine and black, iris black, legs black, feet orange-brown. Adult female (B) as male but brown upperparts, *pale lemon-buff breast, white underparts.* Immature male as adult but lacks white at base of bill and breast only faintly yellow, black less intense. Immature female like pale version of adult. **VOICE/CALL** Male song loud and musical *ti-oli-oli-oli-oh,* call a short, high-pitched *swee*, female a reedy *seet.* **BREEDING** Nest built in a hole in a tree, or in a thick tangle of vines. Up to 6 cream-coloured eggs with brown-purple spots laid September–January, hatching after 2.5 weeks, young fledge after 2.5–3 weeks. Pairs may raise up to 3 broods in a season. **FEEDING** Mainly invertebrates, insects, spiders, earthworms, but some fruit, especially in autumn. **P&R** Throughout SI, including native and exotic forests, but absent from grassland areas, both natural and industrial. **T&M** Loss of habitat is a major threat, as is predation by the many alien mammalian pests, especially Stoats, possums and rats. **BV** Native bush throughout SI and Stewart I.

There are 4 other subspecies of tomtit: **North Island Tomtit** (C) *P. m. toitoi*, or Miromiro, is found only on NI and its offshore islands. It is very similar to the South Island Tomtit, but the male has an all-white lower breast and belly. It is found throughout NI where there is native bush and occasionally in mature exotic plantations. **Chatham Island Tomtit** (D – female, E – male) *P. m. chathamensis* is found only Mangere, Little Mangere, Pitt and South East islands in the Chatham Is, while the **Auckland Island Tomtit** (F) *P. m. marrineri* is found only in the Auckland Is. Both resemble South Island Tomtit. **Snares Island Tomtit** (G) *P. m. dannefaerdi* is found only in the Snares Is; it is the largest of the subspecies and is all black, with the immature being slightly browner.

Black Robin *Petroica traversi* EN E

L 15cm Wt (M) 25g (F) 22g

Very small, upright, all-black bush bird. Adults *all black* with fine black bill, iris dark brown, legs black, or brownish. Immature similar but with some paler streaking on forehead, crown and underparts. **VOICE/CALL** A series of clear liquid notes. **BREEDING** Nest in cavity in stump, among rocks, or in dense foliage. 2, occasionally 3 purple-brown-blotched, cream-coloured eggs laid October–December, hatching after 2.5 weeks, young fledge after 3 weeks. Generally re-lay only if clutch lost. **FEEDING** Entirely invertebrates, taken while foraging on forest floor or from low branches. **P&R** 150–200, found only on Mangere and South East islands in the Chatham Is. **T&M** Driven almost to extinction by the 1970s due to habitat loss and predation by rats and cats. Population of just 5 birds in 1979–81, including only 1 productive female, Old Blue, from whom all today's Black Robins are descended. Subject to a continuing monitoring and protection programme. **BV** Chatham Is, with special permission as the 2 islands occupied are reserves.

C B A / D E F / G

South Island Robin *Petroica australis australis* **LC E**

ALTERNATIVE NAME Toutouwai | L 18cm Wt 30–35g

Small, *inquisitive, upright* forest bird. Adult male (A), *black head, neck, upper breast and upperparts with white spot at base of upper mandible. Lower breast and belly off-white,* sometimes slightly yellowish and with grey on flanks. Bill black, *very finely pointed*, iris black or dark brown, legs very long, and feet grey-black with pale soles to feet. Adult female (B) similar but *breast dark grey and belly grey-white*. Immature (C) similar to female but lacks white spot at base of bill. **VOICE/CALL** Loud, clear song including the phrase *pwee-pwee-pwee,* also a soft chirp. **BREEDING** Nests in the fork of a tree, or occasionally in an old Blackbird or thrush nest. Up to 4 purplish-brown-spotted, cream-coloured eggs laid July–January, hatching after 2.5 weeks, young fledging after 3 weeks. **FEEDING** Almost entirely insects and other invertebrates found on the forest floor. When large prey is captured, it is dismembered and some portions cached for later retrieval and eating. **P&R** SI only, mainly in areas of native bush, most common in the northwest and southwest. **T&M** Loss of habitat and predation by introduced pest predators, particularly rats, Stoats and possums. **BV** Native bush; robins will often come to you, possibly looking for insects disturbed by your presence.

There are 3 subspecies of the New Zealand Robin; the other two are: **North Island Robin** (D – juvenile, E – female, F – male) *P. a. longipes*, which is found on NI and several offshore islands such as Kapiti, Mayor, Little Barrier and Tiritiri Matangi. The male is darker than the South Island subspecies, being black-grey all over except for grey-white belly. The black feathering is striated with grey. **Stewart Island Robin** (G) *P. a. rakiura* is found only on Stewart I. and has the dark coloration of the NI subspecies, with the white belly of the SI variety.

Callaeidae

North Island Kokako *Callaeas wilsoni* **EN EG**

L 38cm Wt (M) 233g (F) 218g

Large, all-grey, *long-tailed* bird of the forest canopy. Adult all dark *bluish grey with black facial mask and large, rounded, blue wattle* on either side below bill. *Bill black, short, heavy and slightly down-curved*, iris dark brown, legs long and feet black. Immature *grey rather than blue-grey and wattle smaller and pink*. Spends most of the time hopping around in canopy; not a strong flyer. **VOICE/CALL** Mainly at dawn, series of low, haunting, mournful flute-like notes *ko-ka-ko-o-o-o*. **BREEDING** Nests in dense foliage in canopy. 2 or 3 spotted pinkish-grey eggs laid October–March, hatching after 3 weeks, young fledge after 4.5 weeks. Adults may continue to feed young for 4 months. In good years may raise 2 or 3 broods. **FEEDING** Mainly leaves and fruit, supplemented with invertebrates, especially when feeding young. **P&R** 1,500–2,000. NI only. Previously widespread, now severely restricted and found in a small number of mainland areas, Puketi Forest, Hunua Ranges, Bay of Plenty and offshore islands such as Tiritiri Matangi, Little Barrier, Kapiti. **T&M** Conservation-dependent due to loss of habitat and alien predators, especially Stoats, possums and rats. Subject to intensive protection through habitat restoration, pest control and developing new populations in sanctuaries. **BV** Very early morning to locate birds by song; observation is tricky as they are almost always in the canopy. Pureora Forest, Hunua Ranges, Bay of Plenty (Otanewainuku), Mount Bruce, and Little Barrier, Tiritiri Matangi and Kapiti islands.

South Island Kokako *Callaeas cinerea*, which was found on SI and Stewart I., was virtually identical apart from having orange rather than blue wattles. It is now considered extinct although reports of sightings are still received.

North Island Saddleback *Philesturnus rufusater* **NT EG**

ALTERNATIVE NAME Tieke | L 25cm Wt (M) 80g (F) 70g

Medium-sized, distinctively plumaged, *very active, ground-foraging* forest bird. Adult (A, B) is all *glossy black with chestnut saddle across back* with a lighter line along the front edge, *and chestnut coverts around base of tail. Bill black, long and sharply pointed with tear-shaped, pendulous red wattles on either side*, iris dark, legs and feet black. Immature lacks pale line along front edge of saddle and has smaller wattles. **VOICE/CALL** Can be very noisy, a strident *cheet-te-te-te-te*. **BREEDING** Nests in hole in tree, in rocks, crown of tree fern or dense epiphytes. Up to 4 grey or off-white eggs laid August–May with up to 4 broods in a season. Eggs hatch after 2.5 weeks and young fledge after 4 weeks. **FEEDING** Invertebrates, by foraging vigorously on the forest floor and in vegetation, but also fruit and nectar. **P&R** 6,500, probably increasing. Previously widespread, now restricted to island sanctuaries plus Karori Sanctuary in Wellington. **T&M** Conservation-dependent. Combination of loss of habitat and alien pest predators, especially rats, Stoats and possums. Subject to an intensive programme to develop populations on island and fenced mainland sanctuaries. **BV** Karori Sanctuary, Kapiti and Tiritiri Matangi islands.

South Island Saddleback (C – adult, D – juvenile) *Philesturnus carunculatus* is almost identical to NI species but the adult lacks the lighter gold line at the front of the saddle, also immature overall brown with only hint of chestnut saddle. This species became restricted to Big South Cape I. and two adjacent islets by the mid-1900s, from where it was exterminated by a rat invasion in the mid-1960s. The current population – in the low thousands – exists on ~16 islands off Stewart and South islands – including Fiordland and Marlborough Sounds. All are descended from 36 individuals rescued in 1964 and propogated on Kaimohu and Big Stage islands.

Meliphagidae

Tui *Prosthemadera novaeseelandiae* **LC EG**

ALTERNATIVE NAME Parson Bird | L 27–30cm WS 40cm Wt (M) 120g (F) 90g

Medium-sized, black, thrush-like bird with unusual and *distinctive song*. Adult (A) largely black with blue or bronze sheen, especially on primaries and tail, *long white filoplumes on nape and shoulders, and a white wing bar, 2 small white tufts on throat look like a bow tie, hence common English name. Bill black, long, finely pointed and down-curved*, iris black, legs and feet black or black-brown. Immature (B) much duller and lacks bow tie and filoplumes. In flight, often makes a distinctive whirring noise with wings. **VOICE/CALL** Can be very vocal. An amazing range of noises, mixture of melodic and guttural tones, wheezes, croaks, coughs and chuckles, varies with time of year and region. Does a very passable imitation of a North Island Kokako. **BREEDING** Nests in the canopy or sub-canopy. Up to 4 white or pale pink eggs laid September–January, hatching after 2 weeks and young take a further 3 weeks to fledge. **FEEDING** Wide variety, but a specialist nectar and honeydew feeder, also takes fruit and invertebrates. **P&R** Widespread, especially in NI, where it is found in all but the most industrial agricultural areas. In SI it is found mainly in the north, west and south and on Stewart I. **T&M** Alien predators and habitat loss; however, it has managed to adapt to human-induced changes to the ecosystem better than most native species. **BV** Widespread, but especially in areas of native bush; quite common in suburban areas with good tree cover.

The **Chatham Island Tui** (C) *P. n. chathamensis* is virtually identical to the mainland subspecies, but somewhat larger. It is found on the Chatham Is and is endangered due to loss of habitat and alien predators.

Bellbird *Anthornis melanura melanura* **LC EG**

A B

ALTERNATIVE NAMES Korimako, Makomako

L 17–20cm WS 22cm Wt (M) 32–34g (F) 25–26g

Small, rather inconspicuous forest bird with *haunting song*. Adult male (A) olive-green, *darker on head*, which may have a purple sheen, *and neck, brighter on flanks, belly and rump; primaries and tail near black*. Bill black, fine and *down-curved*, iris red, legs and feet dark grey. Female (B) similar but generally duller and browner with very *thin, drooping 'moustache', a white line running back from base of bill*. Immature as female but yellow moustache and brown eye. **VOICE/CALL** Quite varied, a series of loud, ringing melodious notes. Alarm call a rather harsh *yeng-yeng-yeng*. **BREEDING** Nest built in fork of tree or similar. Up to 5 red-spotted, pinkish-white eggs laid September–January, but varies on some islands, hatching after 2 weeks and young fledge after a further 2 weeks. **FEEDING** Largely nectar and fruit, but some invertebrates; females tend to eat more invertebrates and young are fed entirely on them. **P&R** Found in most parts of the country apart from Northland, industrial agricultural areas and Otago grasslands. **T&M** Loss of habitat and alien pest predators. Bellbirds have survived reasonably well but their range and numbers have reduced due to predation. **BV** Native bush, central NI and northern and southern SI.

There are 2 other subspecies of bellbird: **Three Kings Bellbird** *A. m. obscura* is virtually indistinguishable from the mainland subspecies, but is found only on the Three Kings Is in the far north, while the **Poor Knights Bellbird** *A. m. oneho* is found only on the Poor Knights Is, though does cross over to the mainland from time to time. A second species, the **Chatham Island Bellbird** *A. melanocephala*, became extinct in 1906.

Notiomystidae (previously Meliphagidae)

Stitchbird *Notiomystis cincta* **VU EG**

B A

ALTERNATIVE NAME Hihi | L 18cm Wt (M) 36–40g (F) 30g

Small, *very noisy* forest bird. Adult (A) male *black head, neck, breast and upper back, with prominent white blaze behind eye*. Lower back and tail brown *with white wing bar and yellow on primaries*. Belly and undertail pale brown. Black breast separated from pale belly by *ragged orange-yellow band*. Bill black, fine and slightly down-curved, iris black, legs and feet reddish brown. Female (B) retains *white wing bar*, but otherwise *largely dull olive-green*, brighter on primaries and outer tail feathers, and pale grey on throat and breast and belly. Immature as female but brown rather than olive-green. **VOICE/CALL** Penetrating, explosive *see-see-ip*. Several together can be deafening. Also a very loud alarm call *yeng yeng yeng*. **BREEDING** Builds nest in hole high up in large tree, 3–5 white eggs laid September-March, hatching after 2 weeks, fledging after 4–5 weeks. On Little Barrier I. they are monogamous, but on Kapiti I. they are polyandrous, possibly due to lack of nesting sites. **FEEDING** Mainly nectar and fruit, but some invertebrates. **P&R** *c.*2,000. NI only, severely restricted, previously widespread but now found only on offshore island sanctuaries, and predator-controlled or predator-free fenced mainland sanctuaries. **T&M** Conservation-dependent. Habitat loss and alien pest predators, especially Stoats, rats and feral cats. Subject to intensive conservation programme, introducing new populations to sanctuaries, supplementary feeding, and predator control and elimination. **BV** Little Barrier I. is their last remaining natural habitat, but reintroduced to Kapiti and Tiritiri Matangi islands, also found at Ark in the Park near Auckland city, and Karori Sanctuary, Wellington.

INTRODUCED PASSERINES In the latter half of the 19th century, a number of acclimatisation societies were established to introduce alien species to New Zealand. While many mammalian species introduced have become serious pests, most of the introduced bird species have not had a serious impact on native species as they were better adapted to the agricultural and urban environment that has taken over much of the country.

Turdidae

Blackbird *Turdus merula* LC I (Eur)

L 25cm WS 34–38.5cm Wt 70–130g

Medium-sized, all-dark bird, common in urban and agricultural areas. Adult male (A) *all jet black apart from bright orange-red bill and orbital ring*, iris dark, legs and feet dark brown. Female (B) *all dark brown apart from pale striated throat, bill dull orange* with dark tip, orbital ring orange, legs and feet grey-brown. Immature (C) as female but rather paler with vermiculations on breast and grey-brown bill. **VOICE/CALL** Mellow flute-like song, a loud scream when alarmed, also an insistent *chink chink* when a cat or other predator is around. **BREEDING** Nests built in a dense shrub, hedge, tree fork or similar. Up to 6 speckled blue-green eggs laid late August–December, hatching after 2 weeks; the young fledge 2 weeks later. **FEEDING** Wide variety of invertebrates and fruit. **P&R** 150–500 million. Native of Europe and Asia, introduced to NZ in 1862–75 and spread rapidly to all parts of the country, including offshore islands. **T&M** No threats, however they can be a horticultural pest, eating berry fruits, though they also consume numbers of insect pest species. **BV** Almost anywhere, including parks and gardens. Not common in dense native bush or alpine areas.

Song Thrush *Turdus philomelos* LC I (Eur)

L 22–23cm WS 34.5cm Wt 70g

Medium-sized, rather upright, brown bird often found in parks and gardens. Adult (A) head, nape and upperparts mid-brown, upper breast and flanks pale cinnamon, lower breast and belly off-white, *and all heavily streaked dark brown*. Bill grey-brown or horn coloured, iris dark brown, legs and feet pinkish brown. Immature (B) similar but rather yellower. **VOICE/CALL** Clear musical song, each note repeated, often from high conspicuous perch. Call a thin *seep* and a shorter *sipp*. **BREEDING** Builds a substantial mud- or rotten-wood-lined nest in dense vegetation, shrub, hedge or similar. Up to 6 lightly spotted blue eggs laid August–December, though can be later or earlier, hatching after 2 weeks; young fledge 2 weeks later. **FEEDING** Wide range of invertebrates, especially snails and earthworms, as well as fruit and some seeds. **P&R** 80–200 million. Native of Europe, Africa and Asia, introduced to NZ in 1862–78 and quickly spread throughout the country. **T&M** No known threats; some potential for damage to commercial crops, but also consumes large numbers of invertebrates, some of which are pests. **BV** Very widespread, common in all areas, especially urban and suburban ones.

3/7/12 Rotorua

Prunellidae

Dunnock *Prunella modularis* **LC I** (Eur)

L 13–14.5cm WS 19–21cm Wt 21.5g

Small, grey-brown, *shy, retiring, inconspicuous* bird. Adult head and upperparts brown, *streaked lighter and darker*, underparts grey or grey-brown, *heavily streaked on flanks; collar and neck soft grey*, grey eyebrow. Bill black, short and finely pointed, *iris red-brown*, legs and feet reddish brown. Immature browner and more heavily streaked, especially on head and neck. **VOICE/CALL** Call a shrill sustained *tseeep* or a trilling *tit-tit-tit* or *i-i-i*. **BREEDING** Nests in thick undergrowth, hedge or similar. Up to 5 deep-blue eggs laid August–January, hatching after 1.5–2 weeks, young fledging up to 2 weeks later. **FEEDING** Largely invertebrates, but some fruit and seeds also taken. **P&R** 36–78 million. Native of Europe, introduced in 1867–82, spread rapidly, now present in all parts of the country but not in large numbers, commonest in eastern SI. **T&M** No known threats. **BV** Widespread; best probably Northland, inland Bay of Plenty, southern NI and eastern SI.

Passeridae

House Sparrow *Passer domesticus* **LC IP** (Eur)

L 14–17cm WS 19–25cm Wt 29g

Small, very urbanised, *gregarious*, brown bird. Adult male (A) has a general grey and brown appearance, *with grey forehead and crown, grey face patch and breast and underparts, black chin and throat, small white stripe behind eye*. Wing has *narrow white wing bar*. Bill black or grey-brown, *short, heavy and pointed*. Breeding plumage rather brighter than non-breeding. Female (B) very much plainer with mid-brown upperparts, pale brown underparts, *pale sand-coloured eye-stripe, white wing bar smaller but still visible*. Immature (C) as female but duller. **VOICE/CALL** Variety of chirps and cheeps, also a double *chissick*. **BREEDING** Builds domed nest in hole in tree, building or sometimes in thickly branched canopy of tall trees, often in small colony. Up to 6 off-white eggs with brown spots and streaks laid late September–January, hatching after 1.5–2 weeks, young fledge after a further 2–2.5 weeks. **FEEDING** Mainly seeds, especially cereals, grasses, and introduced weed species; some invertebrates, which form the bulk of the food for the chicks; fruit and nectar. **P&R** 540 million. Native of Europe, introduced to NZ 1866–71, spread rapidly, now found in all parts of the country, especially NI. Common in urban/suburban areas, not found in native bush or in alpine areas. **T&M** Known pest species, causes significant damage to crops. **BV** Widespread apart from native bush and alpine regions, especially near human habitation.

Finches – Fringillidae There are no native finches in New Zealand; however, four species have been introduced from Europe and are now widespread throughout the country. They have thrived partly due to the abundance of introduced European plants and are a potential problem for agriculture. As seed eaters they are found mainly in open grassland and suburban areas, rarely in native bush.

Chaffinch *Fringilla coelebs* **LC I** (Eur)

L 14.5–15cm WS 25–29cm Wt 175–245g

Small, ground-feeding finch with *bounding flight and double white wing bars*. Adult male (A) *head and nape slate-blue, chestnut mantle, olive rump*, tail and primaries brown *with white outer tail feathers visible in flight. Face, breast and belly rich cinnamon*, undertail grey, *white on wings clearly visible*. Bill blue-grey, quite short, stout and pointed, iris dark brown, legs and feet grey, sometimes reddish. Female (B) much quieter colours, light brown head, nape and back, *pale cinnamon breast and belly*, sand-coloured eyebrow, *white wing bars very visible*, bill and legs browner. Immature like female but duller. **VOICE/CALL** Main call note *pink-pink*, flight note *tsup*, also *wheet* and *tsit*. **BREEDING** Nest, camouflaged with lichen, located in fork in trunk or branch, up to 6 grey-blue eggs with purplish blotches laid, hatching 2 weeks later, young fledge after 2 weeks. **FEEDING** Largely seeds, but also some fruit and invertebrates. **P&R** 500–1,500 million. Native of Europe and Asia, introduced to NZ in 1862–80, now found in all parts of the country. **T&M** Potential pest of cereal crops, horticulture and the fruit industry. **BV** Widespread in all areas; especially common in urban and suburban areas.

Redpoll *Carduelis flammea* **LC I** (Eur)

L 11–13cm WS 19–22cm Wt 8.5–15.5g

Small, rather *dull brown* finch. Adult male (A) *forehead and crown red*, nape and upperparts brown, streaked darker, *breast fawn, streaked darker brown, but pink to crimson in breeding season*, belly and undertail fawn, with heavy streaking on flanks. Bill horn coloured, *short stout and pointed, with black upper ridge*, iris dark brown, orbital ring dark grey, legs and feet dark grey. Female (B) similar but *red on head much smaller and lacks red on breast*. Immature similar to female but lacks red on head. **VOICE/CALL** Flight song a rather metallic *chuch-uch-uch*, call a plaintive *tsooeet*. **BREEDING** Builds nest in fork in a low shrub, up to 6 lightly spotted and streaked, bluish-green eggs laid mid-October–February, normally 2 broods in a season. Eggs hatch after 1.5 weeks, young fledge after 2 weeks and are fed by adult for a further 1–2 weeks. **FEEDING** Grass and weed seeds, some invertebrates. Rather shy bird, often in small flocks. **P&R** 100 million. Native of Eurasia and North America, introduced to NZ in 1862–75, widespread by 1900. Common and widespread throughout New Zealand from coast to subalpine zones, including all coastal and outlying islands. Probably most plentiful in SI; in NI found mainly in the central area. **T&M** Not as numerous as the other finches and less likely to be an agricultural pest. **BV** Open country, scrubland and grasslands in SI, especially to the east and south; also Chatham Is.

Goldfinch *Carduelis carduelis* **LC I** (Eur)

L 12–13cm WS 21–26cm Wt (M) 16g (F) 14g

Small, very *colourful finch* that forms significant flocks known as 'charms' in winter. Adult has *black and white head with bright red face*, nape and mantle mid-brown, *rump white, tail black and slightly forked*. Upperwing black with *broad yellow wing bar and white tips to the flight feathers*. Underparts white apart from irregular, pale fawn band across breast. Female similar but with *smaller red face* than male. Bill greyish white, short, stout and sharp, iris

dark brown, orbital ring dark grey, legs and feet reddish brown. Immature lacks colourful head, largely mid-brown, streaked, with black wings and yellow wing bar. **VOICE/CALL** Call a liquid, twittering *tswit-wit-wit*, song is a musical elaboration of this. **BREEDING** Nest built in fork of branch in shrub or small tree or vine. Up to 6 pale blue eggs with reddish-brown spots and streaks laid mid-October–February, hatching after 1.5 weeks; young fledge after 2 weeks and are fed by parents for a further 2–3 weeks. **FEEDING** Mainly weed and grass seeds, with some invertebrates. **P&R** 75–350 million. Native of Eurasia, introduced to NZ in 1862–83, established and widespread by 1900. Found throughout the country, especially in NI and eastern SI. Not found in native bush. **T&M** No threats, not a known pest species, though they have the potential. **BV** Widespread, especially in open country.

Greenfinch *Carduelis chloris* **LC I** (Eur)

L 15–16cm WS 23–27cm Wt 28g

Chunky, olive-green finch with large bill. Adult male (A) yellow-olive all over apart from dark primaries with *bright yellow flashes, yellow outer tail feathers* and dark tip to *slightly forked tail*. Bill pale, heavy and pointed, iris dark brown, legs and feet pinkish grey. Female (B) similar but browner all over with less yellow on wings. Immature similar but browner and somewhat streaked. **VOICE/CALL** Flight note a rather soft *chi-chi-chi-chit*, alarm call is a high-pitched *tsooeet*, common to other finches, and a long, drawn-out nasal *dzhweee*. **BREEDING** Nest built in fork of branch of small tree, or top of dense shrub such as gorse. Up to 6 spotted pale blue eggs laid October–February, later further south, hatching after 2 weeks and young fledging 2.5 weeks later. **FEEDING** Largely seeds from cereals, brassicas and weeds, some invertebrates. **P&R** 45–150 million. Native of Europe, North Africa and western Asia, introduced to NZ in 1862–68. Not common in native bush although present in Fiordland, West Coast of SI and on Stewart I. **T&M** No threats, some potential for agricultural and horticultural damage. **BV** Widespread, generally in open country.

Emberizidae

Yellowhammer *Emberiza citrinella* **LC I** (Eur)

L 16cm WS 23–29.5cm Wt 18–30g

Small, very yellow bird with *long tail* and very short bill. Adult male (A) has *bright yellow head and throat, upperparts chestnut, streaked darker,* primaries darker with very faint pale wing bar, *rump chestnut,* tail brown *and slightly forked, with white edges to outer tail feathers. Underparts yellow with rufous band on chest* and greyish undertail. Bill bluish horn, short and pointed, iris dark brown, legs and feet pale fleshy brown. Female (B) similar but *less colourful, with more streaking on breast*. Immature duller and browner. **VOICE/CALL** In flight, a sibilant *twit-up*, also well-known song sounding like '*little bit of bread and no cheese*', sometimes missing out the '*cheese*'. **BREEDING** Nests close to ground in thick vegetation. Up to 5 pinkish-white eggs with fine brown scribbling, laid October–February, hatching after 2 weeks with young fledging 2 weeks later. **FEEDING** Seeds, especially introduced weeds, and invertebrates. **P&R** 70–200 million. Native of Eurasia, introduced to NZ in 1862–75. Now widespread but scarce along West Coast of SI. **T&M** No threats, not a known pest species. **BV** Widespread in open country.

Cirl Bunting *Emberiza cirlus* **LC I** (Eur)

L 15–16.5cm WS 22–25.5cm Wt 210–290g

Small, yellowy ground-bird, rather like a dull Yellowhammer. Male (A) *head boldly black and yellow with black throat*. Crown and nape slightly yellowy grey, *upperparts chestnut, streaked darker,* tail brown and *slightly forked with white edges to outer feathers*. Breast grey, becoming streaked yellow on belly, slightly rufous on flanks. Bill blue-grey, short and pointed, iris dark brown, legs and feet pinkish brown. Female (B) lacks striking head pattern and is a *general yellow-brown all over with darker streaking*. Immature as female but duller. **VOICE/CALL** Call a soft *zit*, song a short trilling rattle. **BREEDING** Builds nest in dense vegetation. Up to 4 bluish-green eggs with black streaks, laid October–January, hatching after 2 weeks; young fledge after 1.5–2 weeks. **FEEDING** Seeds, especially cereals; young fed on invertebrates. **P&R** 6–16 million. Native of Eurasia, NZ population 5,000, introduced in 1871–80. Mainly in SI, very few on NI. **T&M** No threats and not a pest species. **BV** Open country in Marlborough and down east coast to Banks Peninsula.

Alaudidae

Skylark *Alauda arvensis* **LC I** (Eur)

L 16–19cm WS 28–36cm Wt 38g

Small, brown ground bird with amazing song and flight habit. Adult *head and upperparts heavily streaked pale to mid-brown, head has distinct crest*. Throat pale, breast pale brown, both heavily streaked, *belly and undertail white*, underwing greyish brown. Bill pale pinkish grey with darker tip, iris dark brown, orbital ring dark grey, legs and feet yellow-brown to orange-brown. Immature similar but duller and lacks head crest. **VOICE/CALL** Male in breeding season ascends to 100m or more and starts a long, never-ending trilling melodic song, and continues singing as he descends. Usual flight call a liquid *chirrup*. **BREEDING** Ground nester in open fields, sand dunes. Up to 5 speckled creamy eggs laid September–January, up to 3 clutches in a season. Eggs hatch after 1.5 weeks, young leave nest at 1.5 weeks, but are not fully fledged for 3 weeks. **FEEDING** Largely seeds of grasses, cereals and introduced weeds; also invertebrates. **P&R** 250–1,000 million. Native of Eurasia, introduced to NZ 1864–75 and rapidly spread throughout country. Now found in all areas apart from native bush and alpine zones. **T&M** No threats, but can cause damage to sown seeds and seedlings. **BV** Widespread in open areas, agricultural land, sand dunes; scarce on West Coast of SI.

Sturnidae

Starling *Sturnus vulgaris* **LC IP** (Eur)

B A C

L 19–22cm WS 32–38cm Wt 75–100g

Medium-sized, *gregarious* bird, well adapted to co-habiting with humans. Adult male (A) has generally *dark, near-black plumage, with a green and purple sheen*, especially during breeding season, and with white spots in winter. *Bill long and finely pointed, yellow in breeding season, dull horn in winter*, iris dark, legs and feet yellow-brown. Female (B) similar but slightly *less glossy and more heavily spotted plumage*. Immature (C) *dull mouse brown* all over with black bill. **VOICE/CALL** Song is a mixture of clipped and bell-like notes, rather like an orchestra tuning up. **BREEDING** Nests usually in a hole in cliff, tree or building, but occasionally in thick vegetation, flax, cypress trees, buildings, chimneys, etc. Up to 6 sky-blue eggs laid mid-October–December, hatching after 1.5 weeks, young fledging after 3 weeks. **FEEDING** Mixture of invertebrates; its long bill is adapted for probing earth, fruit and nectar, especially from flax and Pohutakawa. **P&R** 310 million. Native of Eurasia, introduced to NZ in 1862–83 and rapidly became established, now found in all parts of the country apart from native bush and alpine areas. Known to venture short distances into native forest to take ripe fruit from some species, especially podocarps. **T&M** No threats; does cause some horticultural damage, and deprives native species, especially when it forms very large flocks in autumn, though it does also feed on pest invertebrates. **BV** Widespread throughout NI and SI, especially agricultural and suburban areas.

Indian Myna *Acridotheris tristis* **LC I** (India)

L 22–27cm WS 33–43cm Wt 125–130g

Medium-sized, *upright, cheeky* bird, well adapted to urban and agricultural environment. Adult *head and neck dark glossy black* with purple sheen, rest of body cinnamon brown apart from *white undertail and with large white wing-patch visible at rest and in flight*. Bill and bare skin round eye yellow, *iris yellow*, legs and feet dull yellow. Large white

wing-patch on underside of wing. Immature head browner, bill and facial skin paler. **VOICE/CALL** Very mixed collection of noises, gurgles, melodic notes and chattering. **BREEDING** Nest built in hole in tree, cliff or building. Up to 6 greenish-blue eggs laid mid-October–March, hatching after 2 weeks; young fledge after 3.5–4.5 weeks. **FEEDING** Omnivorous. Invertebrates, fruit, young birds, lizards; scavenges from rubbish dumps and road-kill carrion. **P&R** Native of India, central and Southeast Asia, introduced to NZ 1870–77. Did not survive in SI, but well established in NI, mainly from Central Plateau northwards, also Hawke's Bay and Taranaki. **T&M** No threats; some evidence of pest problems in the horticultural industry. **BV** Northern NI, especially near urban areas.

Pycnonotidae

Red-vented Bulbul *Pycnonotus cafer* **LC I** (Asia)

L 20–22cm

Medium-sized, rather slim, dark-plumaged bird with *long, white-tipped tail. Adult black head, neck and upperparts with white rump*, underparts black, fading to grey on belly and with *red patch on undertail*. Bill dark and finely pointed, iris dark, legs and feet dark grey. Introduced in 1952 from a ship; they were eradicated but reports suggest that some may still exist in the Auckland area.

Artamidae

Australian Magpie *Gymnorhina tibicen* **LC IP** (Aus)

L 41cm WS 65–85cm Wt 350g

Large, obvious, black and white bird. Two forms, white-backed (A) and black-backed (B). Both have *black head, neck and underparts, white rump and 2 large white shoulder patches on upperwing*. White-backed male *has white nape, mantle and back, these with grey vermiculations in the female*. Black-backed has white *mantle and black back*. Bill pale bluish white, large and pointed with black tip, iris red, legs and feet dark grey. Immature resembles female but with dark brown in place of black and with dark bill. **VOICE/CALL** Very unusual soft, flute-like carolling call. **BREEDING** Nest high up in tall trees, often pines, macrocarpa or eucalypts, also on power poles, etc. Up to 5 pale blue-green eggs laid July–November, hatching after 3 weeks, young fledge after 4 weeks. Fiercely territorial in breeding season, may even attack people. Most territories held by pairs, but occasionally form very complex family groups of 3–10 birds. Non-breeding birds form flocks of as many as 80 birds. **FEEDING** Mainly invertebrates, but some fruit, seeds and grains, also carrion. **P&R** Native of Australia, introduced to NZ in 1864–74 but slow to establish. However, now widespread and found in most parts of the country, especially agricultural areas. **T&M** No threats, but having been brought in to help control pasture invertebrates, they are now seen as pests by some farmers because of their aggression towards other birds and people during the breeding season. **BV** Widespread NI and SI, especially agricultural and commercial forestry areas.

Corvidae

Rook *Corvus frugilegus* **LC I** (Eur)

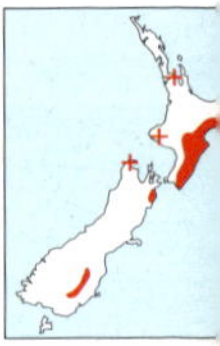

L 45cm WS 81–99cm Wt (M) 425g (F) 375g

Large, all-black bird of open country. Adult *all black with very large, heavy, pointed, pale grey bill with dark tip, iris dark brown*, orbital ring grey, legs and feet black. In flight, broad wings with fingered tips. **VOICE/CALL** Hoarse or raucous *caw*. **BREEDING** In small colonies in tops of tall trees. Up to 7 pale green-blue eggs laid late-August–November, eggs hatching after 2.5 weeks, and young fledging after 5 weeks. **FEEDING** Largely invertebrates, especially caterpillars and grubs, but also seeds and cereals. **P&R** 60–220 million. Native of Eurasia, introduced to NZ 1862–74, very slow to establish and still very localised, found mainly along the eastern NI south of Gisborne, with a few scattered elsewhere and small numbers in the southeast of SI. **T&M** No threats, probably not in large enough numbers now to be a serious pest species following control efforts. **BV** Open country, east coast of NI between Gisborne and Masterton.

Extinct Bird Species

New Zealand has the unenviable distinction of having lost a higher proportion of its native birds, some 50 species, than anywhere else in the world. All of these species were endemic to New Zealand, and so their loss was a loss to the whole world.

Two things stand out from the list below. First, the devastating effect that the arrival of the Maori, accompanied by the Pacific Rat, or Kiore, and domestic dogs had on the moas and adzebills, all gone within 150 years. Secondly, how nearly half (23 species) have become extinct since 1800, with three disappearing within the last 50 years, which is a clear indication of how little we have understood or appreciated the native avifauna. Several other species would have become extinct in the last 40 years, had the Department of Conservation not devoted very significant resources to rescuing them, in some cases from the very brink of extinction.

Extinct by 1400CE

Upland Moa *Megalapteryx didinus*
North Island Giant Moa *Dinornis novaezealandiae*
South Island Giant Moa *Dinornis robustus*
Eastern Moa *Emeus crassus*
Stout-legged Moa *Euryapteryx gravis*
Crested Moa *Pachyornis australis*
Little Bush Moa *Anomalopteryx didiformis*
Mantell's Moa *Pachyornis geranoides*
Heavy-footed Moa *Pachyornis elephantopus*
Coastal Moa *Euryapteryx curtus*
Haast's Eagle *Aquila moorei*
North Island Adzebill *Aptornis otidiformis*
South Island Adzebill *Aptornis defossor*

Most depictions of moa show them with an upright 'Ostrich-like' posture; in reality, the neck was held horizontally, parallel to the ground. Moas were not only flightless but were unique in not having even vestigial wings.

Extinct by 1800

New Zealand Stiff-tailed Duck *Oxyura vantetsi*
New Zealand Musk Duck *Biziura delautouri*
Eyles' Harrier *Circus teauteensis*
Snipe-rail *Capellirallus karamu*
New Zealand Coot *Fulica prisca*
Long-billed Wren *Dendroscansor decurvirostris*
Stout-legged Wren *Pachyplichas yaldwyni*
New Zealand Raven *Corvus antipodum*
Finsch's Duck *Chenonetta finschi*
Scarlett's Duck *Malacorhynchus scarletti*
Chatham Island Duck *Pachyanas chathamica*
Chatham Island Coot *Fulica chathamensis*
Chatham Island Raven *Corvus moriorum*
Scarlett's Shearwater *Puffinus spelaeus*
Hodgen's Waterhen *Gallinula hodgenorum*

Extinct in the Nineteenth Century

Hawkin's Rail or Mahanui *Diaphorapteryx hawkinsi*
Dieffenbach's Rail or Mehoriki *Gallirallus dieffenbachii*

New Zealand Owlet Nightjar
Aegotheles novaezealandiae
Forbes' Snipe *Coenocorypha chathamica*
New Zealand Quail or Koreke
Coturnix novaezelandiae
North Island Snipe
Coenocorypha barrierensis
South Island Snipe
Coenocorypha iredalei
Megapode *Megapodius*
Chatham Island Fernbird
Bowdleria rufescens
Hutton's Rail or Matirakahu
Cabalus modestus
North Island Takahe or Moho
Porphyrio mantelli
New Zealand Little Bittern
Ixobrychus novaezelandiae
Stephens Island or Lyall's Wren
Traversia lyalli

New Zealand Quail: male (lower) and female (upper)

Extinct since 1900

Southern Merganser *Mergus australis* 1902
North Island Piopio *Turnagra tanagra* 1902
South Island Piopio *Turnagra capensis* 1905
Chatham Island Bellbird or Komako *Anthornis melanocephala* 1906
Laughing Owl *Sceloglaux albofacies* 1914
Huia *Heteralocha acutirostris* 1920s
South Island Snipe *Coenocorypha iredalei* 1964
South Island Kokako *Callaeas cinerea* 1967
Bush Wren *Xenicus longipes* 1972

Huia: male (front) and female (back)

Stead's Bush Wren

Notes for the Visitor

This is not a touring or travel guide, nevertheless this section may help you to see rather more native bird species than you would otherwise. The biggest mistake many visitors make when planning to visit New Zealand is not allowing enough time. For while the land area is only slightly larger than the UK's at 269,000sq km, it is over 1,600km long and is not only divided into three islands by the Cook and Foveaux straits, but for much of its length, from Fiordland in the southwest to the East Cape in the northeast, it is divided by a mountain chain with only ten routes across it. There are no significant motorways outside of Auckland and most towns do not have bypasses, so do not be too ambitious and allow a *minimum* of two weeks on each of the two main islands.

Thanks to the impact of alien pest species, such as Stoats, possums and rats, many native species are hard to find, except in areas where these pests are controlled or have been eliminated. Some of the best locations are offshore islands or 'mainland islands', areas that have been enclosed by a predator-proof fence, or have significant ongoing pest-control programmes.

Island Sanctuaries

The most easily visited island sanctuaries are the following:

Tiritiri Matangi Island near Auckland is maybe the best example of an island sanctuary. Pests were eradicated some 30 years ago and over 250,000 native trees planted, and it is now home to Takahe, North Island Kiwi, Stitchbird, Kokako, Tui and Saddleback, amongst others. Plan to stay at least one night there.

Kapiti Island on the west coast north of Wellington is another excellent example of an offshore sanctuary and features Little Spotted Kiwi, Kaka, Weka, Takahe, Bellbird, Tui, Red-crowned Parakeet and more. An overnight stay is also recommended.

Mayor Island/Tuhua is a small volcanic island in the Bay of Plenty noted for its obsidian. It has recently become a sanctuary and you can rent a cabin from Christmas to Easter. Good for Orange-fronted Parakeet, Whitehead and Kaka.

Matiu-Somes Island is in the middle of Wellington Harbour and easily accessed. It also has accommodation and features, among other species, Red-

Tuatara *Sphenodon punctatus* is endemic and one of just two species in the order Sphenodontia. It dates back to the age of the dinosaurs.

crowned Parakeet, North Island Robin, Little Blue Penguin and Spotted Shag. It is also home to eight species of reptile, including the amazing Tuatara.

Ulva Island is situated in Patterson Inlet on Stewart Island, and is home to the Stewart Island Weka, South Island Kaka, Red-crowned Parakeet, Kereru, Bellbird, Brown Creeper, Yellowhead, and the Stewart Island Robin and Brown Kiwi.

Mainland Islands

New Zealand has pioneered the design and use of pest-proof fences, which have been erected in a number of places to provide a safe haven for native species. They have been extremely successful, if expensive, and more mainland sanctuaries are in the pipeline. The following in the North Island are all worth a visit:

Karori Sanctuary in Wellington was the first and is the best-known fenced sanctuary. It is only five minutes from the centre of Wellington and very accessible by public transport. A very good location for Tui, Kaka, Little Spotted Kiwi, Kereru, North Island Weka, Stitchbird, Saddleback, New Zealand Falcon and more than 20 other native bird species, as well as reptiles and amphibians.

Bushy Park is an area of lowland native rainforest near Whanganui, with a 4.6km-long fence enclosing 100ha of native bush. Here you can find North Island Robin, Brown Kiwi, Kereru, Saddleback and Tui, amongst other species.

Maungatautari Ecological Island is an isolated 800m volcanic cone in the Waikato south of Hamilton. It has the longest pest-proof fence of all, 47km. Birds here include Takahe, North Island Brown Kiwi, Kaka, Kereru, Bellbird, Tui, Morepork, Whitehead, Stitchbird, North Island Tomtit and Grey Fantail.

Tawharanui Open Sanctuary is a fenced-off peninsula near Warkworth, north of Auckland, open to the public; being coastal, a wider variety of species can be found here, including New Zealand Dotterel, Brown Teal, North Island Brown Kiwi and Robin, Morepork, Grey Fantail and Red-crowned Parakeet.

Otanewainuku near Te Puke in the Bay of Plenty has a small pest-free enclosure as well as an intensive pest-control programme; birds here include North Island Brown Kiwi and Robin, Tui and Bellbird.

Ark in the Park is a large native-species recovery project in the Waitakere Ranges to the west of Auckland; look out for Stitchbird, Tui, North Island Robin, Morepork, Kokako and Kaka.

Northern Te Urewera Ecological Restoration Project, part of the Te Urewera National Park between Gisborne and Rotorua, is one of the best areas for Kokako and a variety of native forest birds.

Trounson Kauri Park in Northland is a 450ha inland island in Northland, home to the awesome Kauri trees and a good place for many native bush species, including North Island Brown Kiwi, Kereru, Morepork, Tui and Grey Fantail, among others.

South Island has much larger areas of wilderness, but fewer sanctuaries. Among those worth visiting are:

Orokonui Eco-sanctuary just north of Dunedin is a 3sq km sanctuary with a 10km pest fence around it, and includes regenerating native lowland forest as well as wetlands and open water.

Hinewai is a private reserve on the Banks Peninsula near Christchurch. The emphasis here is on plants, but pest control, particularly of possum, has attracted many native bird species to the reserve.

Rotoiti Nature Recovery Project is an area of honeydew beech forest on the shores of Lake Rotoiti in the Nelson Lakes National Park. Here the emphasis is on controlling introduced wasp species that deter native bird species from feeding on the honeydew produced by a scale insect.

Other Birding Spots

NORTH ISLAND

Great Barrier Island in the Hauraki Gulf is free of many pests and so has good birdlife, including Brown Teal, New Zealand Dotterel, Fernbird, Shining and Long-tailed cuckoo, Banded Rail, Spotless Crake, Australasian Bittern, Grey Warbler, Little Blue Penguin, Black Petrel and other seabirds.

Kaipara Harbour and **Manukau Harbour** are two very large west coast harbours; Kaipara is north of Auckland, Manukau is at Auckland, and both are excellent for waders and wetland birds.

Muriwai has a wonderful Australasian Gannet colony on the west coast north of Auckland.

Miranda Shorebird Centre in the Firth of Thames is *the* place for waders, with 43 species recorded here and a total list of over 130 species. This site also has a chenier beach (made up almost entirely of mollusc shells), one of only three in the southern hemisphere.

Whangamarino Wetland is a Ramsar site in the Waikato north of Hamilton, and is a remnant of once very extensive wetlands. Over 56 species have been recorded here; look out for Kingfisher, Pukeko, Pied Stilt, Australasian Bittern and several species of duck.

Tauranga Harbour is a very large, shallow harbour in the Bay of Plenty, and is good for waders, large flocks of Bar-tailed Godwit, also Variable Oystercatcher, New Zealand Dotterel and Caspian Tern, Banded Dotterel and Wrybill in winter. There are also good options for pelagic seabird watching.

Maketu Harbour and **Little Waihi Harbour** are two smaller harbours in the Bay of Plenty, but offer a wonderful selection of waders, including New Zealand Dotterel, especially in the summer when the northern migrants are here. They are also good for spoonbill in winter.

Ohiwa Harbour is yet another wader paradise in the Bay of Plenty, with many other sea- and shorebirds present.

White Island is the most volcanically active place in New Zealand. There is an Australasian Gannet colony and the trip out and back is a good opportunity to spot seabirds, including albatrosses.

Mokoia Island is in the middle of Lake Rotorua, and is good for North Island Brown Kiwi, Saddleback, Stitchbird and Weka. Access is by boat from Rotorua.

Mount Bruce National Wildlife Centre, 30km north of Masterton on SH2, is a breeding centre for endangered species including Kaka, Kokako, Brown Kiwi, Stitchbird and Yellow-crowned Parakeet.

Other birding sites worth visiting on North Island include:
Pureora and Pirongia Forest Parks.
Karikari Peninsula, Whangarei and Ruakaka harbours in Northland.
Waipu Estuary, south of Whangarei, is excellent for waders and other wetland birds.
Manawatu Estuary near Foxton has excellent waders and waterside birds.
Lake Taupo and the **Rotorua lakes** offer good birdwatching opportunities.
Ahuriri Wetlands, close to Napier, has good waders and coastal species.
Nga Manu Nature Reserve, about 50km north of Wellington near Waikanae, good for water and waterside birds, ducks, herons, etc.
Cape Kidnappers is another Australasian Gannet colony, this time on the east coast, near Hastings.
Cook Strait is often a good place for seabirds, including albatrosses.

SOUTH ISLAND

Kaikoura, situated midway between Picton and Christchurch, is a mecca for ocean wildlife. Deep underwater canyons just offshore bring a huge variety of marine life to Kaikoura, including whales, dolphins, several species of albatross and numerous smaller petrels and shearwaters, skuas, gulls and terns. A must for any serious birder!

Twizel, in central Canterbury, is the only breeding ground of the Black Stilt, the rarest wader in the world. There is a captive breeding programme here, and you can watch the birds from the Black Stilt Visitor Hide.

Taiaroa Head at the tip of the Otago Peninsula near Dunedin is the site of the only mainland albatross colony in the world, with some 30 pairs of Northern Royal Albatross. Stewart Island and Spotted shags, as well as New Zealand Fur Seals, can be found on the rocky shoreline.

Farewell Spit at the top end of South Island is another birding paradise, with an Australasian Gannet colony, as well as nesting Little Blue Penguin, White-fronted and Caspian terns. There is a large amount of good wader habitat, offering chances to see Banded Dotterel, Variable and Pied oystercatcher, and Pied Stilt. Over 90 species have been recorded here, many of them migrant or vagrant waders.

Lake Ellesmere near Christchurch is one of the best wader and shorebird locations in the country.

Foveaux Strait between South Island and Stewart Island can be good for a variety of seabirds.

Other birding spots on South Island include:

Wairau Estuary and the **Big Lagoon** near Blenheim.
Bromley Oxidation Ponds and **Avon-Heathcote Estuary**, Christchurch.
Okarito Lagoon and **Waitangiroto Nature Reserve** – White Heron sanctuary, Westland.
Oamaru, north of Dunedin, with Little Blue and Yellow-eyed penguin colonies.
Nugget Point on the Catlins coast, good for seabirds.
Fortrose Lagoon east of Invercargill, good for waders including Royal Spoonbill.
Awarua Bay and **New River Estuary** near Invercargill for waders and waterside birds.

Offshore Boat Trips

If you want to see the many seabirds found in New Zealand, you need to take a boat trip. Crossing the **Cook** or **Foveaux straits** can offer good opportunities, but not to compare with a trip on a smaller boat. **Kaikoura** on South Island has already been mentioned, but trips can also be arranged from **Akaroa** on the Banks Peninsula and from **Dunedin**. North Island offers very good opportunities, mainly on the east coast, particularly from **Tauranga** and **Whakatane** in the Bay of Plenty, **Whitianga** on the Coromandel Peninsula, from **Tolaga Bay** on the East Cape, and from several locations in the **Hauraki Gulf** and **Bay of Islands** further north. Species seen vary during the year, but there is always something out there. The trip to **White Island** from Whakatane can also offer good birding opportunities. Kayaking is also an option in a few places; **Okarito Lagoon** in Westland is a good example.

White Island in the Bay of Plenty is New Zealand's most active volcano, and site of a colony of Australasian Gannets; the trip out is excellent for pelagic seabirds and cetaceans.

National Parks and Protected Areas

New Zealand's national parks cover more than 30,000sq km and are a key element of the overall conservation strategy as well as being excellent areas for birdwatching. When visiting, remember that you are not allowed to remove anything but rubbish or garbage from the parks: **leave only footprints, take only pictures and memories**.

North Island

NATIONAL PARKS The more populated North Island has fewer national parks than South Island, but their accessibility makes them excellent places to observe native birds and other wildlife.

Te Urewera This is the largest area of native forest in North Island, a remote and wild area featuring lakes Waikaremoana and Waikareiti, and large areas of hills clad with native forest, much of it beech. It offers good birding, especially for Kokako, and over 650 species of flowering plant plus ferns, mosses, lichens and fungi.

Tongariro Sacred to the Maori, the three active volcanic peaks that make up this, New Zealand's first national park, were gifted to the nation in 1887 by Te Heuheu Tukino IV, paramount chief of the Ngati Tuwharetoa. The park is an excellent area to observe alpine and subalpine habitats. The park is interesting geologically, especially for its many amazing volcanic features.

Whanganui This is a lowland park on the Whanganui River. Good for podocarp broadleaf forest, with Northern Rata, Rimu, Tawa and Rewarewa prominent, and beech forest on the ridges. The river cuts through soft mudstone, creating a spectacular gorge, and there are some interesting sub-fossil deposits. A good area for birds, especially the Nankeen Night Heron, and plants.

Egmont Centred on the spectacular snow-capped volcanic cone of Mount Taranaki, or Egmont. Walk from lowland and montane podocarp broadleaf rainforest through subalpine bush to alpine herbfields and fellfields and the snow line. Good birdlife, wonderful alpine plants and some good bogs also.

FOREST PARKS There are 14 forest parks in North Island, all in upland areas apart from Northland Forest Park, which includes the finest remaining Kauri trees. Coromandel, Kaimai Mamaku, Whirinaki and Raukumara around the Bay of Plenty offer a wide variety of native forest. Pirongia and Pureora to the west contain large areas of podocarp broadleaf forest and excellent and varied bird and other wildlife.

There are a large number of other conservation areas, conservation parks, scenic reserves and so on, all of which provide an element of wilderness and offer birdwatching opportunities.

South Island and Stewart Island

NATIONAL PARKS

Abel Tasman This is the smallest national park on South Island and is noted for its coastline, especially the beaches, inlets and estuaries. Much of the bush is regenerating. There is both beech and podocarp-broadleaf forest, and areas of geological interest including granite and limestone outcrops, the latter linked to the karst limestone formations found inland on Takaka Hill.

Kahurangi At over 4,500sq km, this is one of the largest parks and contains a wide variety of habitats, birds and wildlife. It is excellent for alpine and subalpine flora and fauna and is the last major refuge of the huge *Powelliphanta* snails.

Paparoa A small park on the West Coast centred on the remarkable limestone pancake rocks at Punakaiki. Inland, the vegetation is a lush temperate rainforest with good examples of podocarp-broadleaf forest along with Nikau palms.

Nelson Lakes At the northern end of the Southern Alps, this park is good for montane forest, especially beech, and alpine habitat, plus the lakes Rotoiti and Rotoroa. There is a wide variety of bird and other animal life; good for kiwi.

Arthur's Pass A mountainous park straddling the divide, with beech forest to the east and podocarp-broadleaf to the west. Braided rivers, alpine plants and wildlife make this one of the best and most accessible parks, a good place for Kea and other alpine birds.

Aoraki-Mount Cook A high alpine and mountainous park including Aoraki/Mount Cook, at 3,754m the highest peak in New Zealand. The park also features the two longest glaciers in New Zealand, the Tasman and Hooker. Little forest, but wonderful alpine uplands with a wide range of flora and fauna.

Westland – Tai Poutini Situated on the west of the divide and including the Fox and Franz Josef glaciers, which are accessible by easy trails. Vegetation includes alpine meadows and fellfields, beech and podocarp-broadleaf rainforest and coastal wetlands and lagoons, with a huge variety of flora and fauna.

Mount Aspiring A very mountainous park centred on the 3,030m Mount Aspiring and great for trampers, the vegetation is beech forest and alpine with a large variety of alpine flora and fauna.

Fiordland The largest national park, but with very limited access. Vegetation varies from alpine to coastal rainforest with rainfall up to 12m a year and so there is a wide variety of plants, over 700 species, as well as birds and invertebrates, including, annoyingly, the sandfly, or namu.

Rakiura Rakiura covers 85 per cent of Stewart Island, and is largely podocarp-broadleaf forest, with subalpine on the highest areas. There are extensive wetlands in the middle and large coastal dune systems to the west, which are ecologically quite distinct. Good for kiwi, Weka, Kaka and other native birds.

PROTECTED AREAS South Island has seven forest parks and four conservation parks. Among these are Craigieburn and Lake Sumner, which offer wonderful upland and alpine experiences, while the Catlins on the southeast coast has some of the least affected rainforest in the country and is additionally right next to a wild and fascinating coastal area. As in the North Island there are too many protected areas to mention all of them, but they are all worth a visit and add to the overall wildlife and wilderness experience.

Mitre Peak is in Fiordland National Park.

Birding Tour Operators

A number of companies offer birding tours of New Zealand; this is not an exhaustive list, but is a good start:

Birding Tours New Zealand
224 Horndon Street
Darfield 8172
Tel: +64 3 318 8557
E-mail: rob@birdingtoursnewzealand.com
Contact: Rob Lawrence

Ecotours New Zealand
PO Box 44, Waipu
www.ecotours.co.nz

Heritage Expeditions New Zealand Ltd
Wild Earth New Zealand
Antarctic House, 53B Montreal Street
PO Box 7218, Christchurch
Tel: 0800 262 8873 (within NZ)
Tel: +64 3 365 3500
E-mail: info@heritage-expeditions.com
www.heritage-expeditions.com
www.wildearth-travel.com

Kiwi Wildlife Tours (New Zealand) Ltd
Postal PO Box 686, Warkworth
E-mail: info@kiwi-wildlife.co.nz
Tel: +64 9 422 6868
Fax: +64 9 422 6362
Contact: Chris Gaskin

Manu Tours
106 Ocean Beach Road
Tairua 2853
Tel: +64 7 864 7475; +64 25 281 3809 (mob.)
www.nzbirding.co.nz
Contact: Tony Wilson and Carol Harker

Nature Quest New Zealand Ltd
PO Box 6314, Dunedin
Tel: +64 3 489 8444
E-mail: nature@naturequest.co.nz
www.naturequest.co.nz

Wrybill Birding Tours NZ
PO Box 8291, Havelock North 4157
Tel: +64 6 877 6388
www.wrybill-tours.com

In the UK

Birdquest Ltd
Two Jays, Kemple End
Stonyhurst, Clitheroe BB7 9QY
Tel: 01254 826317
Fax: 01254 826780
E-mail: birders@birdquest.co.uk

Naturetrek Ltd
Cheriton Mill, Cheriton
Alresford SO24 0NG
Tel: 01962 733051
E-mail: info@naturetrek.co.uk

Sunbird Tours
26B The Market Square, Potton
Sandy SG19 2NP
Tel: 01767 262522
E-mail: sunbird@sunbirdtours.co.uk

Useful Environmental and Conservation Organisations

Bird-oriented Groups

Ark in the Park
www.arkinthepark.org.nz

Birding NZ
Useful online group, good source of what birds are about and where.
www.groups.yahoo.com/group/BIRDING-NZ

Miranda Shorebird Centre
www.miranda-shorebird.org.nz
E-mail: info@miranda-shorebird.org.nz
Tel: +64 9 232 2781

Ornithological Society of New Zealand
www.osnz.org.nz
E-mail: osnzeo@slingshot.co.nz

Other Conservation and Wildlife Organisations

Bushy Park Trust
www.bushypark.org.nz
E-mail: info@bushypark.org.nz
Tel: +64 6 342 9879

Conservation Volunteers New Zealand
www.conservationvolunteers.co.nz
E-mail: ereynolds@conservationvolunteers.co.nz
Tel: +64 9 376 7030

Department of Conservation
www.doc.govt.nz
E-mail: enquiries@doc.govt.nz
Tel: +64 4 471 0726

ECO – Environment and Conservation Organisations of Aotearoa New Zealand
www.eco.org.nz
E-mail: eco@eco.org.nz
Tel: +64 4 385 7575

GreenPages Directory of Conservation and Environment Groups
GreenPages lists a large number of local and national conservation organisations in New Zealand.
www.greenpages.org.nz

Hinewai – Maurice White Native Forest Trust
Long Bay Road, RD3, Akaroa 7853, New Zealand
Tel: +64 3 304 8501

Zealandia Karori Sanctuary Trust
www.sanctuary.org.nz
E-mail: kwst@sanctuary.org.nz
Tel: +64 4 920 9200

Maungatautari Ecological Island Trust
www.maungatrust.org
E-mail: mail@maungatrust.org
Tel: +64 7 823 7455

National Wetland Trust of New Zealand
www.wetlandtrust.org.nz
E-mail: enquiries@wetlandtrust.org.nz

Native Forest Restoration Trust
www.nznfrt@org.nz
E-mail: bdavis@auckland.ac.nz
Tel: +64 9 373 3859

New Zealand Ecological Restoration Network (NZERN)
www.bush.org.nz
E-mail: office@bush.org.nz
Tel: +64 3 338 5451

Orokonui Ecosanctuary – The Otago Natural History Trust
www.orokonui.org.nz
E-mail: info@orokonui.org.nz
Tel: +64 3 482 1755

Pukaha Mount Bruce – National Wildlife Centre for Endangered Species Breeding
www.mtbruce.org.nz
E-mail: emailinfo@mtbruce.org.nz
Tel: +64 6 375 8004

QEII National Trust
www.openspace.org.nz
E-mail: info@openspace.org.nz
Tel: +64 4 472 6626

Royal Forest and Bird Protection Society
www.forestandbird.org.nz
E-mail: office@forestandbird.org.nz
Tel: +64 4 285 7374

Supporters of Tiritiri Matangi
www.tiritirimatangi.org.nz
E-mail: enquiries@tiritirimatangi.org.nz
Bookings: www.doc.govt.nz/tiritiribunk-house
Tel: +64 9 425 7812

Tawharanui Regional Park
www.arc.govt.nz/parks/our-parks/parks-in-the-region/tawharanui

Wellington Botanical Society
www.wellingtonbotsoc.wellington.net.nz
E-mail: juliawhite@paradise.net.nz
Tel: +64 4 938 5102

WWF New Zealand
www.wwf.org.nz
E-mail: sarah.lee@wwf.org.nz
Tel: +64 4 499 2930

Zoological Society of Auckland
www.zoologicalsociety.co.nz

Bibliography and Further Reading

Other Books by Julian Fitter

Wildlife of the Galapagos – HarperCollins 2007.
New Zealand Wildlife – Bradt Publications 2009.
Field Guide to Wild New Zealand – David Bateman 2010.

With Tui De Roy and Mark Jones
Albatross, Their World, Their Ways – David Bateman 2008.

Birds

Brooke, M. and Cox, J. *Albatrosses & Petrels Across the World*. OUP 2004.
Chambers, S. *Birds of New Zealand – Locality Guide*. Arun Books 1989.
Hutching, G. *Back from the Brink – The Fight to Save Our Endangered Birds*. Penguin 2004.
Ombler, K. *Where to Watch Birds in New Zealand*. New Holland 2007.
Onley, D. and Bartle, S. *Identification of Seabirds of the Southern Ocean*. Te Papa Press, ACAP, 2006.
Onley, D. and Scofield, P. *Albatrosses, Petrels & Shearwaters of the World*. Christopher Helm 2007.
Ornithological Society of New Zealand. *Checklist of the Birds of New Zealand*, 4th Edition. Te Papa Press 2010.
Robertson, H. and Heather, B. *Hand Guide to the Birds of New Zealand*. Penguin Books (NZ) 1999.
Tennyson, A. and Martinson, M. *Extinct Birds of New Zealand*. Te Papa Press 2006.

Flora and Fauna

Baker, A. *Whales & Dolphins of New Zealand*. Victoria University Press 1999.
Brownsey, P. and Smith Dodson, J. *New Zealand Ferns and Allied Plants*. David Bateman 2000.
Crowe, A. *Which New Zealand Insect?* Penguin 2002.
Dawson, J. *Forest Vines to Snow Tussock – The Story of New Zealand Plants*. Victoria University Press 1993.
Dawson, J. and Lucas, R. *Nature Guide to New Zealand Forest*. Random House NZ 2004.
De Roy, T. and Jones, M. *New Zealand – A Natural World Revealed*. David Bateman 2006.
Gibbs, G. *Ghosts of Gondwana: The History of Life in New Zealand*. Craig Potton Publishing 2007.
Gibson, I. (ed.). *A Continent on the Move, New Zealand Geoscience in the 21st Century*. Geological Society of New Zealand 2008.
Hunt, J. and Lucas, R. *From Weta to Kauri*. Random House NZ 2005.
Ombler, K. *A Visitor's Guide to New*

Zealand's National Parks. New Holland (NZ) 2007.
Salmon, J. *Field Guide to the Alpine Plants of New Zealand*. Reed 1968.
Salmon, J. *Native Trees of New Zealand*. Reed 1999.
Shirihai, H. *The Complete Guide to Antarctic Wildlife*. Alula Press/Princeton 2002.
Thornton, J. *The Reed Field Guide to New Zealand Geology*. Reed Publishing (NZ) 2003.
Wilson, H. *Stewart Island Plants*. Manuka Press 1994.
Wilson, H. *Wild Plants of Mount Cook National Park*. Manuka Press 1996.

Glossary

Alien Non-native species introduced into the ecosystem
Amphipod Order of shrimp-like crustaceans such as sandhopper
Arthropod Invertebrate animal with exoskeleton, segmented body and jointed limbs
Carpal joint Joint in middle of a bird's wing
Caruncle Wart-like protuberance
CE Common Era (used to be AD)
Cephalopod A class of mollusc, including octopus, squid and cuttlefish
Copepod Small fresh- and salt-water crustaceans
Coverts Small feathers on wing or tail
Crustacea Group of arthropods, including crabs, lobster, shrimp, krill and barnacles
Culmen External ridge along upper mandible
Diurnal During daytime – as opposed to nocturnal
Endemic Found naturally only in that location, or breeds only in that location
Gam/Gamming Mock courtship practised by young non-breeding birds, in small groups
Gular skin Bare skin joining lower mandible to neck
Invasive Introduced or alien species that has become established, changing the ecosystem
Jizz Term used for general appearance or shape of a bird, originally General Impression of Size and Shape, a system developed for pilots in World War II
Kleptoparasite/ism Parasitism by theft; species that steal food from other species
Lamellae Thin plate-like structures on feet of geckos, giving them amazing traction
Loral line Line between eye and bill
Lores Area immediately in front of the eye
Mollusc Phylum of animals including snails, slugs, squid and mussels
Morph Form, plumage variation
Mustelid Family of mammalian carnivores including Stoats, Weasels, ferrets
MYA Million years ago
Nail Small central hook on bill of ducks and geese
Native Found naturally in that location, not introduced
Polyandrous Mating of female with more than one male in any one breeding season
Polymorphic Existence of several plumage patterns, which are not the result of a recurrent mutation.
Primaries Main flight feathers on bird wing
Rictal Hairs around base of kiwi bill
Scapulars Feathers on upperside of wing close to body
Secondaries Flight feathers on bird wing
Speculum Well-defined patch of feathers on secondaries or secondary coverts
Sulcus Upper edge of lower mandible on a bird's bill or beak
Tarsus Lower part of leg
Tibia Upper part of leg

Index